The Tho...

"A shoot-margarita-out-your-nose funny collection ᴏ
travel essays stretching across the globe and into every area of ɛᴍ
rassment that you're thankful didn't happen to you."

—*Playgirl*

Sand in My Bra and Other Misadventures

"A collection of ridiculous and sublime travel experiences."
—*San Francisco Chronicle* Best-Seller List

"These snappy travel stories bursting with candor and crackling humor
are sure to leave readers feeling that to not have an adventure to remember is a great loss indeed. *Sand in My Bra* will light a fire under the behinds
of, as the dedication states, 'all the women who sit at home or behind their
desks bitching that they never get to go anywhere.'"

—*Publishers Weekly*

Whose Panties Are These?

"The whimsy, the weighty, and the wild-eyed. *Whose Panties Are These?*
delivers thirty-one more humorous, sometimes raunchy essays from exotic places, in anatomically correct detail. The writers are mostly professional journalists and they are definitely women of mischief versed in
the first two rules of travel: laugh first and don't ever whine. Like Paul
Theroux, editor Jennifer Leo has strong feelings about travel writing,
aiming 'to go beyond the been-there-done-that stories and bring you
the outrageous.'"

—*ForeWord Magazine*

"*Whose Panties Are These?* isn't niche, it's freakin' hilarious. Jen Leo has
collected destructively funny stories of everything that can go really
wrong on the road to women, from having to buy velour panties in a
very public Indian market, to attacking an exhibitionist in Japan, to having to wonder about the groundshaking question 'Is my butt too small?'
in Senegal. Laughing at, and with, these gals' misadventures is good
karma for everyone. You're probably next."

—*Student Traveler Magazine*

TRAVELERS' TALES
HUMOR BOOKS

Sand in My Bra

Whose Panties Are These?

The Thong Also Rises

Not So Funny When It Happened

There's No Toilet Paper on the Road
Less Traveled

Hyenas Laughed at Me
and Now I Know Why

The Fire Never Dies

Last Trout in Venice

TRAVELERS' TALES

What Color Is Your Jockstrap?

funny men and women write
from the road!

Edited by
JENNIFER L. LEO

TRAVELERS' TALES
PALO ALTO, CALIFORNIA

Credits and copyright notices for the individual articles in this collection are given starting on page 270.

We have made every effort to trace the ownership of all copyrighted material and to secure permission from copyright holders. In the event of any question arising as to the ownership of any material, we will be pleased to make the necessary correction in future printings. Contact Travelers' Tales, Inc., 853 Alma Street, Palo Alto, California 94301. www.travelerstales.com

Art Direction: Stefan Gutermuth
Interior Design: Kathryn Heflin and Susan Bailey
Cover Photograph: © *Ragnarth Sigurdsson/Arctic-Images*
Page Layout: Cynthia Lamb using the fonts Bembo and Journal

Distributed by: Publishers Group West, 1700 Fourth Street, Berkeley, California 94710

Library of Congress Cataloging-in-Publication Data

What color is your jockstrap? : funny men and women write from the road / edited by Jennifer L. Leo. — 1st ed.
    p. cm.
  Includes index.
  ISBN 1-932361-34-0 (pbk.)
  1. Voyages and travels—Anecdotes. 2. Voyages and travels—Humor. I. Leo, Jennifer.
  G465.W46 2006
  910.4—dc22

2006009344

First Edition
Printed in the United States
10 9 8 7 6 5 4 3 2 1

To all the travel love-spawn whose parents
enjoyed the road a little too much.

Table of Contents

Introduction

Men. We love them for making us smile, and hate them for breaking our hearts. They're good for carrying our bags, and I swear, one day, we'll invent a way to convert their natural gas into useable power for our hybrid cars, laptops, foot spas, and anything else we'd rather be using than an air freshener. I know some of you would prefer to live without them, but I never could.

I entered the travel writing world because of Tim Cahill and have since made room on a bookcase for signed Bill Bryson books, driven from San Francisco to Santa Barbara for a Pico Iyer reading, and gotten drunk with Rolf Potts on three different continents. In short, I love our traveling smellier half. That's why, after Bra, after Panties, after Thong, those with the bulge in their pants asked when they would be able to write for one of my books, I couldn't say no. In fact, everyone at Travelers' Tales thought it a fabulous fun way to complete this scantily clad underwear empire.

Boxers and briefs weren't going to cut it. Heck, I wear those to bed. But I've never worn a jockstrap, and since we had so much fun playing with a Hemingway title, we thought we'd put a cheeky spin on a modern-day career classic. Hence, *What Color is Your Jockstrap?*

Inside you'll find a diverse cross-section of misadventures. Some share the bizarre stories of travelers who went to the ends of the earth only to have the cosmos spit in their face, while others are the tales of typical travel challenges—just the sort of thing even rookie travelers can relate to. There are even plenty of laughable journeys that were taken on purpose. We did not separate the women's stories from the men's, but you'll find the front half of the book occupied by gross bodily function mishaps, and the back of the book holding the sweeter, more reader-friendly stories. Whether they're about suffering through diarrhea in Cabo San Lucas or figuring out how to get along with French women while working in Bordeaux, these travelers are globetrotting super heroes!

Eavesdrop on Jim Benning's phone call with a Chinese prostitute in "Lust in Translation," spend all your money shooting off heavy weapons with Eben Strousse in "Guns and Frivolity in Cambodia," hit on a smoking hot Argentinean with Elliott Hester in "Love and the Bad Empanada," or fight a mob of Nepali taxi drivers with Rachel Thurston's mother in "Mama Chihuahua, World's Fiercest Travel Partner."

There are so many outrageous accounts of vacations gone wrong that by this fourth book, you just have to wonder, do all trips go bad? No, of course not. But I guarantee that if you are someone who wants to return with a brag-worthy story to amuse your friends or write up for the press, it's best to hope that the tarmac *does* get pulled out from under you. After all, if you're crying on your trip, someone else is laughing about it later. Bottom line, get out and get lost. There's a great big world out there—just waiting to fart on you!

ELLIOTT HESTER

* * *

Love and the Bad Empanada

What's that smell?

THE DOUBLE-DECKER ANDESMAR BUS TO SALTA DEPARTED midafternoon and arrived twenty-two hours later at a depot in the dusty northwest region of Argentina. The ride was a surprisingly smooth one, not the cramped back-roads bumpathon I'd imagined it would be. My seat, one of only seven or eight on the lower deck, was as large and relaxing as a first-class throne on a small commercial aircraft. In fact, the cabin resembled the premium cabin of a McDonnnell-Douglas MD-80—albeit smaller and not as clean, with worn seat covers, inoperative reading lights, rattling windows, and, instead of a curtain separating the first-class cabin from tourist class, a wall dividing our cabin from the cargo compartment. Still, this was comfort. The majority of passengers had been accommodated in the lengthy upper deck, but smaller seats and a dense configuration allowed less personal space. All were served soft drinks by an unsmiling attendant and entertained by three successive movies, the last of which, *Remember the Titans,* starred my favorite actor, Denzel Washington.

I watched the first film, gazing intermittently out the window at grazing cows and dusty pueblos backlit by a slanting sun. It was the very best of bus rides. A discount traveler's dream come true. It might have been perfect if not for the tainted empanada.

The empanada is Argentina's most popular food. The farther north you travel from Buenos Aires, the more often empanadas appear on restaurant menus. Stuffed with ground beef, mine had been purchased at a greasy diner in a greasy bus depot somewhere north of Sante Fe. Even before I tasted it, I knew this particular empanada was bad. The dough crunched as my teeth sank into it. That's when I noticed the meat. Hard as pebbles, it had been fried beyond recognition. But common sense gave way to hunger. While a smirking cook eyed me from behind the counter, I sat on a stool chewing gravel-meat and washed it down with warm Coca-Cola. The fact that I was the only customer should have told me something.

Soon after boarding the bus and settling in for the second movie, my bowels became engulfed in a four-alarm fire. I sprang for the lavatory, prepared to battle the blaze. Right then and there I remembered a warning from the "Getting Around" section of my *Lonely Planet Argentina* guide. "Carry water, a healthy snack, toilet paper…" Toilet paper? I was smart enough to bring water, but the healthy snack had been substituted with the bad empanada. And toilet paper—the strength and quantity of which is inextricably linked to the digestion of bad meat—had been forgotten. I scanned the lavatory, hoping beyond hope…

Bursting from the lavatory, I poked the dangling arm of the woman sleeping in the nearest seat. She fixed me with a sluggish eye. "Excuse me," I whispered. "Do you have toilet paper I can borrow?"

The question made me roll my own eyes even before the woman frowned and said, "*¿Que?*" After using the toilet paper, was I actually planning to give it back?

"*Por favor, señora. Yo. Necesito. Papel. ¡Muy importante!*" I stood there in the aisle, my buttocks clenching mightily beneath hastily buttoned Levis, the volcanic eruption mere seconds away. The woman nodded sleepily. She reached into her bag, pulled out a pen, a notepad, and then—

"*No, no, no, señora. Necesito pa-pel,*" I said, stretching the word and tilting my head toward the lavatory. She shook her head, reached into her bag, and produced a flimsy roll. Instead of offering it, she snatched off a few sheets and thrust them into my trembling hand. Economy would be the spirit of the moment. I leapt into the lavatory. The fire burned. The bus rolled on and on.

Sometime later, when the fire had been doused, when passengers no longer winced and retreated to their seats after making the mistake of opening the lavatory door, a beautiful woman boarded the bus. I kid you not. Everywhere you look in Argentina, there's a beautiful woman. Eyeballing the unsuspecting tourist on a city street. Accompanying him to a soccer game. And yes, walking toward him on the Andesmar bus to Salta. During the various plane, train, and bus rides in a life defined by departure time, I have never had the privilege of sitting next to a woman as provocative as the one standing in the aisle. This trip was no exception. The tall, casually dressed Argentinean sat across the aisle from me. Too close to admire without being obvious, but not so far as to restrict conversation.

I smiled.

She said, "Hello."

"Oh, you speak English."

In the darkened cabin, lit only by the flickering of the

Denzel Washington movie, I got to know Isabella Tortellini. The twenty-nine-year-old sales rep worked for a multinational textile company with offices in Buenos Aires. Of the many aspects of life she said she was thankful for, grueling long-distance bus rides were not one of them. "After the *corralito*," she said, referring the government's recent economic meltdown, "my company, they make…how you say, cutback?"

"My company is doing the same thing," I said.

"Before, I fly across my territory. Now," said Isabella, shrugging her shoulders and releasing a sigh, "I must take a bus."

I felt for her. Really. And during the next hour or so, as the bus rumbled across the darkened countryside, as the conversation deepened and our eyes locked in short flirtatious interludes that were acknowledged with bashful smiles, something stirred inside me. I *felt* for her. Really. Isabella proved to be smart, beautiful, gainfully employed, and according to her bashful confession, she was single and exceedingly available. Comparatively speaking, I was…well, single and exceedingly available. I leaned across the aisle and whispered something to her. She leaned across the aisle and whispered back. We were close enough to sense what appeared to be happening. Close enough to kiss. Mere inches from her moistening lips, seconds away from the most erotic bus ride of my life, I discovered Isabella's one irrepressible flaw. Bad breath. Hog's breath. Halitosis *muchas!* Hers was not simply a case of unbrushed teeth and the aftereffects of a carnivorous dinner. As Marcellus proclaimed in *Hamlet*, "Something is rotten!"

Back in Miami, there was this flight attendant named Ronnie Hamilton who always seemed to show up on my crew. Ronnie was a nice enough guy, but his breath smelled like shit. I'm not exaggerating. He'd walk up to you and say, "Hello," or, "How's it goin'?" and you'd turn away wondering if he'd licked a turd before putting on his uniform and driving to the airport. Pity the passenger who made the mistake of asking Ronnie for assistance. He liked to get right up in passengers' faces, the way stinky-breath people often do, and blabber away tangentially until the victims reached for the oxygen masks. Flight attendants disappeared whenever Ronnie approached. Pilots refused to let him into the cockpit. He must have suffered from a glandular thing, because every time I ran into him—in airport operations, on the airplane, even at an airline party in Fort Lauderdale—his breath smelled exactly the same. Like shit.

Maybe Isabella suffered from the same ailment as Ronnie Hamilton. Or maybe it was something else. Either way, her breath hit me like a Tyson punch. I fell back across the aisle, dazed and utterly bewildered. Try though I did to sustain tête-à-tête from a safe distance, the sudden change in logistics forced our conversation to falter. Dialogue that once flowed as robustly as the Colorado rapids had been reduced to a trickle from a drainage ditch. Ultimately, she turned her eyes away and focused on the Denzel Washington movie I had all but forgotten about—even though he's my favorite actor.

A troubling thought occurred after she leaned away so promptly and settled into her seat. The question nibbled at my consciousness. As discreetly as possible, I cupped one hand in front of my mouth, exhaled once, twice, a third time for good measure. It was then that I realized, with no small measure of embarrassment, that my own breath—tainted by the bad empanada—smelled as skanky as a baby's day-old diaper. I stole a glance at Isabella. She stole a glance at me. Never were two people in greater need of breath mints. But the rancid winds had done irreparable damage. When Isabella disembarked an hour later in Where the Fuck Are We, Argentina, we simply waved goodbye, choosing to keep our breaths to ourselves.

Elliott Hester is a flight attendant, magazine writer, and newspaper columnist. He is the author of Plane Insanity: A Flight Attendant's Tales of Sex, Rage and Queasiness at 30,000 Feet, *and* Adventures of a Continental Drifter, *from which this story was excerpted. He took a year off to travel the world and is now living in Barcelona, Spain.*

JIM BENNING

* * *

Lust in Translation

Was it a call or a call girl?

I'VE ALWAYS CONSIDERED MY HOTEL ROOMS TO BE
refuges—places where, no matter how foreign the culture
around me, I could retreat and unwind, free from the challenges and confusion of the outside world. That was particularly true in China. I'd arrived with only a few words of
Chinese at my disposal: "hello," "thank you," and, as a result
of an ill-fated attempt at a community college Mandarin
course, "I like to eat rice." While I had little trouble procur-
ing a bland, starchy lunch, other tasks, such as asking for directions or buying a train ticket, often devolved into
exhausting games of charades. The language barrier felt as in-
surmountable as the Great Wall, and at the end of each day,
my well of patience having run dry, I would escape into the
safe confines of my hotel room.

That's exactly where my wife, Leslie, and I wound up,
beat, after exploring the northern city of Xi'an late one afternoon. So when the telephone suddenly rang, intruding
upon our sanctum, I was in no hurry to answer it. None of

our friends knew where we were. Not a soul at the hotel's front desk spoke English. And I had no interest in proclaiming, yet again, my great love of rice.

I considered ignoring the phone, but when the caller didn't relent after nearly half a dozen rings, I flopped down on the bed and picked up.

"*Ni hao*," I said.

A woman at the other end uttered something in Chinese, her voice rising in a way that suggested a question.

"I'm sorry, but I don't speak Mandarin," I replied in English, assuming that would put a quick end to it.

As I was about to hang up, she said something else, this time exhaling between words, as though she were pedaling an exercise bike.

"What's that?"

She offered a few more words in a warm, soft voice, and then breathed into the phone, this time in a way that evoked not a sweaty gymnasium but a romantic, candlelit bedroom. I had no idea what she was saying, but I liked the way she was saying it.

Leslie, standing across the room, shot me a quizzical look. I pulled the receiver away from my lips and whispered, "I think it's a prostitute, but I'm not sure. She doesn't speak any English."

Leslie shook her head, then wished me a good time and disappeared into the shower.

I'd remembered reading something about Chinese prostitutes occasionally calling hotel rooms to seduce potential clients, but I'd never received such a call myself.

On the streets around our hotel, amid the noodle joints and mom-and-pop markets, we'd seen a number of curious shops with barber poles, hazy pink lights, and young women inside. Was this woman calling from one of them? Was she hoping to lure me in?

"I'm sorry," I said, "but I just don't understand what you're saying."

She said something back, her breathy voice rising and falling seductively.

I cursed the Great Wall of language barriers. What to do?

I summoned my most charming, debonair voice and said, "*Wo xi huan chi fan.*" *I like to eat rice.*

My phone friend giggled with delight and cooed, as though I'd just whispered a sweet nothing in her ear.

I felt as though I'd unlocked the door to some alternate Forbidden City where gibberish was an aphrodisiac and young women had nothing better to do than to giggle and coo and flirt on the phone with strange men. I liked it.

I picked up my Mandarin phrasebook and rifled through it, searching for another *bon mot.*

"*Wo yao zu yiliang zixingche,*" I said. *I want to hire a bicycle.*

My friend laughed. Then she whispered something else, her soft voice revealing, I was almost sure, a deep and heretofore unspoken yearning.

A picture was forming in my mind of a young woman who looked not unlike Lucy Liu, flaked out on a sofa in one of those pink-lit rooms, twirling a finger in her long hair, smiling coquettishly. When she replied this time, I could swear she was telling me, "I know a great place where we could share a bowl of rice." Or "I will be your bicycle." Then again maybe she was just saying, "My prices start at a very reasonable three hundred yuan." Whatever. The important thing was that she seemed to be into me.

I scoured the transportation section of my phrase book for another enchanting line.

"Moban qiche jidian kai?" I said. *When is the last bus?*

My friend giggled. I laughed.

Just about then, Leslie stepped out of the bathroom, a towel wrapped around her, patting her damp hair. She looked puzzled.

"You're still on the phone?" she said.

I smiled and shrugged.

Leslie furrowed her brow and then cracked a smile. She couldn't decide whether to be annoyed or amused. I wasn't sure myself whether to feel guilty or stupid.

It was, in an odd, small way, not so different from the confusion I've often felt traveling in a country where the culture and language are not my own. I arrive eager to make sense of everything. But the more time passes, the more I'm reminded that this is not so easily accomplished, and that the world is an impossibly complicated place. And then, as hard as it is, I try to make peace with my confusion, and even, on rare occasions, embrace it.

I decided it was time to get off the phone. I searched my phrase book for a few parting words. Then, in my best Mandarin accent, I said, "Is there a lifeguard on duty?"

My friend giggled. We giggled together. Then I gently hung up the phone.

Jim Benning is a San Diego-based writer and co-editor of the online travel magazine WorldHum.com.

ESSA ELAN

✦ ✦ ✦

The Butt Reading

There's more than one kind of lottery.

O.K., SO I'VE NEVER ACTUALLY KNOWN ANYONE TO PICK up a dog and bring it back home only to discover that it was, in fact, a rat. And I've never been chased down the highway by someone trying to tell me that there was a serial killer stashed away in my backseat. If I hear a story that happened to my best friend's uncle's cousin's sister-in-law's nephew and later discover that it also happened to my neighbor's dog-walker's brother's ex-girlfriend's English professor's wife, I quickly dismiss it as urban legend.

So when Rita, a girl working at a gas station off I-75, told me about this guy named Hector (known to her by eight degrees of separation) having his penis read, and then her co-worker, Lele, chimed in with her recount of someone named Marie getting her butt read, I got severely suspicious.

"Yeah girl," Rita whispered as if she were telling me a secret, when I knew she'd probably told twenty folks before me, "There's a fortune teller across the street who can read anything: a penis, your breasts, or your butt."

"What does that mean? Like palm reading?" I asked.

"Like palm reading, but better. She says the lines along your other body parts are more intense, and she can tell you about your family, destiny; she helped one guy win the lottery."

The lottery, huh? I looked at my watch, and realized that I was actually making pretty good time between Atlanta and Orlando, I was already well into Florida.

"Does she have to touch you?" I probed.

"Touch you? Girl, I don't know, I haven't gone to her. I don't want no one looking at my big ol' butt," Rita said as she turned to straighten the potato chips. I could see her point, she had an ass like a $4 mule.

I decided to try this palm reader, Mama Dee, and see what she could tell me. I walked across the slow street to the building, which looked a bit shady, somewhat like a road-house. There was one dusty sign that stated, "Discover Your Future" in the window.

I knocked on the door as I entered to see a matronly black woman seated on a Victorian chaise.

"Come in child, and drop your pants." She surprised me with how quickly she wanted to get down to business.

Usually, I'm highly disobedient, but Mama Dee reminded me a little of my grandma, so I was scared to piss her off, thinking she might take a switch to my behind. I dropped my pants, turned around, and showed her my butt. She informed me that the shape and highness indicated that I'm energetic and high-strung (all true) and then she told me that I would come across an unexpected obstacle on my way to Orlando. She told me that when my CD fell to the car floor, to leave it and not pick it up.

"What about the lottery?" I pleaded with hope and anticipation.

Mama Dee burst into laughter, as if that were the most ridiculous question anyone had ever asked in the history of questions. "No lottery for you, child. You got other worries."

I paid her a ten spot and went back to my car, eager to make it to Orlando before sunset. I shook my head as I realized I gave someone money to look at my butt, when in Atlanta I knew plenty of men who would gladly pay me to just see my underwear. It all seemed wrong, I'd been scammed. She didn't even tell me anything useful, and there was no lottery for me.

I had two more hours of driving left. Miles down the highway, I began fidgeting with the radio, but nothing good was on. I decided to listen to a CD instead. As I pulled it from the holder, it slipped from my hand and fell to the floor of the car. I was about to pick it up when I remembered Mama Dee and her warning to let it be. Just then, I rounded a blind turn of the turnpike and had to swerve my car off the highway. The car in front of me was also skidding, as well as the car behind me. Before us was a huge accident, and two tractor trailers were stretched across the road, completely impassible.

Shocked and sweating, I realized that if I had reached down for that CD, I would have hit the trucks head on. Dang, Mama Dee was right, and who would have thought my ass could save my life?

Essa Elan is an Atlanta writer with work appearing in Amoret, Reading Divas, Personal Journaling, CLAMOR Magazine, *and* Age Ain't Nothing But a Number. *She is editor of an online newsletter,* Virgin Ink, *hosted on Topica.com.*

JULIA WEILER

* * *

Be Grateful,
Not Hateful

Togetherness takes on a whole new meaning.

I SHOULD HAVE KNOWN OUR THANKSGIVING TRIP TO Mexico was doomed as soon as I stepped out onto the tarmac and my brother-in-law was nowhere in sight. "We're looking for a white convertible VW Bug…right?" I asked my husband as he scanned the desolate landscape. "And you're sure Mike said he'd pick us up?" I continued shooting him the hairy eyeball.

"Yeah, yeah…he's supposed to pick us up here at the airport, and we're on time and everything," James finally replied sounding agitated. "I bet that bastard forgot us."

With that he stormed off towards the pay phones while I guarded our bags and kept an eye out for our missing ride.

A couple of L.A.-looking blondes wearing silicone-filled tube tops sat down on the bench next to me. "Oh my Gaaawwd Stacy, can you like…beeelieeeve we're in Cabo?" one of them squealed, her boobies bouncing with excitement. "It's like, going to be sooo totally cool."

She pulled a bottle of tequila from her shiny, hot-pink beach bag and poured herself a shot. She threw it back with gusto and turning to me, shrilled, "Don't you just looooove Cabo San Lucas?"

"Oh, um…sure," I replied, feeling flat-chested and terribly unhip.

Truth was, I'd never been to Mexico before. In fact I hadn't even been outside of the Pacific Northwest that much, but I was *hoping* to looooove Cabo. James and I had just gotten married a year earlier and, unable to have a proper honeymoon at the time, we had settled for a weekend of camping instead. Although I had enjoyed myself, it hadn't exactly been what I'd call romantic and so I saw this vacation, despite the inclusion of relatives and a holiday, as our second chance. I was looking forward to a week of luxurious spa treatments, candle-lit dinners, and long walks on the beach.

As I sat there trying to come up with something cool to say to the tube-top girls, James returned from the phone booth looking frustrated and unsuccessful. "Well, I can't get a hold of Mike," he reported.

"Like, who's Mike?" one of the tube-tops chimed with enthusiasm, "He sounds like, waaay cute."

Mike was James's older brother, and he and my mother-in-law had arranged and financed the entire trip. They had flown in a few days prior and were supposed to be here to meet us. Without their guidance, we were pretty much clueless as to what to do next.

"Did you see if the resort could send us a shuttle or something?" I asked James.

"Yeah…I mean no…well sort of," he stammered. "They couldn't really understand me. I think maybe their English is a bit rough."

"Rough," I yelped. "What do you mean rough? Like they totally don't speak English *at all*?" I demanded, slipping into valley girl. "They MUST understand shuttle. Did you try taxi? How about car, *el coche…el Camino…el* SOME-THING?" The tube-topped Boobsie Twins looked at us with sympathy and batted their fake eyelashes.

"You can like totally share our shuttle!" they exclaimed in bouncy unison.

A white minivan pulled up to the curb just then, and we climbed inside with the bubbly Boobsies. James gave the name and address of our hotel to the driver, who appeared to recognize neither. Although he claimed he could get us there "*ningun problema*," his reassurance failed to comfort me.

As I watched the van fill with happy vacationers, who knew where they were going, one of the Twins elbowed me playfully in the ribs. "Oh my Gaaawd, aren't you like sooo totally excited," she jiggled, offering me a shot of tequila.

"Totally," I replied and downed the liquor.

We passed one beautiful resort after another and released a few lucky passengers every so often, until, finally we came to a small dirt and gravel road. "*Este es su hotel,*" the driver announced happily taking the forlorn turn.

"But there's no sign or ANYTHING!" I cried, certain that he was mistaken.

"*Si,* no sign," the driver concurred as he continued down the dusty trail.

I looked to the Boobsie Twins for consolation. I needed them to say something perky…something like, "Don't stress, it's going to be totally awesome!"…or maybe even a cheerful round of "You'll looooove it!" but to my dismay, even they were perplexed beyond optimism.

We pulled up in front of a sun-bleached stucco building with a three-tiered fountain sputtering pathetically in the

center of a small courtyard. The place had the look of a resort that had probably been something in its heyday but was
now, perhaps, better suited for containing *actual* hay. I
downed a quick shot of tequila from the Boobsies as the driver unloaded our bags.

"Like, good luck," one of the Twins said looking at me
with pity.

"Yeah, like…for sure," added the other handing me one
last nip of Cuervo.

"*Buena suerte de hecho*," I agreed, stepping out onto the
cracked Saltillo tiles.

As we made our way up to the lobby, dragging our own
bags and looking for some sign of the staff (or even another
guest for that matter), Mike appeared. "Oh, there you guys
are," he said *waaay* too casually. "I was just coming to get you."

If not for the tequila swirling in my bloodstream, and the
fact that it was Thanksgiving Day, I might have said something
sassy, but subdued by both mild intoxication and holiday, I allowed myself to get checked in without a struggle. As we
were led to our room, I reminded myself that I was only in
Cabo at the generosity of my in-laws, and I began my mantra
of "be grateful, not hateful." I decided from that point forward that I'd maintain a positive attitude, no matter what.

We made our way along overgrown garden paths past
nice-ish looking two- and three-story buildings. By the light
of the setting sun, their peeling orange paint, highlighted
with bands of yellow caution tape, almost looked romantic.

"Room has nice sea view," our escort announced with an
unctuous grin as we continued down narrow stairways and
tangled footpaths.

Finally, we came to a dark, damp, tunnel-like corridor. I
hadn't seen anything quite like it anywhere else on the prop-
erty, and now our guide was motioning toward it as though

we should enter the forgotten passageway. "Grateful not hateful," I reminded myself as I entered the dimly lit hall.

I opened the door to our room and noted an odor reminiscent of stale seawater and a port-a-potty. Despite the unfavorable smell, I looked around the room for something positive to focus on. It appeared to be clean and spacious, and, although not readily apparent, there was still the promise of a "sea view" to look forward to. James tipped the gentleman who'd escorted us, and at last we were alone.

"Well," I crooned, patting the bed seductively. "This sure looks inviting. You wanna give it a try…stud?" I plopped onto the rock-hard mattress with a thud and tried to strike a sexy pose.

Just then there was a knock at the door, and Mike waltzed into the room, sniffed the air once, and pronounced…"Weird." With the expression of one who'd just detected a fart, he added, "How long till you guys can be ready for dinner…fifteen minutes enough?"

So much for my early evening love-in.

I rummaged around in my suitcase in search of my slinkiest outfit, and devoid of tube tops, I settled for a sexy little "tank top-miniskirt" number. In tribute to the Boobsie Twins (whose clones appeared to have been let loose all over Cabo), I flashed several pedestrians (who seemed most grateful for my giving), from the back of Mike's convertible on the way to the restaurant.

The Thanksgiving dinner was fantastic—an exciting night of mariachis, margaritas, and merriment—and I was starting to feel just like one of those girls gone wild. When Mike suggested we continue the good times over at the dance-on-yer-table, drink-'til-ya-puke, all-night party bar, El Squid Roe, I couldn't think of a better idea.

We took a short walk down the street toward a neon palace of lights pulsating with techno-rap and bursting with young, hard-partying hipsters. I could already smell the alcohol and sweat oozing from the place before I even got through the jam-packed doors.

I summoned my inner party girl and squeezed my way into the chaos. Almost immediately, I felt someone grinding against my backside. Meanwhile, a woman with unbelievable cleavage and a tray of purple wobbly things quickly approached me from the front. So enraptured was I by her plentiful décolletage, that I barely noticed her slide one of the jiggly squares down my throat. She slipped me one more, and with an alluring smile, she disappeared into the deafening madness.

Feeling a bit disconcerted, I looked around at the three stories of wild, pelvis-slamming dirty dancers and asked myself, *What would the Boobsie Twins do?* Working my miniskirt, I wiggled over to my husband and grabbed his butt. His face lit up, and we joined the orgy of gyrating hip-thrusters up on the table. Some guy with a water gun tangoed by and shot streams of tequila into our mouths as we got our groove on, while, elsewhere the crowd cheered as booze was ejected from a bong into the gaping maw of a liquor-thirsty patron.

The bar was writhing and throbbing in hedonistic excess. Indeed the whole place was turning into one giant, unabashed hump-fest, and I began to wonder if anyone would even notice if James and I just started doing it right there on the dance floor. As I was about to find out, a deluge of icy, cold water from above crashed down upon us. This "cool-down treatment" was courtesy of Mike, who, holding an empty bucket one dance floor above us, was laughing uncontrollably.

"Too close," he hollered down over the noise at us in-between fits of hysteria.

Drenched to the bone and experiencing a moment of sobriety, I looked to James whose fire had also been extinguished, and I knew that we were definitely over our limits on cheap drinks and tawdry behavior. Still, I was impressed that we had been too hot for El Squid Roe! …and I was ready to move on to a much more intimate setting. James and I sloshed our way toward the exit, and slipping outside into the crowded street we promptly caught a cab which carried us back to the seclusion of our semi-dilapidated hotel.

By the time we made it back to our room, our hangovers were already setting in, and my libido began to diminish. I was no longer feeling very girly or wild, and the offensive mystery smell permeating our quarters had grown even stronger.

"I don't want to do it while that smell is still in here," I told James. "You know, I don't want to develop any…strange associations," I added as I approached the glass doors of our "sea-view" balcony. "James, come over here," I said summoning him to my side. "It's time for the big reveal and some fresh air!"

I pulled aside the drapes and threw open the doors. To my horror, the fresh gust of wind I'd expected only carried in more of the terrible smell. "Oh, God," I gagged, "there must be something rotting on the beach."

Trying to breathe through only my mouth, I stepped outside to appraise the night view. There was light glinting off a reflective surface just beyond our balcony, almost blending with the sea. "What do you suppose that is?" I asked.

James who was holding his nose and making a face replied, "Maybe ibt's one ob thobe endless horizon pools or sombting?"

"Mmm…sounds fancy," I said dreamily. "We'll have to check it out tomorrow after they've cleaned up whatever is responsible for that stench." With that I closed the doors, gulped down some tap water, and immediately passed out in bed.

Sometime in the very small hours that following morning, I was jerked from slumber by an uncontrollable urge to shit my guts out. I tried to sit up in bed and was immediately overwhelmed by a wave of nausea massive enough to catch a ride on. My head was throbbing as though a million Mexican-hat dancers were using my brain as their sombrero, and I was seriously running the risk of throwing up and crapping simultaneously. If I didn't want this to happen in bed, I would have to move swiftly.

I put one hand over my mouth and the other across my backside, and just like the little Dutch boy, I hoped not to spring any leaks. I rolled out of bed onto the floor, and I continued rolling myself toward the bathroom where I realized I would be faced with a painful dilemma. Do I sit down to shit first and risk puking on the floor or do I bend over to puke first and risk shitting on the wall?

After a moment of tense deliberation, I decided to sit down on the toilet and barf into the wastebasket. As I sat there violently expelling fluids from nearly every orifice, in walked my husband who, alerted by my retching, came to see if I needed some assistance. "You going to be O.K., sweetie?" he said looking at me as though I were the possessed little girl from *The Exorcist*. "You need me to hold your hair back or anything?" he added, fully expecting my head to start spinning around.

Eventually, when I was devoid of all bodily fluids (which I was very, very thankful for), James carried me back to bed and gently tucked me in under the covers. There were little schools of fish molded into the plaster on the wall above me, and I stared at them wondering where they had come from and why they were swimming. "Do you see fish on the wall?" I asked him meekly.

"Yes, they are really there," he said reassuring me. He wiped the sweat from my brow.

"But…are they moving?" I asked feverishly wishing they would stop.

As I lay there hallucinating, there was a loud knock at the door. A few minutes later Mike walked in, took one look at me, and pronounced, "You look hung-over…and what the fuck is that smell?" He eyed me accusingly.

The putrid stench, to which now I truly was a contributor, was being generated just outside our balcony. You see, it turned out that the thing we had thought by last night's starlight to be a fancy, high-end swimming pool was actually by the light of day the hotel's nasty, low-end open-air sewer treatment system. With the breeze coming in off the Sea of Cortez, the rancid scent blew directly into our room which added insult to my misery.

Late that night, things went from bad to worse, and James became horribly sick, too. It was the same vile, terrible shit that had turned me into a human salad-shooter and now we were two of the same brand. I crawled over to the bathroom to assist my sick husband, and immediately needing to puke, realized our lack of facilities. There was poor James sitting on the pot with the wastebasket between his knees barfing and shitting himself into oblivion, and all I could think about was stealing his throne.

"OFF THE POT," I groaned trying to knock him over.

I really wanted to be there for him in his time of need, but my ass was about to explode, and I simply had no time for courtesy.

"MOVE," I cried again in a panic, trying not to blow it out both ends.

My tortured delirious husband was clearly not going to give up his seat, and with the toilet bowl and garbage can both permanently occupied, my options were limited. I had no other choice. I had to throw myself into the bathtub, close the doors, and hope for the best.

The following morning we woke up on the bathroom floor, and I decided it was time to summon a doctor. Being the stronger of the two at this point, it was left to me to make the call. I picked up the phone but there was no dial tone. I wiggled the cord and checked the connections, but the damn thing just wouldn't work. If we wanted medical help, I would have to make the long trek up to the front desk.

I am grateful for legs that can walk, I told myself as I gathered up my willpower.

I set off to save the day and by the time I bellied up to the front desk, I was winded and ready to puke again.

"*Necesito a doctor por favor*," I huffed. "*Soy muy enfermo*," I continued in terrible Spanish. The guy at the counter stared at me like I was an idiot.

"*Tengo una fiebre…y…mi estomago es muy, muy malo*," I said, trying to remember how to say, "I'm dying!" *en Español*. He continued to stare at me blankly. Suddenly, he smiled and mimicked downing a shot.

"*¡Demasiado tequila!*" he exclaimed proudly.

"Noooo," I cried desperately.

I scribbled my room number onto a piece of paper and drew a skull and crossbones with an arrow pointing to the word "*enfermo*." I added "*el doctor*" and "*por favor*" next to a smiley face and shoved the note at him before retreating to my sewage-, barf-, and shit-scented room.

By some miracle, James and I received a house call from the doctor later that day. He diagnosed us with severe gastroenteritis and gave us shots in the ass. Despite delivering a rather nasty Charlie horse, the drugs quelled our bodily eruptions and put us into a narcotic, dream-like stupor for the rest of the day. During our moments of semi-lucidity, James and I cuddled and consoled each other that if we had to get sick on our first romantic vacation together…at least someone else was footing the bill.

On the last day before our departure we finally felt human enough to get out and explore the hotel grounds. We set off to find the three hot tubs and sculpted swimming pools touted in the hotel's brochure. Although the setting was lovely, and you really could see Los Arcos, only one tub was actually operational and the term *hot* had been used way too loosely. The swimming pools, built right into the dramatic and eroding cliffside, looked as though they might, at any moment, fall into the ocean. The sunbathing areas were festooned with more of the bright yellow caution tape which cordoned off evidence that something along those lines may have already happened.

> We had bat soup in Indonesia one evening, and the following day went out for a surf. My friend's stomach had already started churning, then somehow, due to some huge rise in his intra-abdominal pressure and the tight-fitting wet suit, the contents of his gut came out and managed to fire out the back of his wet suit neck seal, into the air.
>
> ◆
>
> —Rob Conway, from *How to Shit Around the World* by Dr. Jane Wilson-Howarth

Our curiosities sated, we returned to our room where we discovered copious amounts of water pouring down through our ceiling and pooling up dramatically on the floor. Our television, which had somehow turned itself on in our absence, was taking the brunt of the deluge and beginning to spark. Confused and still somewhat prone to hallucinations, we were both at a loss for how to react.

Afraid to enter the electro-shock hazard zone, and feeling especially hateful, we decided to simply close the door and proceed to the front desk. Once there, I performed a rather ungrateful display of charades for the guy behind the counter while my husband did his best between expletives to explain our situation in Spanish.

That evening, in our nice, new room, the doom and gloom finally lifted. We were well enough to make love, and although too wiped out to get it on honeymoon-style, I was ten pounds lighter and probably looked really hot. As the sun went down that evening we relaxed on our jasmine-scented balcony, sipping frosty cold Coronas, and celebrating our close victory over death. Our vacation hadn't been romantic, we decided, not as much as camping, but the palm trees were sure nice, and we were thankful to be in love.

I looked over at James and smiling, held my beer up in the air. "How about a toast?" I cried.

"To projectile vomiting," he replied ceremoniously.

"To uncontrollable shitting," I added, breaking into giggles.

"To romance, sewer smell, and squid roe," James continued, tears welling in his eyes.

"Don't forget the Boobsie Twins," I added in merriment.

Suddenly James became very serious, then breaking the silence in perfect valley girl replied, "Toooootally." With that we clinked our bottles in celebration and watched the impossibly red sun slip into the sea.

★

Julia Weiler is an aspiring documentary filmmaker who recently discovered that if she were to focus solely on writing, she could eliminate her need to upgrade to HD equipment, plus have a lot more room in her luggage for tube tops. She met her husband James more than a dozen years ago while learning to skydive and the two have been falling in love ever since. She has dreams of someday rescuing him from his grown-up corporate job so the two can engage in uninterrupted journeys around the world, where she hopes he will always be willing to hold her hair back when she gets sick. Her very first story was published in The Thong Also Rises *and has been embarrassing her ever since.*

TAMARA SHEWARD

* * *

Day Trip to Chechnya

They don't have this ride at Disneyland.

THE MOST POPULAR LAST MEAL REQUESTED BY THOSE meeting death in the morning is a cheeseburger and fries. Facing my last night on earth, I got flat champagne and salted yogurt.

Condemned by audacity, curiosity, and flat-out idiocy, I had created my own destiny. Instead of sitting in a ramshackle cell, gagging on saline curds, I could have been cavorting, *après ski*, in one of the world's most beautiful resorts. But I'd thrown it all away to hop into a rusty Lada with a pistol-waving lunatic who promised he wouldn't kill me before smuggling me into the Most Dangerous Place on Earth.

"To your health!" Rashid cried, smashing his mug of tepid bubbly into mine. "*Na zdorovia!*"

"*Na zdorovia,*" I replied, feebly. To my health indeed. The toast seemed both ironic and moronic; if I cared so much about my well-being, what the hell was I doing going to Chechnya at dawn?

✳

Known to the outside world through breathless news anchor staples as "war-torn breakaway republic" and "al-Qaeda training ground," Chechnya isn't exactly the type of place that screams "day trip." With abduction, guerrilla warfare, and decapitation topping the list of "Things to See and Do," Chechnya reeks of menace and bloody mayhem. Conscripted Russian soldiers have been known to do themselves an injury rather than face a front in which up to seven of them are killed each day, and those who do go have a hand in making Grozny the most heavily bombed capital city on the planet. Intrepid reporters after a rare glimpse of the carnage are either escorted by thugs and spinmeisters loyal to President Putin or are forced to pay insurgent border runners thousands of dollars to ensure their dubious safety. And "Chechen tourism" is a cruel oxymoron.

I'd been on my way to the glitzy slopes of Mt. Elbrus when I met Rashid, one of Russia's so-called taxi mafia and denizen of the largely Islamic Karachay-Cherkessia Republic. My Elbrus-bound bus had turned out to be a work of fiction, but Rashid could get me there at a surprisingly reasonable price. But when I joked about a day trip to Chechnya—a mere 250 kilometers to the east but a million miles from Elbrus's ski-bunny glamour—he simply nodded and pulled out a pistol, concealed in a chamber beneath the Lada's battered dash.

"Why not?" he shrugged, waving the gun.

I stared at him blankly. Why *not* go into a violent, anarchic hellhole where I'd most likely wind up hooded and chained to a radiator for the rest of my short life?

"*Pashlee,*" I said. "Let's go."

★

We spent the afternoon driving maniacally through contentious territory marked in every traveler's guidebook with forbidding exclamation marks, stopping only to admire the eerie, cragged Caucasian scenery. Rashid was known to local soldiers for his artful graft, so we glided past military checkpoints with relative ease. In the tinderbox that is the North Caucasus, "relative ease" meant I didn't get shot for telling a leering, heavily-armed soldier to "Get the fuck out of my face" after he insisted I be strip-searched, but he didn't understand English anyway.

But the carefree attitude that characterized the day morphed into a throbbing pall by the time we detoured in Vladikavkaz, the capital of North Ossetia, at sundown. Chechnya by night was impossible, and Vladikavkaz wasn't much better:

———— ☽ ————

It is the nature of certain books—the travel, adventure, humor, memoir kind of book—to offer some reason, some driving force, an irreproachable motivation, for undertaking the odd journey. One reads, *I had long been fascinated by the Red-Arsed Llama, presumed extinct since 1742, and I determined to find one;* or *I only feel alive when I am nearly dead, and so the challenge of climbing K2, alone, without oxygen, or gloves, and snowboarding down, at night, looked promising;* or *A long career (two-and-a-half years) spent leveraging brands in the pursuit of optimal network solutions made me rich as Croesus, and yet I felt strangely uneasy, possibly because I now own 372 (hardworking) kids in Sri Lanka.* And typically, the writer emerges a little wiser, a little kinder, more spiritual, with a greater appreciation for the interconnectivity of all things.

◆

—J. Maarten Troost, *The Sex Lives of Cannibals*

Out in the streets, men were sharpening knives beneath shot-out streetlights and from behind our jammed door I could hear husky voices cooing my name with muted malice.

"I'm scared," I told Rashid.

"*Da*," he said. "Very big danger."

I gawked at him in disbelief. "You said it was O.K.!"

"For me. Not you." He waved the yogurt at me. "More *ayran*?"

It was one hell of a last supper.

Dawn snuck up on me like the bandits I'd spent a sleepless night waiting for, and far from lifting my spirits, the sunny morning fumed with dread. In the hotel corridors, random men with guns eyeballed me balefully, and out on the street, it felt like everyone was staring at the crazy Australian who'd come to be kidnapped. Even Rashid seemed to have gotten cold feet.

He hadn't paid his bribes to the "*Russki soldat svinya*" controlling the area and, he said, if we tried to drive across the Chechen border, these "soldier pigs" would kill him. I couldn't be sure if Rashid had come down with a case of melodrama or if this was simply border protocol, *Kavkaz*-style.

Getting around in a war zone is never easy, but when your driver is too afraid to drive and you're dressed in a glittery red jumper that screams "Decadent Infidel," it's a right hassle. We hitched a lift with the first Lada whose winking occupant didn't try to buy me from Rashid, then caught a local bus through the badlands of decrepit mosques and gutted housing estates until it reached its terminus, a vacant no-man's land just meters from the Ossetia/Ingushetia border. Crossing the gate, with its concrete-and-Kalashnikov décor, was harrowing enough, but by the time we got to the Nazran taxi depot, I didn't know who to be afraid of anymore. After getting into a cab with Rashid and three brooding, hulking Chechens, I opted for "everyone."

Our new driver, Hussein, had been hired by Rashid on the premise that he wouldn't sell me to any wannabe ransom-hunters on the 100-kilometer journey to Grozny. While an admirable statement—Rashid had taken an hour to find a driver willing to give such an assertion—I couldn't help being more than a little discomfited by Hussein's propensity for narrowing his eyes at me in the rear-vision mirror. And even if his death glares weren't indicative, I wasn't sure about the other passengers, a stiff-backed, glowering man in the passenger seat who refused to acknowledge me and his *hajib*-covered wife who shrunk from my accidental touch as if I were already a corpse. Even Rashid was unnerving me; in the dawning horror that I'd done something awesomely fool-hardy, I was riffling through my Russian dictionary, pointing out words in increasingly panic-stricken nudges. "*Zalozhnik?*" I whispered. "Hostage?"

Rashid shrugged and nodded out the window. "Al-Qaeda," he said. "Boom, boom."

Heavy silence filled the cab for the two interminable hours to Grozny. Outside, the North Caucasus passed in an undulating reel of green hills, ramshackle timber cottages, and the occasional wild fox. It was a scene of peace and whimsy, seemingly incongruous with my fears of being added to the sixty people who are abducted from the region each month. But with every click of the speedometer, the tension in the car mounted and—arcadian surrounds or not—my guts churned with the certainty that I'd finally run out of luck.

As we neared the Grozny demarcation, the woman finally turned to face me. Fixing me with a cold eye, she asked: "*Korrespondent?*"

"*Nyet,*" I trembled. "*Touriist.*"

A quizzical look furrowed her brow and suddenly, alarmingly, she started screaming. *I'm doomed,* I thought, transfixed by her wailing and her mouth full of gold teeth. This war-crazed babushka is going to eat me alive.

"*Touriist!*" she cried, smacking my knee. "*Touriist!*" After a stunned pause, the car erupted with gales of laughter and great hoots of hilarity. The man in the front seat was chortling and shaking my hand, and Hussein's eyes now watered and squinted with amusement. As wartime Chechnya's first ever day-tripper, it looked like I had cheated death with nothing more than outlandish foolishness.

Idiocy pays.

Nothing can prepare you for entering a live combat zone. I've lived across from Belfast's notorious Sandy Row and gotten into fisticuffs with an armed and amorous Cambodian soldier in Khmer Rouge territory, but Grozny made everything else look like War-Lite.

The ravaged outskirts of the city were an apocalyptic paean to war and destruction. The idyllic countryside had given way to scarred flatlands littered with the detritus of a decade's worth of ferocious bombings. Piles of rubble that vaguely resembled buildings were draped in camouflage netting and topped with huge Russian flags in blatant displays of triumphalism. Soldiers manned heavily fortified checkpoints every hundred meters along the widened road, roughing up anyone of Chechen extraction who didn't have the rubles to pay them off.

But if the fringe was devastated, then downtown Grozny

was obliterated. The Putin Government has told the world that Chechnya is under a policy of "normalization," but central Grozny was about as normal as Dresden, circa 1945. Troops in full combat gear stalked the desolate streets alongside massive tanks protecting them from snipers, while Chechen "police" in balaclavas fingered their weapons and looked the other way. There was not a single building that hadn't been shelled repeatedly, and erstwhile grand façades—Grozny was once a revered center of culture and the arts—were now, with their gaping maws and sagging foundations, pitiful caricatures of a people under siege. It was in this squalor, sans–electricity, sanitation, or potable water, that Chechens made their homes.

We pulled up by a bullet-riddled "peace memorial" to drop the couple

———☽———

On clear days in Yerevan, Mount Ararat would loom on the horizon like a beautiful hologram. By night an overcrowded streetcar rumbled up a nearby hill, showering sparks down from its overhead power line like the Frankenstein monster of mass transportation. But the night air was also filled with the sound of automatic weapons as criminal groups carried out vendettas against one another in the lobby of a neighboring hotel and opposition groups sprayed gunfire along the perimeter of the presidential compound, which bordered our residence and a wooded park along the Hrazdan River. At an informal gathering I asked the Armenian Foreign Secretary about all the shooting. He looked me in the eye and said in the sincerest of tones, "I think those are picnickers."

◆

—Lee Forsythe, "How I Got My Diplomatic License Revoked"

off. Unthinking, I opened the car door to get out, but was immediately flung back inside by the terrifying blasts of a nearby skirmish.

"Don't worry," said Hussein, revving the engine. "The worst happens at night. If you stay in the car, you should be fine."

"Should?"

"If you go outside, you will not see inside again. Look, slowly." He casually nodded his head towards a clump of brush beside the memorial. "Do you still want to go out?"

I squinted into the vegetation and nearly choked on my heart. Barely visible in his camouflage, a Russian soldier was on his stomach, his rifle trained directly at my head. Where the locals had been free to alight, I, as an unknown element, would be toast. Highly-concentrated combat zones are like inbred hillbilly hamlets: survival depends on the grapevine, and folks don't take kindly to strangers.

But while the Russians appeared keen to bump up their body count, the separatists seemed quite happy to keep me alive. For a suitable fee, that was. As we splashed down a boggy street lined with an insanely haphazard market, I noticed a lack of anyone trying to kill me and wondered if I might be able to have a wander around.

"*Nyet*," Hussein barked. "They probably won't shoot you, but they will take you to al-Qaeda. Or maybe you want to meet Bin Laden?"

"You're kidding."

"Who knows? But I tell you, you'll meet some of his friends if you move from that seat."

Not feeling overly social, I stayed put, gawking at the hectic scene outside my window. Before a tortured backdrop of ruined buildings and barbed wire, vendors displayed their measly wares—counterfeit Marlboros, greasy bottles brimming with recycled petrol, the occasional radish—on card tables sinking in a morass of mud and trash, while a weatherworn woman protecting a dribbling hose was mobbed by filthy toddlers clutching grimy ewers. Teenage boys squatted over soggy shoes, watching impassively as men darted in and out of mysterious alleyways. I knew I was being watched, too, but nobody said a word to me. Nobody, in fact, seemed to be saying much at all: For all its chaos and activity, the marketplace was devoid of human sound. No hawkers cried, no men argued, no children laughed. The only constant was the drone of helicopters and the rumble of tanks. It suddenly seemed very apt that the Russian word for "sad"—*groozny*—was almost identical to "Grozny."

I turned to Hussein. "When did all of this happen?"

He laughed bitterly. "When? It's happening now. It happened last night. It will happen tonight. *Svinya*," he spat. "It happened a month ago, when they destroyed my home." He and his family had been visiting a relative the night the Russians bombed his block of flats, killing many who had been unlucky enough to be home. He, his wife, and their two daughters had since been moved to a refugee camp in Ingushetia.

"But I will come back." A fierce glint came to his eye. "Chechen people are like the wolf, our symbol. We will always fight for our home."

His face relaxed. "And you are Australian. You have kangaroos, not wolves. Why did you come?"

It was a bloody good question. Why? Because I wasn't supposed to? Because I wanted to see what life was like where *mujahids*, not marsupials, bounded across the fields?

Hussein finished my thoughts. "Because you are crazy!" he laughed. "You are the first woman I know to come alone to Grozny. Crazy woman!"

I smiled. "As crazy as this place?"

He shook his head sadly, his eyes sliding over every bullet-riddled wall, every burnt-out building, every wild-eyed child scurrying past sandbags and submachine guns. "Nothing," he said. "Nothing is as crazy as this."

Tamara Sheward lives in Far North Queensland, Australia. In addition to being a traveler and journalist, she has tried stints at being a toy spider salesman, Guinness packer, slum lord's subordinate, Rugby World Cup streaker, and smut peddler. She is the author of Bad Karma: Confessions of a Reckless Traveller in South-East Asia.

* ✲ *

Pumpkin

Were they an odd couple or just odd?

FLYING TO INDIA SEEMS NOT A TRIP FOR THE WEARY. I feel some anxiety, as I am not the best long-distance traveler. I wonder if this trip might be different, somehow. I had many difficult things happening in my life and I thought a trip to India might allow some quiet from the noise in my head. I was teased by many about my lack of tolerance to spices outside of cinnamon. Everyone had ideas to make this trip pleasurable. The idea to bring a lot of my own food was a good one. Unfortunately, I ate most of that while flying over Cleveland.

It's not that I'm afraid of the spices of India, and it's not that I am a bad traveler. I like to think of it as being *sensitive* to the environment. Not everyone is born with intestinal fortitude. Some of us just got good looks and a poor digestive situation. O.K., some of us didn't get either of those. I was just trying to stay positive.

Now I am on the plane to Amsterdam, with my eyes closed, thinking positively about the next eight hours. We have not yet taken off so I am trying to get into some groove. As time passes no one comes to sit next to me. The flight attendants are doing their pre-flight routine, and seemingly people have stopped boarding. Can this really be? I would get two seats to Amsterdam to myself? I am almost giddy, practically singing out loud. Sadly the only song that comes to me is "Delta Dawn." (I don't understand this either.) So, I'm smiling, I'm humming, I may even be doing a little two-step under my seat. The doors are nearly closed…when I see a man come toward me. My head quickly starts to spin around, with no less intensity than Regan in *The Exorcist*. I now have this mood swing from pure joy and amusement to anguish and torment.

He is clearly coming to sit by me. It is clear. The problem is I'm on the aisle; he is about six-foot-four, husky, in his fifties. It's not looking pretty for him or me. I give him a big smile, he says, "Sorry." I say, " About what? Are you apologizing ahead of time for stealing my food?" He says, "No, I just think we're going to be a little tight." I say, "It's fine, look I'm small." Well, that may not be true, but I could be playing shortstop for the Red Sox and still seem small compared to him. But I say, "You sit on the aisle, that will help a little." So he sits there, we chat a little, plane takes off, and he is getting squished. I see some perspiration on his forehead. So after like an hour, I say, "Let's put the arm up, that will give you more room." He protests (but not really) and he lets out this sigh of relief.

So there we are in our little love seat together on our way to Amsterdam. We share names, little work stuff, family, and it's all quite pleasant. About two hours into it, I call him Phil. He says, "Actually Donna, I prefer to be called Phillip." I start to laugh and say, "Phil, this is a helluva time to be so sensitive. Quite frankly in about thirty minutes I'm bound to start calling you Pumpkin, cuz if we were sitting any closer we'd be sharing a mortgage." He stares at me for about ten long seconds, breaks into this huge grin, and says, "Well, I'd prefer Pumpkin to Phil or Phillip." Then Pumpkin it is. I find out that Pumpkin doesn't travel a lot internationally, and had been dreading this trip for weeks. Because of his size, he says he seems to make enemies quickly on planes. I tell him I love that he is big, I am sure we'll get extra food thrown our way. Extra everything, pillows, blankets. He laughs and says he has not thought of it this way. I tell him I assume everything that comes his way is going to be shared with me 50/50. "Absolutely," he says. And so it comes.

I tell him I think the extra perspiration on his head will bode well for us. Don't dab it off so much. Flight attendants might be worried about him and that will give us a fair amount of attention. I suggest that when they are near that perhaps we should talk loudly about his "recent" bout with tachycardia or hypoglycemia or something meaty but not fatal. And so we do. Of course, we laugh the whole time, given that neither of us knows anything about either one of those illnesses. We go in and out of conversation like every *couple,* I guess. Oh, that's right, we just met. As the idea of sleeping comes to all of us I ask Pumpkin if I can sleep on his arm. Of course he says yes. So I sleep for the first time ever on an international flight. I wake up about four hours later shockingly refreshed.

He's gone to the bathroom, and the flight attendant comes up and asks what I and my husband would like: "Coffee, tea?"

"Hmmmm," I say, "I *think* my husband would like coffee."

"Cream?"

"Hmmmm. Yes, cream, too."

"Sugar?"

"Hmmmm. No, we're trying to cut down." I go on for a second about his past health problems, and we had made a promise to each other to decrease our sugar consumption. So Pumpkin comes back and informs me he isn't a coffee drinker. Well, of course, I am shocked, almost hurt, but say, "See how well we're communicating? People wonder why we've been together so long, it's all about the honesty. You tell me what you need, I tell you what I need. It's fabulous."

> A vulture boards an airplane carrying two dead raccoons. The stewardess looks at him and says, "I'm sorry, sir, only one carrion allowed per passenger."
>
> ♦
>
> —International Pun Contest

He says, "Donna, I don't think I've ever had a flight like this in my life." Then he says, "My wife would never believe this, and probably wouldn't like it." I ask why. He says, "Well you're a pretty woman who shared a seat with me and ended up calling me Pumpkin, which I like."

"Oh, it will be fine. Just tell her I'm a lesbian. That always helps."

He says in shock, "You're a lesbian?"

"Well yes I am."

"But you don't seem like one, and you're so pretty."

"Oh honey, do you want to re-think that like really quickly? What do lesbians seem like exactly? And quite frankly, lesbians are good-looking girls."

He looks at me horrified, and says, "I didn't mean to offend you."

"If you told me you were voting for George Bush, now

that would offend me. What the other comment tells me is you need to get out of the damn suburbs and meet some other people. I'd show you my lesbian membership card but it's packed away with my pistachios. Didn't the sensible shoes give me away?" Well, all those references were lost on my guy. But then he turns to me and says, "I guess I am not as forward thinking as I like to give myself credit for."

I can't believe the potential of the conversation as well as the timing as they announce that we are getting ready to land. I say, "We all fall into assumptions and stereotypes. For in-stance, I just assume that everyone is gay unless I'm told otherwise...and I am so surprised you are married to a *woman*." He loves that, and says "Touché." We sit quietly through the landing both thinking: *What just happened on this plane*? He helps me get my carry-on out of the overhead, and we proceed to get off the plane. We walk quietly down the hall, and get to the point where it is clear we are now going to walk in different directions. He looks and smiles at me; I say, "*Ciao* Pumpkin." He leans way down and we embrace. He says, "Thank you." I say, "No, thank you." He turns and walks off slowly, I get a little misty-eyed and head for Bombay.

Donna DiMenna did stand-up comedy before spending a small fortune to attend grad school and becoming a psychologist. Her private practice was short-lived, as she found her clientele was just too depressing. She turned to consulting at a global HR firm which allows her to travel, and began a sideline as a writer. She lives in St. Paul, Minnesota.

✳

A woman called and asked, "Do airlines put your physical descrip-tion on your bag so that they know whose luggage belongs to who?"

I said, "No, why do you ask?"

She replied, "Well, when I checked in with the airline, they put a tag on my luggage that said FAT, and I'm overweight. Is there any connection?"

After putting her on hold for a minute while I "looked into it" (I was actually laughing), I came back and explained that the city code for Fresno is FAT, and that the airline was just putting a destination tag on her luggage.

—Anonymous travel agent

SUSAN ORLEAN

* *

Skymalling

It's retail therapy with altitude.

ONE CHARACTERISTIC OF THE SKYMALL CUSTOMER
seems to be an excess of body hair. In fact, as you leaf
through the hundred or so pages of the Skymall catalog, you
begin to suspect that its customers have luxuriant growth
everywhere, sprouting out of their noses, ears, cheeks, legs,
underarms, and what is always delicately referred to as "the
bikini area." In the world of Skymall, though, hirsutism is
not an obstacle: It is a challenging and market-exploitable
opportunity, with exciting products attached to it. Just look
at last summer's issue of the catalog. On page 23, you are offered the Turbo-Groomer 5.0, with superior Swiss surgical
stainless-steel blades, for those hard-to-reach nose and ear
hairs; on page 42, the immersible long-use travel shaver, for
hair removal underwater; on page 74, the Igia Forever Gone
Plus, "the permanent solution to hair removal;" on page 81,
the Discrette Plus by Epilady, which announces itself as
"Always one step ahead in hair removal." There are also line
extension hair-removal associated products, such as Chrome-
Plated Fog-Free Shower Mirror and the AM/FM Shower

43

Radio with Lighted Mirror, which allows you to listen to traffic reports while you shower and shave, satisfying another Skymall trait, the desire to do more than one thing at a time, especially if one of the things you're doing is removing hair. I never used to think about hairiness when I flew, but then I began to read Skymall regularly, and as a result, much of my air time is now devoted to wondering if I have too much hair, and, if I do, what system I should use to get rid of it. I also wonder, persistently, whether or not I should at least surrender and order myself a solar-powered cascade fountain or a jewelry organizer with sixty-six pockets or a Pop-Up Hot Dog Cooker—three Skymall items I have thought about buying time after high-flying time. I have dog-eared enough copies of Skymall to fill a kennel. I fly all the time, and even on those overscheduled days when I fly somewhere in the morning and somewhere else in the afternoon, I always pull Skymall out of the seat pocket and browse through it, savoring each and every brass guest towel holder and hand-painted Russian balalaika and foldaway closet ladder and pocket pepper mill. For me, Skymall is the land of products I never think I want, serving needs I never thought I had, and which I can't quite bring myself to buy but can't help considering once they have been brought to my attention.

Skymall is a weird entity. It is a go-between that packages other mail-order companies and offers them in a virtual shopping mall in the virtual megalopolis of the sky. In the trade it is known as a "multi-channel specialty retailer." It actually has no products of its own: It doesn't produce anything or manufacture anything or even customize anything it offers for sale. Its closest precedent is probably the Yankee Peddler. Skymall is offered in some hotel rooms and airport lounges and on some Amtrak trains, but its singular and fundamental microenvironment is the airline seat pocket—that grimy pouch sagging from the seat back, where it is tucked between the evacuation-slide instruction card and the airsickness bag and whatever previous travelers' rubbish the ground crew failed to clean out. Skymall debuted in 1990. It is now distributed in nineteen airlines, including American, Delta, Southwest, United, Continental, and Alaska. More than five hundred million air travelers see the catalog every year; its sales in 2000 were a whopping 62.5 million dollars—that's 62.5 million dollars' worth of garden toad ornaments and FM radio/ballpoint pens and Old Fashioned Nachos & Cheese Makers, ordered, in a few instances, from the Skymall website but in most cases purchased while at the comfortable cruising altitude of 35,000 feet. According to a company spokesperson, the founder of Skymall, Robert Worsley, came up with the concept of the catalog when he was on a flight and noticed how bored passengers were. In the words of the corporate legend, Worsley "decided to start a business that would alleviate the boredom factor and give passengers something useful to do with their time." Skymall gobbled up another in-flight catalog along the way and then was in turn gobbled up by Gemstar-TV Guide International in 2001. The Skymall vision, though, has remained the same from the day the company began. "Passengers tell us they think we have something for everyone," the spokesperson e-mailed me recently. "Their reaction to products in the catalog range from 'Wow! That's something cool that I must have!' to "Who on earth would buy that?'"

I began reading Skymall during a period in my life when I had developed a ferocious fear of flying. Because of the itinerant nature of my work, I have to travel all the time, regardless of the state of my nerves. Like all sissy fliers, I gorged compulsively on airplane disaster news, became fluent in traffic controller lingo, and developed a self-taught genius in diagnosing aircraft thumps and rattles. During takeoffs and landings, in particular, I was very busy assisting the pilot. At the same time, of course, I was scared witless and needed to distract myself or I would have jumped out the emergency exit. There were also a few unfortunate episodes of me clawing the arm of the stranger in the next seat when I thought the plane was moments from hurtling out of control. I always carried dozens of magazines and books with me, but honestly, who can concentrate on reading when at any moment she might be called upon to pull a 767-200 jumbo jet out of a nosedive? No, the reading I wanted to do during my flying phobia days was not actual reading: I just wanted to flip through something, the pages sticking slightly to my clammy hands, while running my eyeballs over text. This is how I discovered, and grew to deeply love, Skymall.

My discomfort in the air reached its peak—or was its nadir?—on a flight between Cleveland and New York some time ago. In addition to pawing through Skymall, I often tried to calm myself by jabbering to my seatmates, and on this particular flight I was next to an older gentleman who told me that he was a magazine publisher. Pay dirt! I was just starting my writing career, so I considered the chance to schmooze a real live publisher a major opportunity—major enough for me to put aside my Skymall completely and focus on cultivating my bit of good fortune. Things were, in fact, going very nicely. The gentleman told me that his magazine was distributed all over the United States and was published in scores of languages as well. He even suggested that I come by the office and meet the staff. I was so excited and so afraid of looking too eager that I didn't dare ask him the name of the magazine. Then, somewhere over Altoona, we hit what felt like an air trampoline. I say this not as the sissy

I was then but as the flying strongman I am now: It was really wild turbulence, with service carts clattering down the aisle, overhead compartments flapping open, flight attendants tumbling like tenpins. In the midst of the commotion, my seatmate/future editor/publisher swiveled to face me. "Susan, are you ready to meet your Maker?" he gasped. "Have you accepted Jesus Christ as your personal savior?" Well, I wasn't, and I hadn't, and I twisted away from him, fumbling in the seat pocket to find my lucky Skymall and silently repeating nonsense verse to drown out the sound of his prayers. At last, the plane stopped bucking, and we wafted uneventfully down toward New York and onto the runway. At this point my neck was practically dislocated from craning it away from my seatmate, but he still managed to push his business card into my very sweaty hand before we got off the plane. "I do hope you'll come visit," he said sweetly. "I think you'll find that the *Watchtower* is a wonderful magazine."

Right after that ride, I signed up with a hypnotist and got myself bedazzled into thinking airplane rides were fun—or, at the very least, nonlethal. It worked, and I soon abandoned most of my flying anxiety behavior, but my attachment to Skymall endured. What had started as a palliative had become a passion. Mostly I found myself a little obsessed with the idea of the Skymall customer—the person the catalog evoked. Even when catalogs don't include pictures of people with the products, they do bring to mind a particular individual: they really need to, since there is no salesperson at your elbow giving you the narrative that all retail experiences imply—the story of who you are and who you will be by acquiring a particular item. I can decode a lot of other catalog personas, such as, say the horny trust funders of Abercrombie & Fitch; the nerd-ball pipe-smoking Levenger guy; the swingers who live and die by

Design Within Reach. But Skymall? Who was this person that Skymall described.

Well, there's the hairiness, as I mentioned previously. In fact despite those bikini-area shavers, I would say that there is, overall a distinctly masculine aura in the catalog. Skymall man is a businessperson—maybe a middle-level database administrator or regional field sales trainer. He lives in a house and has a backyard. He is the intrepid traveler but is afraid of fire (for which Skymall provides smoke hoods and fire escape ladders), insects (no problem: he can use the Bug Cap to protect his face and neck, or better still, the Keep Your Distance Insect Vacuum), and germs (besides the Daisy-Lift toilet-seat lifter, Skymall offers vibrating tongue cleaners, ultra miniature personal air purifiers, and bacteria-resistant utensils—"Your old wooden cooking spoon may be teeming with bacteria—replace it with the new-tech ExoGlass Spoon!"). The Skymall man also worries about driveway alert systems, and a listening device detector— "Find Out Who's Eavesdropping on You!") and mean dogs, who, thank goodness, can be stopped in their tracks up to fifty feet away using Dog Off, a great gift for joggers, walkers, repairmen, and postal delivery people." (Just one question: Are we supposed to be giving gifts to repairmen these days? Maybe Skymall men are raising the generosity bar.)

Mean dogs aside, the Skymall man is a pet lover, forking over a fortune for automatic pet dishes, deluxe dog beds, ramps to help older dogs into cars, wheelie bags for pet transportation, and most touchingly, pet headstones made of Vermont slate. (Skymall also features a garden stone of composite granite, cement, and resin with a prewritten "sentiment" of either "My Beloved Pet" or a four-line farewell that is generic enough to use for either a pet or a human buried in the backyard.) The Skymall man likes a drink. He appreciates the value of having a martini atomizer and a Barmaster Electronic Mixing Assistant ("It's the PDA of the Cocktail Circuit") close at hand, as well as, appropriately enough, two different digital Breathalyzers. He likes to barbecue (see the array of tools and grills and even the personal steak-branding iron with up to three initials, "to show your guests the pride you take in a great barbecue!"). But, as much as he likes to be the boss of the backyard grill, he likes to relax while doing it, which he can do once he orders the Remote Cooking Thermometer, which allows him to sit inside and, say, practice his golf game on the amazing Divot Matt until the remote alarm beeps to let him know that his personally branded steaks are ready.

Commitment to utter laziness is another signature Skymall attribute. The Skymall man may make gestures of activity by purchasing the appurtenances of the sporting life (digital golf scopes, electronic fish finders, and a luxuriously padded, synthetic leather motorcycle-seat bar stool, which is particularly desirable, since it is both a sport-related item and a drinking necessity), but the quintessential Skymall sport product may be the ExcerCHIzer. "If regular aerobic exercise is too strenuous, try the ExcerCHIzer for health, fitness, and stress reduction!" the catalog suggests, explaining that the device "helps you perform vital aerobic exercises with minimal effort."

Skymall does celebrate items that perform more than one task at a time—for example, the binoculars that are also a camera, or the Fire & Ice Grill, which is both a barbecue and a cooler, or the world's first digital camera/recorder/PDA stylus pen—but it really exalts in the single-function product, the thing that does one thing and one thing only and is wholly useless otherwise. It's a bold move to tout products like battery-operated automatic eyeglass cleaners and

five-foot-tall popcorn poppers when doctrines like volun-
tary simplicity, arguing that we could live very well with one
blanket, one frying pan, and a knife, are in vogue. What kind
of house could accommodate not only a five-foot-tall popcorn popper, but also a carnival-style snow-cone maker and
soft-serve ice-cream maker, and the Old Fashioned Carnival
Cotton Candy Maker, and the Nachos & Cheese Maker, and
the plastic salad-bar set (The Mother of All Salad Bars!)? Is
it the biggest house in the known universe? Does it have a
storage room just for makers of specific foods? Does Skymall
represent the ultimate in human ingenuity—the ability to
devise a machine that makes cotton candy—or is it address-
ing our lack of ingenuity in not being able to figure out a
way to make cotton candy ourselves?

I am not totally immune to Skymall's beckonings. I once
bought a little handheld scanner after seeing it in the catalog, and fell for not one but two sets of vacuum-sealed storage bags that were going to banish forever—or at least
compress—the clutter in my closets. And this Christmas, at
last, my husband got me a Pop-Up Hot-Dog Cooker. I used
the scanner approximately once; the vacuum bags just added
to my closet clutter. The hot-dog cooker will probably get a
brief work out and then be retired, first to my even more
cluttered closet and then to my neighborhood Goodwill
collection center. This is perhaps proof that the ultimate, best
product of Skymall is Skymall itself—this document of the
misbegotten inventiveness of humankind; the magical thinking that leads us to believe that some material item, however
nutty it is, will improve our existence; and the heartwarm-
ing, affirming fact that we humans are the only life force that
would—or could—conceive of, market, and purchase goods
such as French Maid toilet paper holders, talking Christmas
ornaments, dryer vent brushes, Tan Thru bathing suits, CD

Shredders, World's Largest Write-on Map Murals, and personal neck-mounted cooling systems. In the words of another Skymall product—those framed instructional thought inducers, known in Skymallese as Inspirational Artwork That Shares Your Values—this takes CHARACTER (aluminum or wood framed), EXCELLENCE (double matted), and the ESSENCE OF LEADERSHIP. Or you can just—wood framed and double matted—DREAM.

Susan Orlean is the author of The Orchid Thief, The Bullfighter Checks Her Makeup, Saturday Night, *and* My Kind of Place, *from which this story was excerpted. She has been a staff writer at* The New Yorker *since 1992 and her articles have also appeared in* Outside, Rolling Stone, Vogue, *and* Esquire. *She lives in New York.*

. * .

Birthday Boy

The author devises a very special day for himself.

IT WAS NEARING 3 A.M. WHEN THERE WAS A QUIET, almost apologetic knock at the door of my guesthouse room. I knew what it was all about—I think everybody in the hotel knew what it was all about. The fact was that I was not a discreet puker. When I got sick, I had the embarrassing tendency to shriek like a pterodactyl, and that drew a fair amount of attention from anybody within about a two-mile radius. I have to believe that Americans with food poisoning were nothing new to the good people at the Haveli Guest House in Jodhpur, India; I imagine, however, that the staff was more accustomed to pressing one ear against the door to listen for the telltale sounds of a guest with stomach trouble, rather than, say, sandbagging the door and draping the corridor in yellow caution tape.

Clinging to a toilet for twenty-four hours has a way of screwing up one's best-laid plans. Just a few weeks into my solo round-the-world tour, I would be turning thirty, and I was determined to be somewhere memorable to mark this occasion. I had selected the Taj Mahal based on the fact that most Americans had actually heard of it and that it sounded interesting enough that it might distract attention from the fact that I was alone on my birthday.

A bad bowl of fish curry had changed all that. Now, according to my calculations, I would be in the tiny desert town of Jaisalmer, India in far western Rajasthan, and I was pretty sure that nobody had heard of that. People would likely assume that I had simply made up a place on the far side of the world to cover the fact that I was sitting alone in my apartment eating Apple Jacks out of the box.

In a potential saving grace, it seemed that Jaisalmer was famous for camel safaris. This sounded, if not exactly appealing, at least exotic. On the other side of the coin, however, reports on camel safaris from returning backpackers seemed to be decidedly less than enthusiastic. Travelers spoke of the event in the same halting voice that they might speak of surviving a multi-car pile up on the freeway: stunned disbelief, gaps in their memory, and abrupt adjective-dominated sentences ("hot...painful...fetid...").

"Still, pretty cool to ride a camel, huh?" I would offer hopefully, quickly mentioning that I was already committed to spending my birthday in this fashion in hopes of softening the response and encouraging them to find the positive. It seldom worked. It was as if I had enthusiastically proclaimed my intention of spending my birthday licking dog shit off the sidewalk. Worse, it only served to announce the fact that I would be spending my birthday alone, my only hope of companionship being to hire a beast of burden and riding it around.

Thus it was that on the last morning of my twenties, the other four souls who would be going on the camel safari and I met up at the local German bakery in Jaisalmer. (The ubiquitous "German bakery" is one of India's great mysteries. How Germany managed to swoop into a country of 1 billion and claim credit for the croissant, I'll never understand.) The group consisted of two French Canadians, a brother and sister named Justin and Marianne, one Israeli named Shlomi, and me. It took us about forty-five minutes in a jeep to get to where we would start the safari, of which I spent the first twenty-five dropping atomic hints regarding my birthday until I finally had to coyly admit that I was, in fact, turning thirty the next day. And how embarrassing that everybody knew!

Less than an hour from Jaisalmer we were piling off the jeep and onto our respective camels. (My camel's name was apparently Sandy. It occurs to me now that maybe they were all named Sandy.) We started off all excited and asking the camel drivers all kinds of questions, until Marianne asked what the camels were constantly chewing on.

"Their own vomit," he answered matter-of-factly. That put an end to the Q&A for a while.

With nobody talking anymore, it was dead quiet out there in the desert—one was left alone with one's own thoughts. My thoughts that morning mostly focused on trying to come up with another time in my life when I had been this uncomfortable. The heat was astonishing—the last time I had felt heat like this was when I was an eight-year-old fat kid and fell onto a campfire trying to retrieve a marshmallow. In addition, my legs, straddling Sandy's broad back, were being torn apart like the wishbone of a Thanksgiving turkey. To add further insult to my misery, my camel was third in the line, meaning that I was caught in the flatulent slipstream of the two lead camels. My brain was reviewing the emergency evacuation procedures through the ear canal should things get much worse.

An impossibly long two hours later, we came to a halt. Our camel driver unhooked the chain of camels, handed Sandy's reins to me, and informed me I would be controlling him from here on out. I believe I replied, "I don't think so," not as a matter of defiance, but more as a simple prediction. Camels are, after all, just about the weirdest domesticated animal on the planet—riding one feels about as natural as strapping a saddle on a giraffe. To make matters worse, Sandy was not happy about this transfer of power, and took the opportunity to voice his displeasure.

Let me just say that I had always expected camels, in keeping with their comical appearance, to make a noise like a cute variation of a farm animal. So when Sandy opened his mouth, I expected to hear some kind of yodeling moo or a maybe a sweet trilling *baaa*.

Camels do not make this kind of noise. They make the kind of noise that you will be familiar with if you have seen the T-Rex scenes from *Jurassic Park* and had your ear pressed against the speaker. It sounds less like a child's barnyard animal toy and more like the last sound a person would ever hear before losing a torso. And this is whom I would be spending my birthday with.

Nevertheless, I now had the reins of this ridiculous beast. And much to my surprise, Sandy did exactly what I wanted him to do, which was basically to not whirl his neck around and projectile vomit in my face. In fact, after a while, the whole thing was like riding a bike—specifically, an eight-foot-tall bike with exploding square tires that had been dipped in camel vomit. After a while, controlling him was a breeze, especially if you wanted to go exactly where he wanted to go, which I did.

In the late afternoon, we arrived at an area of massive Sahara-style sand dunes, maybe a couple hundred meters long by a hundred meters wide, just sitting in the middle of the landscape as if it had been poured from the sky. In the late afternoon sun it looked like billowing silk, the finest and softest sand you can imagine, and from there we watched the sunset and ate dinner.

It was the first real chance for Justin, Marianne, Shlomi, and me to talk to each other. We quickly discovered that we had almost nothing in common, and yet it was exactly because of that that we got along so well. It is a fascinating thing to meet people who lead absolutely different lives and learn about how they came to live those lives. When the campfire took its last quiet breaths, we laid out our blankets on the top of the highest sand dune and stared at the star-studded night, all wrapped up in the pale band of the Milky Way like a Christmas ribbon.

I woke up just before sunrise on October 24th, just as the sky started to glow a faint blue in the east, gradually rinsing away the stars until the sun blazed up over the dunes. It began to heat up quickly after a surprisingly cold night.

It was now my birthday. I was thirty years old, and my friends and family were thousands of miles away. Still, it was a nice thing to be wished a happy birthday by people I barely knew, albeit after I had dropped some more subtle hints (i.e., "It's my birthday today…remember I told you? In the jeep?"). My day with Sandy, however, could have started off better. As it turned out, the sand dunes on which we slept were too steep to ride our camels down, so we had to lead them down. I started down the steep dunes, but found it was difficult to navigate. To compensate, I started taking large loping steps, in order to get down faster and stay upright.

It did not occur to me that this technique would not play to Sandy's strengths as an awkwardly designed quadruped.

He did not have much of a choice, however, since I was pulling him down, oblivious to his distress. I paused because I felt a curious gust of putrid wind on the back of my neck, and stopped to turn around.

Camels are not small animals—they tend to measure about seven or eight feet tall and weigh up to 1,500 pounds. They are built for survival, going for weeks at a time without water in an unforgiving environment. They are not given to prancing gracefully down a hill any more than they could skim across the water like a trained dolphin. When I stopped to turn around, I was so close to this beast barreling down on me that his face actually butted my head.

It was a terrifying sight. I thought I was going to die, crushed under this terrific weight, and I did not want to die. Moreover, I sure as hell didn't want to die like *this*, on my thirtieth birthday in India, in a manner likely to make international headlines that spawned terms like "camelanche" and employed the word "pancake" as a verb.

In retrospect, of course, the smart thing to do would have been to stop. I was not about to stop. Humans did not get this far up the evolutionary ladder by simply stopping in front of 1,500 pounds of out-of-control camel flesh. So I gripped those reins tighter and tried to zigzag out of the path of destruction, which of course only pulled this camel along with me. At every swerve, I caught a glimpse of Sandy, legs splayed out in four separate directions like a "Slippery When Wet" sign for camels. I could see the camel drivers calling at me to do something, but it was drowned out by the terrified ear-splitting guttural roar coming from two feet behind me.

How this looked to others, I cannot be sure. I do know that when we reached solid ground, Sandy's eyes blazing wildly, my companions were doubled over in laughter. I didn't care—I decided that the gift of life, the freedom from a horribly gruesome and unbearably embarrassing death, was my first birthday present of the day.

From that point on, quite unexpectedly, things began to improve. For Sandy and me, I think that brush with death (mine) served to bring us closer. He and I got along just fine after that. In fact, more often than not, we took the lead in front of the other camels. Sandy was in his element now. By that afternoon, we had hit a wide, flat expanse of desert, and the two camel drivers called up and asked us if we wanted to race.

"Race? Race what?" asked Marianne.

"I think he means the camels—race the camels," Shlomi responded.

"He can't mean race the camels—what would we do, just wait here for them to come back?" said Marianne, looking into the distance.

"He means with us on top, Marianne," said Justin. "We'd race them. You know? Like a race?"

"Ah. I see. No, I don't want to do that."

"Me neither," I chimed in.

"Yeah, there's no way," Justin started. "My legs feel like they're being…"

"O.K.!" Shlomi called over to the camel guys. "Yes, we want to race!"

So with that funny brand of Israeli democracy deciding our fate, and a few loud wild clicking noises from the camel drivers, we were off, four of us in a line, racing across the desert.

It turned out to be a thrilling experience, despite the uncanny sensation of somebody shoving a chainsaw up your ass. But here's what counts: Sandy and I, we won that race. You could argue that the others let me win, but that would be assuming two impossibilities: 1) that they had any control at all over those beasts, and 2) that they even remembered it was my birthday. I celebrated our victory by patting Sandy on the head.

We stopped for the night on another set of sand dunes, and for the first time in my life, I watched the sun rise and set on the same day. One of the camel drivers had taken off, reappearing about four hours later, just in time for dinner. As usual, they cooked up a nice feast for us over an open fire under the stars, with one difference: at the end of the meal, he brought out one more thing that they had cooked and handed it to me. I looked up to see Shlomi, Justin, and Marianne wearing excited grins.

"What is this?" I asked him.

"Birthday cake!" said our camel driver with a huge smile.

It turned out he had been informed by the others that it was my birthday, and they had chipped in to buy butter, a very expensive commodity in the desert, and quietly bribed him to ride two hours across the desert to a village where he could buy it. "It's a surprise party!" Justin explained, handing me a Fanta.

I took a bite of that cake thing. Whatever it was, it sure wasn't cake—but at least it tasted far better than it looked. The taste, however, was far less important than what these guys had done for me, knowing me less than two days.

And then they all sang "Happy Birthday" in every language they knew, and once again we laid out next to each other on the top of the dunes, huddled together for warmth. One by one the others fell asleep, but I didn't want this night to end just yet. So I lay there on my back in the desert of western India, gazing up at the endless night sky, that magical moment when you are looking at everything and nothing at the same instant, and wondered how anybody could feel insignificant with friends so close by you can hear them breathing.

Conor Grennan is an American who spent eight years after university living in Prague and Brussels, where he worked in the field of international public policy. He quit in 2004 to travel the world so that he would have something to talk about at parties. He writes far too much, as evidenced by his ongoing round-the-world travel blog, located at tblogs.bootsnall.com/conor.

* ✳ *

Total Immersion

How a quiet expatriate became
the life of the party.

I HAD BEEN LIVING IN PUERTO VALLARTA FOR ALMOST three months and was, like many new arrivals, feeling somewhat frustrated by my inability to connect with the local culture. Part of the problem was my lack of language skills. Because I was unable to communicate with the many marvelous Mexicans I met, most of my new friends were turning out to be Americans and Canadians whose greatest concern was how many English language channels they could receive with the illegal black boxes attached to their satellite dishes. My wife, to whom I expressed this frustration on a daily basis, counseled me to be patient, that opportunity would soon knock.

And knock it did, in the form of an invitation to attend a wedding in the tiny pueblo of Las Gardenias, some two-and-a-half hours north of Vallarta. "It's kind of rustic out there," Lucy warned me. "Are you sure you want to go?"

"Are you kidding?" I cried gleefully. "This is what I've been waiting for: a chance to totally immerse myself in Mexican culture!"

Las Gardenias was little more than a long dirt road dotted with shacks. But despite its simplicity it possessed, for me at least, a great deal of charm. Chickens, pigs, dogs, and burros wandered the village freely, while an abundance of banana and palm trees gave the place a lush, tropical air. As we pulled up to the tiny adobe-walled church, I felt as if we had entered an enchanted dream, as if we had gone back in time to a more pure, more innocent era.

The interior of the church was heartbreakingly humble: dirt floor, a patched-together roof, unadorned walls, and no pews. But it was packed to bursting with chattering people, bouquets of colorful flowers, and a quintet of confused doves, who had flown in through a hole in the roof and couldn't find their way out again.

Since the poor church contained no furniture of its own, everyone had brought wooden folding chairs from their homes. By the time we'd arrived all of these chairs were occupied, including several pairs which had been placed before the altar. Standing between these last chairs were Paco and Eva, the bride and groom, so small they looked like children. And facing them was the padre, who had just cleared his throat and was about to begin the ceremony.

Our arrival, for some reason, brought everything to a grinding halt. Paco and Eva seemed surprised, even alarmed, by our presence. After consulting briefly with the padre, Paco approached my wife and they held a short conversation in Spanish.

"He wants us to be *padrinos*," she said, turning to me. When I shrugged with incomprehension, she added, "A *padrino* is a godfather."

"You mean, like Marlon Brando?"

A vision flashed briefly before my eyes of a long line of Mexican bakers waiting to kiss my ring, and then asking me to have their neighbors' legs broken.

"Not exactly," Lucy said. "It's a big honor."

"But why us?" I asked. "Why now?" She explained to me that all the available chairs were taken, so Paco wanted to bump two of the *padrinos* out of their exalted seats before the altar in order to make room for us.

"He feels bad about us having to stand up for the whole ceremony," she added.

"That's very nice," I said, touched by the young man's thoughtfulness. "Tell him we accept."

"Being a *padrino* can be expensive," Lucy warned me.

"How expensive?"

"It's hard to say."

"Well," I said, "if it's going to cost more than fifty bucks, tell him we'd rather stand."

In the end, without a plausible excuse for refusing the honor (except that we were too cheap), we graciously accepted Paco's offer.

The ceremony, accompanied by lots of sweet-souled singing from an impromptu chorus, was, despite my inability to understand a single word, beautiful. Babies and very small children crawled freely about on the floor throughout the entire Mass, which gave the proceedings a wonderfully natural and down-to-earth quality. Much to my delight, one child, who had somehow escaped his diapers, even peed on my shoe.

When the ceremony was over, we all walked two blocks down the street to the house of Paco's parents. This, like most homes in Las Gardenias, was really a small *ranchito*, with a fenced-in vegetable garden, a miniature orchard, and small enclosures for the livestock. The entire compound had been gaily decorated with brightly colored strings of *picapapel* (cutout paper squares), balloons, and flowers.

Night had fallen now, and since Las Gardenias lacked electricity, our hosts had been obliged to procure a generator in order to provide illumination, and to power the four enormous speakers stacked up just inside the garden. Unhappily, this generator ran on gasoline and produced, along with the electricity, voluminous clouds of fumes and a sound not unlike that of an outboard motor revving up inside a shower stall.

But the noise from this generator, it turned out, was a mere whisper, like the sound of a feather falling, compared to the awesome, brain-crunching, *unbelievably* loud music which abruptly exploded forth like thunder from the titanic speakers.

The onset of this cacophony was the signal for the start of a series of beautifully quaint and typically Mexican customs. They began with a waltz, the bride and groom moving gracefully around the dusty yard as the several hundred guests applauded wildly. After a while, the couple broke off dancing in order to switch partners. The bride's new partner, after half a minute, took out a bill and pinned it onto her wedding gown. Across the yard, the woman who had been dancing with the groom did the same. Then they departed, to be replaced at once by another couple.

"What in the world is this?" I asked my wife.

"It's the *money dance*," she said. "Everybody takes turns dancing with the bride and groom and pinning money on their clothes."

"You're joking!" I said.

"It's no joke," she said. "No money dance, no honeymoon."

Several minutes later, a woman approached and handed each of us a pin. It was then I noticed that quite a few people were staring at us expectantly. With a heavy heart I fished two twenty-dollar bills out of my wallet and handed one to my wife.

I've always been a spectacularly bad dancer, and when my turn came my ears began to burn with embarrassment. To make matters worse, there was a dramatic height differential to be reckoned with; I am only moderately tall, but the diminutive bride was almost as short as Dustin Hoffman. In order to hold my partner I was therefore forced to stoop grotesquely, making me look like the Hunchback of Notre Dame trying to tie his shoes.

When, after a few seconds of this torture, another man mercifully tapped me on the shoulder, I put the pin through the twenty-dollar bill and attempted to attach it to the dress. But I was never very good with pins. My shaking hand missed the mark entirely and I wound up sticking the tiny bride, who gave out a little yelp. In the end, she plucked the bill from my hand and pinned it on herself, as above the deafening blast of the music could clearly be heard the sound of the entire wedding party laughing uproariously at my ineptitude.

The money dance was followed by a curious ritual in which the groom put on an apron, picked up a broom, and began to dance by himself all around the yard.

"Why is he dancing with a broom?" I shouted into my wife's ear.

"Quiet!" she shouted back. "We're going to miss it."

"Miss what?"

Many of the groom's male friends and relatives gathered around him now, whistling, jeering, and hurling insults. This activity went on for a surprisingly long time. I later learned that the entire business was supposed to symbolize the groom's imminent emasculation—something like a reverse bar mitzvah.

Then, suddenly, the groom swooned melodramatically into the arms of the same group of young men, who proceeded to pick him up and carry his limp body around the yard like a corpse. In the midst of the wild whoops, shouts, and general hysteria which accompanied this puzzling spectacle, I turned to my wife and demanded an explanation.

"Now what are they doing?" I shouted.

"He died," she shouted back.

"I can see that he died," I said. "But what's the point?"

"How should I know?" my wife replied. "What do I look like, an encyclopedia?"

I never did precisely ascertain what this macabre custom was supposed to symbolize, though according to known authorities on the subject, it is in many ways reminiscent of infertility rites performed to this day in certain sections of New Jersey.

But I've forgotten the beer truck incident.

Halfway through the money dance a big beer truck pulled up to the front gate and Paco's father went out to talk to the driver. Then, hat in hand, he approached my wife and me and explained that since we were the *padrinos* of the beer, could we please fork over three hundred thousand pesos (around two hundred dollars at the time), so that he could pay the driver.

"Three hundred thousand pesos," I fumed. "Just to sit in a folding chair!"

"I warned you," my wife said.

"For two hundred dollars, I would've stood in the street," I moaned. "I would have stood on my head!"

In the end, I paid the driver, who gave me a terrible exchange rate, the entire amount in dollars.

With the arrival of the beer and the conclusion of the money dance and the mock funeral, the party really got under way. The lugubrious waltz was replaced by lively Ranchero music and soon everyone was laughing, hollering, and kicking up their heels, and along with them an extraordinary amount of dust. Before long, all the dancers, including my wife and me, were covered from head to toe with a festive film of fine brown powder. But none of us minded in the least; we were having far too much fun.

Then someone handed me a bottle, and in the spirit of the occasion I took a healthy slug. It was *raicilla*, a lighter fluid-like form of homemade liquor. After I got over the near-death experience of it napalming its way to my stomach, I realized that this drano-esque beverage produced a rather pleasant effect. So I sought out the man with the bottle, who seemed to take an instant liking to me, and took another pair of painful pulls.

"That's *raicilla* you're drinking," Lucy cautioned me. "You better take it easy. I don't think they're transplanting duodenums yet."

"Sure, baby, whatever you say," I said, swilling down some more.

As the party progressed, the dust, the fumes from the generator, and the Liquid Plumber I had been imbibing set off a dangerously synergistic reaction in the vicinity of my brain, causing me to partially lose consciousness. As my awareness shriveled to the size of a sunflower seed, the only thought to which I could consistently cling centered on my need to find a bathroom.

Apparently there wasn't one, or else it was hopelessly

occupied. So I sought out my *raicilla* connection, with whom I had now established a strong fraternal bond, and the two of us, utilizing gestures which in other circumstances could have gotten us both arrested, held a short wordless conversation. Raoul—I believe that was his name—seemed to be telling me that I should wander off into the bushes and take care of my necessities there.

Dizzy, disoriented and, not to put too fine a point on it, drunk, I proceeded to do just that. Because I did not want to relieve myself too close to the festivities, I wound up wandering rather far afield, into areas of near-total darkness. Which was how, stumbling about uncertainly, I tripped over a low wooden fence and fell full-length into a pigsty.

For several moments I was unable to determine exactly what had happened to me. I spent this confused time rather unprofitably, I'm afraid, thrashing about in the muck like a beached fish. The pigs, meanwhile, startled by my abrupt entrance into their domain, began to make excited (possibly angry) snorting sounds. Visions of voracious man-eating swine tearing me to pieces flooded my imagination, which, along with the impressively disagreeable odor, impelled me to hurriedly navigate my way out of the pen and back toward the lights and sounds of the party.

Lumbering through the overgrowth, there was no way to ignore the fact that large portions of my person were now covered with what I tried to think of as mud, but knew deep in my heart to be sheer pig slime. This knowledge naturally made me reluctant to rejoin the other guests.

So I circled cautiously around the party's perimeter until I spotted my wife.

"Oh my God!" she said. "What *happened* to you? You look like you've been swimming in pig shit."

"Never mind," I said. "Tell Paco and Irma I got sick. I'll meet you at the car."

At that moment, as my excremental luck would have it, Paco himself came trotting up to inform us that it was time to eat. Then, becoming aware of my unusual appearance, he said, "What happened to him?"

Holding her nose, my wife replied in that strange pinched-nose way, "It looks like he fell into a pigsty."

An utterly horrified expression transformed Paco's handsome young face as, holding his own nose, he grabbed my arm and began to yank me towards his house, nasally sobbing incomprehensible apologies.

"What's he saying?" I asked frantically. "Where's he taking me?"

"He's really upset," my wife said. "He's taking you to the bathroom so you can wash up."

"I don't want to wash up," I cried. "I want to leave."

Just as I was about to break free of Paco's surprisingly strong grip, his father came along, was informed of the situation and immediately grabbed his nose with one hand and my free arm with the other. Together, the two men, continuing to pinch their noses, escorted me forcibly across the yard, with my hysterically laughing wife trailing close behind. All around us, partygoers stopped what they were doing to stare at us with mystified expressions on their faces.

Struggling and cursing in English (which fortunately no one understood), I was dragged into the small house and up to the bathroom door, before which stood a long line of urine-swollen individuals.

One look at me and the entire room full of people broke into unbridled laughter, catcalls, and whistles. "I want to go home," I whimpered.

"Oh, come on, honey," my wife chided me, "you're the life of the party."

Whoever was inside the bathroom was taking an awfully long time. Soon everyone was holding their noses. Then people began to demand that I leave the room. Finally, Paco barged into the bathroom, removed its occupant, who had apparently fallen asleep, and dragged me inside. Lucy and Paco's father squeezed in behind us and secured the door.

With the four of us crowded into the tiny rustic bathroom, it was difficult to breathe and almost impossible to move. Paco, gagging and choking, attempted to wipe off my face with a tiny hand towel. His feeble but valiant efforts succeeded only in clogging both of my nostrils with pig slime. It soon became apparent that, short of stripping me naked in front of a fire hose, there was little that could be done in the way of tidying me up. So I dove for the nearest exit.

Out of the house I ran, through the yard, past tables full of partygoers chewing chicken *mole,* past all of the neighbors in the street who hadn't been invited, but who were having their own party anyway, down the road and up to my car. All along the way I passed astonished-looking people, all of whom began at once to sniff fearfully at the air, certain some environmental catastrophe had befallen their village.

Naturally, a small crowd was gathered around my car, why, I have no idea. In a moment I was joined by my wife who pointed out that it would not be wise in my current state to get inside the car. Then, as the incredulous on-lookers stared with their mouths agape, Lucy dug a pair of large black garbage bags out of the trunk. Poking a hole in the first bag she slipped it over my head. Then, poking two holes in the second bag, so that I would be able to walk, she slipped it over my feet and up to my waist.

"I'll drive," she said.

"Good idea," I said. "I've never driven with both my arms stuck inside a garbage bag before."

Halfway back to Vallarta, small round unidentified objects suddenly began to fly past our car. Then two of them smashed into the windshield and stuck there. Out of the corner of my eye, I noticed a garbage truck racing past us in the opposite direction.

"Pull over!" I screamed.

Parked safely on the side of the road, we inspected the windshield. The objects plastered against the glass turned out to be a pair of tortillas, which had struck our vehicle with a combined velocity of 120 miles an hour. Freeing an arm from the garbage bag, I attempted to peel them off with my fingers. But to no avail: due to the incredible force of the impact the tortillas had just about fused with the glass.

As I stood there prying away with my fingernails, saturated with super-viscous effluent and dressed shoulder to ankle in hefty-sized garbage bags, a federal highway patrolman cruised to a halt behind our car. The policeman climbed cautiously out of his vehicle and approached, hand on holster, to within ten feet of where I was standing.

For a full minute the dismayed policeman stood staring silently at what had to be the first American he'd ever seen up close covered in pig filth and dressed in matching black plastic trash bags. On and on he stared, never uttering a word. Finally, I felt compelled to say something by way of explanation. So I pointed to the windshield and uttered one of the few Spanish words I could pronounce without difficulty.

"Tortillas," I said.

The policeman, apparently concluding that this was not a situation he wished to become involved in, shook his head, climbed back into his patrol car, and sped away.

Having nothing better to do, I resumed clawing away at

the tortillas, while my wife resumed her fit of maniacal laughter.

It took my wife nearly a week to get over her giggling, and the birds in our yard even longer to finally peck away the last remnants of the tortillas from the windshield of our car.

Gil Gevins has lived, worked, and traveled extensively throughout Mexico for the past twenty-two years.

★

All exotic lands have their native traditions. Hawai'i, for example, has its hula dances and luaus. Some places in Mexico have cliff diving. St. Maarten has a time-honored tradition that, for lack of a better term, can be called "jet washing." (I have not actually heard a name for this practice, but jet washing is the kindest I could come up with.)

Here's how it's done: Grab a case of beer, park your car on the road at the end of the airport runway, and wait.

When one of those big 737s comes lumbering down the runway for takeoff with its ear-splitting roar, climb (or stagger) halfway up the barrier fence and hang on for dear life. Experienced jet washers (yes, they brag, as in, "This is my tenth time") wear long shirts, long pants, and hats, which are to protect participants from getting burned, scorched to baldness, or to reduce the scattering of body parts, I assume.

Amateurs and the especially daring climb up the fence when planes are landing (versus when they are taking off), which can be a big mistake, since incoming jets have been known to blow people off the fence, across the road and into the lagoon. (No, I am not making this up.)

In casual conversations and based on personal observations while driving past the airport, I have noticed that the typical jet washer is male (though females in halter tops and very short shorts also participate), under age thirty, or Australian of any age, with a Heineken beer in hand. (Note: St. Maarten is a Dutch colony; hence, the choice of beer, which is very inexpensive here.)

I have not personally heard of any actual deaths from this time-honored tradition, though I was told that a Volkswagen once got tumbled about some.

So, try to picture this from the participant's perspective. Imagine sitting cross-legged on the hood of your car at the end of a runway drinking beer and chatting with other like-minded souls. As a huge jet revs up, rather than run away, you laugh with delight and, with all the others, climb up the barrier fence like a convict making his break. Then, as if participating in a good crucifixion, you cling to the wire as the largest and noisiest machine ever invented in the history of the world comes roaring down the runway heading right for you. (Now picture at the last moment thinking: "My hat? Where's my hat?")

Seems to me that throwing yourself into a volcano in Hawai'i makes more sense; however, I am trying not to be critical or judgmental of local customs and traditions. Still, as my father would say, "What a world! What a world!"

—John R. Ingrisano, "Jet Washing"

TIM CAHILL

* ✳ *

Fear of Floating

He just knows they're down there, waiting...

I HAVE THIS IRRATIONAL FEAR. I DO NOT LIKE SWIMMING in freshwater lakes. Strange, because I am, I think, otherwise free of phobias. I don't mind high places; I've been in the water with all manner of sharks; I drive too fast and once even contradicted my wife in public. Fearless!

Except that I'm scared of swimming in freshwater lakes. This is a dread that proved problematic during my late teenage years, when I worked as a lifeguard at a public beach on a small lake. The setup was no different than what you've seen on Baywatch: guard towers, a sand beach, a line of ropes that mark the swimming area. We made a lot of rescues. You could see children getting into trouble and you'd go get them, and pretty girls swooned at your feet. Still, I didn't let people get too far out, and not because I didn't think I could save them at any distance. No. I did a lot of whistle blowing because I didn't want anyone to get beyond the ropes and out into the lily pads. I sincerely did not want to have to rescue anyone out there. Lily pads creep me out.

Once or twice I had to swim outside the ropes and into the floating green pads in order to save some pygmy or another. I use the word *pygmy* because the distressed swimmers were usually children. In that less politically correct day, my fellow lifeguards and I referred to kids as pygmies. We made up a poem about it, the "Rhyme of the Ancient Pygmy." It had a verse that read: "Pygmies, pygmies everywhere, and every one a dink." We lifeguards called ourselves "sun gods," but actually we were babysitters. If one of the kids drowned, we'd look bad. We endeavored not to let that happen.

So when one of the pygmies was floundering around out beyond the ropes, I leapt down off the stand, ran into the water, and swam out to the potentially drowned person. Stupid pygmy. I felt myself shudder even as I pulled the child's head above water and cradled it under my arm, even as I sidestroked for shore and said things like, "I got you now, don't fight, you're safe, I got you," even as I made those remarks in a calm voice as we'd been taught to do, even then, another part of me was saying, "They're going to get you, they're going to get you now, they're right here." And I felt my body bloom in gooseflesh.

You may reasonably infer that I was a good swimmer. I learned early, before I could walk, in the lakes of Wisconsin, and I didn't become phobic about those lakes until sometime after I was ten. That was the first year I went to camp. In our orientation classes, the camp counselors informed us that the lake before us contained snapping turtles.

Common snapping turtles can be found in shallow waters east of the Rocky Mountains all the way from southern Canada to the Gulf of Mexico. They can live for decades and weigh up to seventy-five pounds. In short, nothing to be scared about—unless you went to the same camp I did.

There, on my first or second day, a counselor held up a greenish-black turtle about the size of his palm. He'd grabbed the creature at the edges of the shell, halfway between head and tail. The thing seemed to be sleeping. The counselor dangled an ordinary pencil before the turtle, and the animal took it, *wham*, like that. There was no movement of the body—everything came from the neck—but the pencil grab was as quick as a snake strike. The pencil broke. Then the counselor said we had another lesson. He picked up a green elm twig, a little thicker than the pencil, and the snapper took the twig in another flashing strike. It wouldn't let go. The counselor carried the twig around, with the turtle dangling tenaciously at the end of the branch, until we got the impression that snappers are the pit bulls of the lakes. They'd snap your finger like a pencil; they'd grab your big toe and never let go.

Worse: This was just a small turtle. The camp counselors had captured a giant snapper for our education and edification. The horror of that turtle's fate troubles my thoughts even today. It was big: The shell on the creature was as large as a manhole cover. (I just walked out of my house and measured the manhole cover in my street: twenty-seven inches across. Big snappers have shells that are up to eighteen inches across. I'd still say this unfortunate animal was manhole-cover-size. He must have been forty years old, about as old as snappers get.)

Having been taught to fear the turtles—this was for our own safety—we were now shown that they were mortal. Counselors roped our turtle up by his hind legs on a high crossbar at the rifle range and fired half a dozen .22 rounds into the blameless creature's head.

The image has haunted my dreams for several decades.

Nevertheless, we, as campers, got our boating badges, we were allowed to row over into the lily pads. I found a need to capture snappers. It was easy enough from the boat: just lift a lily pad. If there was a snapper under it, you could pick him up by the shell, as the counselor had done with the smaller turtle. I'd look the snapper in the eye—I never saw anything there other than total reptilian indifference—then carefully put him back. Perhaps I was trying to apologize to an entire species.

The years went by, and somehow puberty got all mixed up with everything, including snapping turtles, so that I imagined the turtles would take their revenge on my manhood, such as it was. Such as it is. Believe me, this fear has taken a lot of the joy out of skinny dipping.

I am not afraid of snapping turtles. What I fear are *unseen* snapping turtles, coming up from below, to seek their ultimate retribution. Perhaps this is not irrational at all. Maybe it's just damn scary.

Tim Cahill is the author of many books, mostly travel-related, including Hold the Enlightenment, Jaguars Ripped My Flesh, Pecked to Death by Ducks, Pass the Butterworms, *and* Dolphins, *as well as the editor of* Not So Funny When it Happened: The Best of Travel Humor and Misadventure. *Cahill is also the co-author of the Academy Award-nominated IMAX film,* The Living Sea, *as well as the films* Everest *and* Dolphins. *He lives in Montana, and shares his life with Linnea Larson, two dogs, and two cats.*

* * *

Pissing on Dave's Feet

Liquid healing in Polynesia.

IT WASN'T A PISSING CONTEST. WELL, NOT REALLY. BUT I noted my husband's studied stance, feet shoulder-width apart, heels lifting and settling like an NBA player at the line. I watched the subtle movements of his shoulders, hunching then easing as his hands found their position. His head was lowered but then, with a hint of cockiness, he lifted it and looked out to sea. To wait. His entire body emanated confidence. And I felt one thing: penis envy.

Behind me stood a handful of Polynesian locals sporting well-worn shorts and flip-flops, no doubt riveted by the spectacle unfolding on their heretofore peaceful public quay. The tourists had landed. And now four white guys were preparing to piss in chorus (I could almost hear the smiles slipping across the locals' faces behind me) while five white women looked on in fascination, horror, and, yes, envy.

Beyond the quay lolled the humble village of Vaitahu, the largest settlement on the Marquesas' smallest inhabited island, Tahuata. Boxy wooden and concrete houses, which had long ago replaced the naturally air-conditioned homes of thatch, marched up the green valley. In the town's center burst the high red roof of the Catholic church like a flashy stamen on an otherwise unfussy flower. Tonight I would watch men playing *pétanque* on the laned lawn, women gossiping in flowered dresses the likes of Laura Ashley on steroids, and children running and climbing and tumbling like the race of children everywhere.

But for now I stood transfixed on the scorching cement quay; a gray cliff wall blazed to my right, Polynesia lazed behind me, and my determined husband was a blot on this otherwise idyllic tropical bay before me. I breathed in the mixed scent of sea and hibiscus, knowing that a more acrid odor would be rising from the quay. Soon. I stared at my husband's back; he looked down again. I waited for the golden arc to appear between his legs. No arc. His butt cheeks clenched briefly; his knees creased forward. I crossed my arms and tapped my foot and swore I could hear the smiles galloping now across the islanders' faces behind me. And, out of the corner of my eye, I noticed Judy, standing next to me, gripping the top button of her khaki shorts as if to say, *If these boys don't get over their stage fright soon, I'm going to have to SQUAT.* It was then that I knew: I should have paid more attention to Shirley.

"First, you must have impeccable control of your sphincter," Shirley intoned like the matron of a girls' finishing school. The ladies corralled around my sailboat's tiny table had come over, ostensibly, for a game of hearts—an agreeable pastime for sailors anchored off Mexico's Baja peninsula. But no longer was anyone looking at their cards. I lay down my hand—it was a shitty one anyway—and topped off everyone's wine. For this curly-haired, pleasantly plump, middle-aged Canadian mother was about to disclose the art of pissing like a guy.

"O.K., let's start by everyone doing a few Kegels," said Shirley, switching to the voice of an aerobics instructor.

A couple sets of eyebrows went up. "Kegels?" Knowing a thing or two already about the lady's secret workout, I sur-reptitiously changed the CD to something more appropri-ate. Meanwhile, Shirley explained the ins and outs of Kegels with a colorful description of their urinary, natal, and, of course, sexual benefits. Within minutes, five ladies (who'd known each other all of a few weeks) were clenching their eyes shut, throwing their heads back, and singing at the top of their lungs: *Come on and squeeeeeeze me.* Little did the neighbors know it was a sing-along! Five ladies' vaginas were also humming the tune, lip-synching, if you will, to an oldie but a goodie—*Mama's got a squeezebox; Daddy never sleeps at night.*

Our neighbors that night included the Mexican towns-people ashore who, in this acoustically perfect bay, were get-ting their fill of *vocabulario inglés* for the human anatomy. Our talk of penises and pelvises was also broadcasting to our hus-bands playing poker aboard *In The Mood*, a boat whose name we women had clearly taken to heart. Abandoning all pre-tenses of serious card playing, the ladies, aged thirty to sixty, were dealing with what really counts: sex, love, sex, relation-ships, and sex. And now, just when our numerous cups of wine were threatening to runneth our bladders over, we had stum-bled upon a topic that, in our new lives as full-time sailors, affected us each and every day. The politics of pissing at sea.

Why, you ask, would a well-adjusted group of intelli-gent, mature women deign admit to an acute sense of penis envy which, everyone knows, is a Freudian throwback based on deluded theory and unsound research? CLEARLY, YOU HAVE NEVER PEED ON A SMALL SAILBOAT. The stench. The endless manual pumping. The tiny seat that squeezes your ass. The abrasive biodegradable toilet paper that clogs and overflows the toilet despite unhygienic rationing. And worse, the calisthenics of pissing while sailing—on the tilt—trying to predict the next swell…the slosh of the bowl…WHOOPS!…the douche.

It is for these reasons—and others too unsavory to mention—that men, instead of pissing *on* a boat, choose to piss *off* a boat, over the side, standing up. (Though sometimes, admittedly, they miscalculate wind direction and get a WHOOPS of their own.) So, when Shirley said she had to go pee, and I apologized preemptively for our toilet's stench, and she said, "No problem, I'll piss over the side"—the discarding stopped and the disclosing began.

"The next step," Shirley continued brightly as though imparting a new tuna recipe or a trick for getting stains out of cockpit cushions, "is mastering the appropriate stance." She slid out of her seat into the boat's narrow aisle, turned and planted her feet wide. "It's all about the pelvic tilt." Shirley gripped the edge of the table and leaned back like a kid on a playground merry-go-round or a stripper on a pole. Bumping her ass on the oven door in the process (my boat is small, Shirley's backside less so) she squealed. Then added, "Now, watch my pelvis."

It's true that as Shirley bent her knees, rocked back on her heels, and tucked in her buns, her pelvis tilted skyward. But, from my vantage point, sitting next to where she was standing, all my mind could register were Shirley's butt cheeks clenching, her snug jeans shorts puckering and climbing her crack. Shirley's blue ass now resembled the top lip of an old lady's pursed mouth.

It was at that unfortunate moment that Shirley chose to toss her head back and crow, "Russ thinks it's AMAZING I can piss over the side. He says it turns him ON!"

At this, the dam of women's voices broke. Shrieks of laughter and shouts of disbelief flooded *Dragonfly's* cabin and overflowed the bay. Shirley kept her ground (still gripping the edge of the table), maintaining that learning to piss standing up was a boon to one's sex life. Our bosoms heaved, our heads shook, our eyes watered. Seeing she was losing credibility, Shirley tried to restore order with a sensible discussion of attire—skirts were best, she said, but panties and loose shorts could be hitched over to one side to make way for the urinary stream. Shirley's audience, however, still marveling over her kinky revelation, was diverging into talk of fetishes and fantasies instead. It was time for drastic measures.

"Now for the real-life demonstration!" Shirley yelled over the din. She pointed outside. "Who wants to try?" No one could deny their need for a bathroom break—we'd consumed enough wine to piss an ocean—so ladies began weaving toward the cockpit, nervous and giggling like girls at cheerleader tryouts. Shirley had already started unbuttoning her body-hugging shorts.

Just then a sound familiar and ominous crashed our consciousness: the sound of dinghies full of drunken husbands. It was well past midnight and the boys had thoroughly redistributed their wealth gambling. They were ready to fold. We ladies tried to shoo them away with shrieks and admonitions, but the dinghies bumped against *Dragonfly's* hull, the men insistent about retrieving their wives and heading home.

It was a clear instance of premature evacuation.

Shirley shrugged her shoulders, buttoned her shorts, and stumbled into her awaiting chariot.

❋

Back on the quay in the middle of the Pacific, prematurity was not the issue. The men were still fighting stage fright, the women were loath to hang their bums in the breeze, and our expert pisser, Shirley, was thousands of miles away, still cruising Mexican waters. But we had a crisis on our hands. We needed urine and fast.

That morning, our fleet of sailors had dinghied to Vaitahu, eager to visit this quaint Polynesian village, only to find a bouldered beach and pounding surf. How would we get ashore? The public wharf was old and craggy, not amenable to mooring inflatable skiffs. Luckily, Cap'n Dave, a firefighter with the matching physique, volunteered to ferry us in, anchor the dinghies in the bay, and swim ashore.

Everything was going as planned until a loud group of brawny Polynesians pushed past us to the edge of the quay. Conferring in Marquesan, they shook their massive heads, waved their tattooed arms, and glared at Dave, who was approaching in an easy crawl. As Dave reached the wharf, the locals, big as linebackers, shouted—"Attention! Attention! *Uhr-SHAN! Uhr-SHAN!*"—and pointed menacingly down at him. Whether they were angry or drunk or out of their minds no one could tell, until Dave, tiring of treading water, clambered up the side of the quay. Immediately, he got the point.

Hidden just below the water's surface, clinging to the cement steps, were dozens of poisonous sea urchins (*"Uhr-SHAN! Uhr-SHAN!"*) whose toxic quills were now embedded in Dave's bare feet. Dave collapsed in pain as French and English voices alike screeched the well-known but less-than-pleasing solution: "PEE-say! PEE-say!" "PEE-onit! PEE-onit!"

Which brings us back, finally, to the seamen struggling

with stage fright, and their impatient and amused onlookers. Doug, looking down dejectedly, complained he'd just gone an hour ago. Jim—his penis poised perilously close to Dave's quills (not that I was looking)—had produced nary a drop. And Michael, the oldest of the group, was still fumbling with his shorts.

But Graeme, my husband and the day's hero, had (as I've already described) prepared himself with precision. Unbeknownst to the spectators behind him, who were watching for the golden arc, Graeme had picked up a large blue mayonnaise lid from the litter on the quay and was, after an initial case of nerves, successfully filling it to the brim with his precious potion. One hand tucking his one-eyed star offstage, the other hand trembling with his petri dish, Graeme presented the prize to Dave, triumphant.

Immediately the other guys took the hint. One offered a half-crushed Hinano beer can of antidote. Another filled an old water bottle golden ("Bottled at the Source" the tattered label read). And Michael's wizened fingers, now clutching a rusty tin can, continued to fumble with his zipper. Splayed on the quay, his feet awash in piss, Dave sighed with relief.

More quickly than it had begun, the show was over. Our island spectators pounded the shoulders of our proud sailors, who, in turn, readjusted their trunks and double-checked their zippers. Someone had flagged down a tired old van (the only vehicle we ever saw in Vaitahu), and the Marquesan hulks lifted Dave to the tattered front seat; we women cooed and fussed. Soon Dave was sitting in the local infirmary just a few hundreds yards down the bay, where the motherly clinician expressed surprise that Dave wasn't in more pain. I, the appointed translator (even though I'd missed the French pronunciation of "urchin"), thought of redeeming myself with something erudite like, *Our firefighter's agony was extinguished by his friends' hoses.* Instead, I said, "The guys pissed all over him." She nodded knowingly—sea urchin cases in the islands were nothing new—and began to first wash, then nurse Dave's bruised feet. Dave nursed his bruised pride.

The next evening, sailing away from Tahuata, I couldn't shake the feeling of frustration I'd felt on the quay the day before. Sure, I could have added my urine to the cause. But, since I hadn't practiced the art of pissing à la Shirley—standing up, undies and shorts hitched to one side—it would have been a true exhibition. I would have had to drop my drawers and *squat,* spraying in the general direction of a cup and my hand holding it. Or worse, hover my white ass (and everything else) over Dave's writhing, porcupined feet. Imagining it, I could hear the blood crawling up our Polynesian spectators' brown cheeks—at the blinding sight of my white ones.

So there in the cockpit, sailing away from Tahuata, my mind returned to the only solution—however unpalatable—it could find.

"Ya' know," I said to Graeme, who was sitting erect, his back against the mizzen mast, "I really wish I'd gotten the chance to watch Shirley." Graeme, having no idea what I was talking about, kept his eyes on the sails. Until I added, "I have to pee—maybe I'll practice Shirley's technique over the side right now. Give me some pointers?"

At that, Graeme's eyes clopped shut, his lips rolled back, and his head shook like a Labrador after a bath. A low growl of disgust gurgled from his throat. (Shirley had definitely been wrong about one thing: Graeme was not going to find this sexy.) But then a thought occurred to him. He opened his eyes grinning. "Hey! If it makes you feel any better, just remember the *number one cause of death*," his index finger wagged, emphasizing the stat we'd heard so often, "for men on cruising boats."

I blinked twice and a slow smile spread my cheeks. Standing in the cockpit, I grabbed Graeme's safety harness and tossed it at him. "That's right," I said, triumphant. "Don't fall overboard tonight taking a piss."

Then I went below to sit down and pee.

Janna Cawrse taught literature and writing in Seattle, Washington, before setting sail with her newlywed husband (and expert pisser), Graeme Esarey. The couple currently lives aboard their sailboat in Hong Kong's Victoria Harbor, and is writing a travel memoir about their misadventures across the Pacific. Janna's work has appeared in several U.S. sailing magazines, including Blue Water Sailing *and* Cruising World.

SETH STEVENSON

Trying Really Hard to Like India

There is pleasure in pain, no?

IT'S O.K. TO HATE A PLACE.

Travel writers can be so afraid to make judgments. You end up with these gauzy tributes to the "magic" of some far-off spot. But honestly, not every spot is magical for everyone. Sometimes you get somewhere, look around, and think, "Hey, this place is a squalid rat hole. I'd really rather be in the Netherlands." And that's O.K.

For example, the last time I went to India I just haaaaaaated it. Delhi was a reddish haze of 105-degree dust. And while, of course, the Taj Mahal was great...the streets outside it were a miasma of defecating children. I could not wait to go home. (Disclosure: I was there on a previous writing assignment. And actually, I loved Ladakh, which is in northern India—up in the Himalayas. But I don't really count Ladakh, because it's more like Tibet than like India. Anyway...)

Now—mostly because my girlfriend wants to come back—I'm back. I'm giving this dreadful place a second chance. And this time I vow I will try really hard to like India.

I'm convinced it's a reachable goal. My plan involves: sticking to South India, far away from Delhi, staying exclusively at beach resorts and luxury hotels, and stocking up on prescription-strength sedatives. But there are other important steps as well, which I will outline for you.

Step 1: Making Peace with Poverty and Parasitic Worms

After flying into Bangalore and acclimating for a couple of days, we visit a town called Mysore (rhymes with "eyesore"). There's a famous temple here and an opulent palace—big tourist attractions both. But to me, the most interesting thing to see (in any place I visit) is the daily life of the people who live and work there.

For instance, from our hotel window in Mysore, we look down on a pile of garbage. Every night, this pile becomes dispersed as it is picked at and chewed on by rats, then crows, then stray dogs, then cows, and then homeless people. Every morning a woman dressed in a brightly colored sari sweeps this masticated garbage-porridge back into a pile. It is the worst job I can imagine. (Previously, the worst job I could imagine was navigator for a rally-car driver, because I get nauseous when I read in cars. But this woman's job is much worse than that. And really, with this added perspective, rally-car navigator doesn't seem so bad anymore.)

When we leave the hotel and walk down the (urine-soaked) street, we get assaulted by auto-rickshaw drivers, by hawkers, by tour guides...and by tiny children pointing to their own mouths. This last one is rough—at least the first few dozen times. Sometimes these kids are part of a scam. They're forced to beg by adults who run panhandling teams. (We've read stories about teams that cut out kids' tongues, to make them seem more pitiable.) But sometimes these kids are just honestly looking for food. Because they're starving. They might eat out of that big garbage pile tonight. Once the dogs are done.

On the train ride back to Bangalore, monsoon rains slap at the window. I gaze out on wet, destitute slums. Wherever one can build a shanty, someone has. Wherever one could be pissing, someone is. The poverty's on a mind-blowing, overwhelming scale, and you feel so helpless. The money in your pocket right now, handed to any one person out there beyond the window, would be life-changing. But you can't save a billion people and turn the fortunes of this massive country. (You're not Gandhi, you know.) And after all, back in Bangalore we hung out with highly paid IT guys who worked for Infosys. There's a lot of wealth in India, too.

The thing is, if you go to India as a tourist, you'll have to make some sort of peace with all this. Because it's one thing to see poverty on television, or to get direct mail that asks for your charity. It's different when there are tiny, starving children grabbing your wrists and asking for money wherever you go.

For my part, I've resolved to send a check to some worthy Indian charity when I get home. (Suggestions are invited.) It's the best solution I can come up with. Because I'm not going to get

---

Mahatma Gandhi, as you know, walked barefoot most of the time, which produced an impressive set of calluses on his feet. He also ate very little, which made him rather frail and with his odd diet, he suffered from bad breath. This made him a super calloused fragile mystic hexed by halitosis.

♦

—International Pun Contest

through this trip until I've reached an understanding with myself…and until I take some Pepto-Bismol, because my stomach is just killing me. Which brings me to the other thing you'll have to be prepared for.

You will get "Delhi Belly" soon after touching down in India. And you won't enjoy your trip until it's gone. My illness takes hold on the train ride back to Bangalore, as my intestines suddenly spasm into a clenched fist full of acid. The restroom—should this come into play—is a hole in the floor of the train. (A sign on the door requests that we not use the hole while the train's in a station—for obvious reasons.)

For the next day or two, I find myself playing a game I call "Could I Vomit in This?" The idea is to pick a nearby object and then decide if, in the event of an emergency, it could be puked into. For example, potted plant: Certainly. Water bottle: Sure. Magazine: Iffy, but worth a try.

The good news is that it won't take long before your stomach adjusts to these new microbial nasties, and you're back to feeling fine. Unless, of course, like my friend who was here a few years ago, you've got a parasitic worm and you lose forty pounds and need medical attention.

Step 2: Escaping Backpackers, Traveling in Style, and Once Again Coming to Terms with Rampant Poverty

I have a problem with backpackers. The problem is that wherever they are, I don't want to be.

Partly, it's that I don't go somewhere like India so I can hang out with a bunch of nineteen-year-old German dudes (though I'm sure they're lovely people). Also, it's that I look at all these backpackers…and I see myself. And frankly, I don't like what I see.

For one, I'm not properly washed. And for another, I've got this massive, geeky pack on my back, which dwarfs my torso and bends me near double under its weight. (Because of this, I have, I'll admit somewhat irrationally, refused to use a backpack on this trip. Instead I've brought a wheeled carry-on suitcase, which has worked quite nicely. Just try to call me a backpacker now! No backpack here, Heinrich!)

But above all, I hate the ambience that forms around a backpacker enclave. The ticky-tacky souvenir shops. The sketchy tour guides. The rabbit-warren hostels. And the way the locals start to eye me like I'm nothing but an ambulatory wallet.

There are two ways to escape the backpackers. The first is to get off the beaten path, wander around, and discover a private Eden not yet ruined by backpacking hordes. This takes more time than my vacation will allow. So I've opted for the second (much quicker) method: money.

Yes, the simplest way to find solitude is to buy it. Thus we've arrived here at the Casino Group Marari Beach Resort.

This idyllic spot is on the west coast of India in the state of Kerala (the setting for *The God of Small Things*). The resort's lovely bungalows are tucked between groves of palm trees. The beach is wide, empty, silent. Each evening the sun melts down into the Arabian Sea. By day we lounge around a heated pool eating big plates of samosas. Nearby, in the recreation area, an older Italian woman is playing badminton in a bikini.

Wait, you say, why bother to go to India for this? If a beach resort's all you want, there are plenty back home, right? I assure you this is different for several reasons, such as...

The food: Each night, we enjoy delicious Indian specialties, prepared by actual Indian chefs, in India. (Pause to lick tandoori chicken from fingers.) You just can't get that at home.

The cost: We're paying about $70 a night for our bungalow. Pretty much anywhere in the States—for a luxury resort with a private beach—you'd pay at least quadruple that. Consider the fact that Sir Paul McCartney once stayed here. When I can afford a hotel Paul McCartney stays at, you can be certain it's a bargain.

The sheer solitude: You'll rarely find a beach this nice that's also this utterly empty. There's nothing here (as my pictures attest). Several hundred yards away are a few wooden fishing boats, which haul up their catch on the beach each afternoon. Also—and I swear this is somehow charming (remember, it's hundreds of yards away)—you'll see a few village folk squatting amid the tides. This is because they don't have indoor plumbing.

The world beyond the hotel gates: Walk outside your beach resort in Florida…and you're still in Florida. Walk outside your beach resort in India and…oh, man, you are unmistakably in India. Lots of heartbreaking rural poverty. Lots of sad-yet-edifying tableaux (which is no doubt what you came here for, correct?). It's sort of the best of both worlds for the tourist who fancies himself culturally aware: Live right next to the picturesque misery—but not in it.

Before you condemn me to hell, please see again *Step 1: Making Peace With Poverty.* Again, unless you're Gandhi—and you're not—you can't come here without diving head first into a salty sea of unpleasant contradictions.

For yet another lesson on this theme, take our last night at Marari Beach. We somehow end up drinking in the bar with a thirty-something American woman—let's call her "Debbie"—who is six stiff drinks ahead of us. Between sips of some tropical concoction, she delivers a slurry monologue explaining that she has come to India on business. Her business: designing doormats. No joke.

One of Kerala's big industries is coir—a textile made from

coconut husks. On a bike ride we took around the village (yes, "the world beyond the hotel gates"), we could see into huts that had looms and people weaving coir into simple mats. These mats get trimmed and finished (by some big export factory) to Debbie's design specs. Then they get shipped to North America and end up in some middlebrow home-furnishings catalog where you can buy them for $26.99.

Debbie is drinking heavily because her job here is wicked depressing. She buys in bulk from the big exporter, who pays a shady middleman, who (barely) pays the villagers here. The villagers can make about three mats per week—all of excellent quality—and for this they get paid a few cents per mat. The middleman of course takes all the profit.

Debbie, goodhearted human that she is, is on the verge of drunken tears as she describes all this. She knows the whole thing is grossly unfair. And that she perpetuates it. But if she wants to keep her job with the American firm she works for, and still make deals with Indian exporters, there's not a damn thing she can do about it.

And unless you have carefully avoided buying any products made by Third World labor—and chances are you have not—you're really no better than Debbie. Let's drink to that. Believe me, Debbie already has.

Step 3: Getting Spiritual and Getting Medicated

You often hear tourists call India a "spiritual" place. It seems as though half the Westerners here either a) come with the intent to live on an ashram; or b) somehow end up at one anyway.

I appreciate the drive to find deeper meaning. I honestly do. And I'm a huge fan of pantheism. Why limit yourself to one god, when instead you could pick and choose from a

sampler of gods? It spices things up. The Brahma-Creator/
Vishnu-Preserver/Shiva-Destroyer thing is a badass meta-
phor, too, even if I don't fully understand it.

But the truth is, I'm not quite wired to surrender my will
to a higher power. And, getting back to my main point, I
certainly don't see why India should corner the market on
spirituality. Why do we get all mystical and fuzzy-headed the
moment we hit the subcontinent?

Look at *The Razor's Edge*—the W. Somerset Maugham
classic I've been reading over here. Protagonist Larry Darrell
begins as a run-of-the-mill Midwesterner. Then he goes to
India. By the time he gets back, he's received illumination
and communed with the Absolute. Also, he has telekinetic
powers.

I'm not sure I believe in the Absolute. But I do think I
would enjoy having telekinesis. Mostly so I could alter the
outcome of sporting events. (Oh, wide right! Too bad!)

To this end, I've decided to get me some spirituality here.
It seems there exists a sort of Hindu metaphysics known as
Ayurveda, which aims to heal both body and spirit (and,
most important, has been championed by Deepak Chopra).
I figure this will do the trick. And since they happen to have
an Ayurvedic spa at our beach resort, I also figure: Why not
seek deeper meaning on a massage table?

I arrive at the Ayurveda center and ask for an appoint-
ment. Maybe thirty seconds later I'm buck naked in a small
room with a smiling Indian man. His name is Sajan. He
hands me a loincloth and helps me tie it. Then he guides me
to the table, lays me down, pours a healthy dollop of oil on
my chest, and begins to rub his hands all over my body.

Understand that I get slightly uncomfortable when I'm
made to hug a person I've just met. I've got a thing about

strangers touching me. And when it comes to strangers rubbing oil on my upper thighs, well, I get even more ill at ease. (Perhaps if the stranger were French actress Julie Delpy? But does she count as a stranger? I feel I know her so well from her films.)

Still, I've had professional massages before, and I've mostly enjoyed them (once I'm past the initial squeamishness). The key in the past has been the kneading of my knotted muscles—thus dispersing any stored-up tension. But as best I can tell, there is no kneading in Ayurveda. Just rubbing—and gallons of oil. While I hesitate to use the term "molestation" (and there was nothing sexual about it), I will say that Sajan's hands were not at all shy. I will also say that my loincloth seemed unnecessarily small and loosely fastened.

At one point—while my eyes were closed—a second pair of hands came out of nowhere and jumped in the mix. This alarmed me, insofar as it was sudden and unexpected. Like an ambush. Also, soon after this, the soothing tabla music that had been playing came to a stop, and left us in silence…save for the sound of four well-oiled palms, briskly sliding over my torso.

In the end, my spirit remained undaunted, but in no way was it illuminated or healed. This was the first massage I've had where I felt less relaxed walking out than I'd felt walking in.

Anyway, if I want to relax here, I've found a much better method: prescription-strength sedatives. I'd like to thank Lord Brahma for creating benzodiazepines. And also Lord Vishnu, for preserving a loosely regulated Indian pharmaceutical system. I can walk into the "Medicines" shop in pretty much any town over here, plunk down fifty rupees (a little more than a dollar), and walk out with a great big bottle of two-milligram Ativan tablets.

This becomes especially key on the overnight train ride from Kerala to Goa. There are cockroaches perched on the wall above my head; across the aisle a man is coughing up phlegm (in a manner that suggests a highly communicable and highly fatal tropical disease); and I'm still trying to shake my traumatic memories of the massage. All of which is making it hard for me to sleep.

I suppose I could call on Lord Shiva to destroy all the roaches. Or the phlegm. But instead I just call on Lord Ativan, destroyer of consciousness. Cockroaches could scurry up onto my face, oil their many legs, and administer an Ayurvedic massage to my eyelids. I'd sleep right through it, given sufficient dosage.

Step 4: Acceding to Chaos

Our first day out in Mumbai (formerly Bombay), we were approached by a man who—I'm fairly certain of this— planned to kidnap us. He gave us this carefully polished spiel about needing to cast a few extras for a Bollywood movie and how we'd be perfect for this scene he was shooting, so if we would just hop into his car with him.... Tempting, but no dice. (It sort of cooled our jets when, in the middle of the pitch, this other Indian guy ran over and shouted, "Be careful with this man! This is a dangerous man!")

I'll admit, this Bollywood scam was brilliant. It played on my vanity and my long-held desire to appear in a Bollywood movie (preferably in a dance scene). I salute you, my would-be abductor.

But other pitches were not as well crafted. For instance, there was this guy who smiled weakly and asked us, with a half-hearted shrug, "Monkey dance?" Our eyes followed the leash in his hand, which led to the neck of a monkey. The most jaded, world-weary monkey I've ever seen. The Lou

Reed of monkeys. He looked like he was about to sit down, pull out his works, and shoot a big syringe full of heroin into his paw. Needless to say, we declined the monkey dance—which I'm guessing would have been some sort of sad, simian death jig.

The upshot of all this: Mumbai is not the place to go for a carefree, relaxing vacation. Just stepping out on the streets can be a difficult ordeal. The air smells like twice-baked urine, marinated in more urine. The sidewalks are a slalom of legless beggars and feral dogs. Hundreds of times each day you walk right past something so unfathomably sad, so incomprehensibly surreal, so horribly unfair...

The only way to cope is to stop resisting. Embrace the chaos. If you see a woman rolling around in the gutter clutching at the massive, bulbous wart on the side of her face and moaning loudly...well, that's part of the scenery. No one else here (certainly no native Mumbaian) will pay her any attention. So why should you? Just say to yourself: *Wow, that's crazy stuff and marvelously edifying.* Doo-dee-doo, keep on walking.

That's harsh and simplistic. The truth is, the chaos can be wonderful sometimes, too. There's a goofy sense of freedom that comes with it. A sense of unknowing.

Back home in the States, it can feel like we've got life figured out, regulated, under control, under wraps. But here in India, nothing seems even close to figured out. Nothing seems remotely under control. You're never quite sure what will happen next, and you're working without a net.

Terrifying? Yes. But also invigorating. On the train ride up from Goa, I perused a women's magazine (sort of an Indian *Cosmo*) that we'd bought at a newsstand. The cover story was about women who'd lived abroad—mostly in the United States and Britain—but moved back because they liked India better. All these former NRIs (Non-Resident Indians) had gotten homesick...for the chaos! Yes, the West was clean and orderly. But that was sort of boring. They missed the hubbub, the craziness, the randomness of India.

I see what they're saying. But in honesty, I prefer to see it from several stories up, in the air-conditioned cocktail lounge of the Oberoi Hotel. Ahhhh. Soft music. Lovely view. No legless beggars.

From up here, sure, all that chaos is beautiful. It's amazing to ponder (while calmly sipping a stiff rum and Coke) how 1 billion people manage to coexist in a single, sprawling democracy. It truly is impressive that this country keeps chugging along—massive, bulbous face warts and all.

In fact, I've come not just to like, but to love India—in a way—from afar. It's the underdog. It's dirty, and hectic, and insane...and I find myself rooting for it.

Seth Stevenson is a frequent contributor to Slate.

J. MAARTEN TROOST

* * *

Your Ambassadors to Butaritari

*On remote Pacific islands, it is easy to make
a spectacular fool of yourself.*

AFTER BOWEL MOVEMENTS, THE STATE OF AIR KIRIBATI
was the favorite topic of conversation on Tarawa. Did you
hear about when the plane ran out of fuel midair and had to
glide in for a landing, someone will say. Or…about when
the engine died, or about when the pilot passed out mid-
flight, or about when they forgot to turn the beacon on at
the airport, or, my favorite, the pilot let me fly the plane.
Distressingly, these were not mere rumors. I had never been
so uneasy about boarding a flight. It did not help that the
shoeless airport official was not pleased with my weight. The
expression on his face, which just moments earlier had revealed only benign indifference, contorted into something
approaching a scowl. As I stood on a rusting, antiquated
scale, fulfilling my role in a pre-boarding ritual meant to in-
still anxiety in travelers, I watched the creases on his forehead burrow deeper, saw his eyes recede in a squint of deep
concentration, and listened to the strange clucking noises
emanating from his mouth. "Tock, tock, tock," he said. He

seemed personally affronted by my weight. And I must add, I was not a fat man.

Indeed, standing on the scale, I was startled by how much weight I had lost—twenty-five pounds—with absolutely no effort at all on my part. I was fit when I arrived on Tarawa, so this wasn't a loss of excess baggage. This was a withering away, and I had once been proud of my iron gut. The Tarawa diet is the ultimate weight-loss plan—hookworm, round-worm, dash of salmonella, hint of dysentery, season with cholera to taste—results guaranteed, except for women. Sylvia lost not a pound, which confirmed for me that when challenged, women have a much stronger constitution than men. This makes sense, of course. Life in Kiribati has a strong Darwinian cast to it, and men, except for one brief glorious moment, are pretty useless from an evolutionary perspective and can therefore be allowed to whither, whereas women are hard-wired to survive. The weaker-sex moniker may apply to the bench-press, but Nature isn't a gym-rat.

And I nearly lost a few more pounds when I contem-plated the plane we were about to fly. This would be an old Spanish prop-plane that predated Franco. It tilted ominously, exuding an air of exhaustion. As the airport official clucked and fretted over our small, feather-light backpacks, I watched the pilot stand on a stepladder and tug at a wing until it aligned with the other wing. Then I smoked eighteen ciga-rettes. Even Sylvia asked for a cigarette. Sylvia doesn't smoke. She's from California.

I did not want to cause a scene, but walking across the tarmac I did feel it was my duty to highlight to the mem-bers of *Te Iitibwerere,* the theater troupe we were traveling with to Butaritari, that the two engines were connected to the wings with *masking tape*. Really. They regarded this as very funny, and I knew then that the I-Kiribati would remain forever unfathomable to me. It was explained to us that the masking tape wasn't actually connecting the engines to the wings, but merely covering up the parts of the plane that were corroded through with rust, and strangely, as I regarded the swaths of masking tape elsewhere on the fuselage, I didn't really feel that much better.

The interior of the aircraft, a CASA, resembled that of an aging, decrepit school bus, complete with benches, though it was not nearly so large or comfortable. As we taxied, I hoped that someone was restraining the dogs, pigs, and children that usually occupied the runway. Pigs, let it be said, are stupid animals, though they do make landing a plane on Tarawa a uniquely interesting experience. Once we were in the air, a cool breeze was felt inside the

——☽——

A woman called to make reservations. "I want to go from Chicago to Hippopotamus, New York." The agent was at a loss for words. Finally, the agent asked, "Are you sure that is the name of the town?"

"Yes, what flights do you have?" replied the customer. After some searching, the agent came back with, "I'm sorry, ma'am. I've looked up every airport in the country and can't find a Hippopotamus anywhere."

The customer retorted, "Oh, don't be silly. Everyone knows where it is. Check your map!"

The agent scoured the map of New York and said, "You don't mean Buffalo, do you?"

"That's it! I knew it was a big animal."

◆

—Anonymous travel agent

cabin and it would have been pleasant had it originated from an air-conditioning unit. Clearly, more masking tape was needed. Two men, wiser than I, sought comfort on top of the luggage that was strewn haphazardly in the back of the plane, and as the engine coughed and sputtered and the aircraft trembled, I found myself envying them their alcoholic stupor. The Pacific Ocean below appeared placid and lush and impossibly vast, like a blue universe unraveling toward infinity. It seemed presumptuous to fly over something so expansive and grand as the Pacific Ocean in a flying contraption so pitiful as ours, and I thought it ominous that when we began to descend we could see in the near distance the island of Makin, a small atoll traditionally regarded as inhabited by the spirits of the I-Kiribati no longer residing in the temporal world.

Te Iitibwerere were the island equivalent of Hollywood stars. True, they didn't have any money, nor did they live in fancy houses, and they weren't stalked by paparazzi and autograph hounds, and Botox and personal trainers didn't figure very prominently in their lives, but in the entertainment world of Kiribati they were stars. On Butaritari, they were to perform plays in each of the island's villages. They were five women and one man, whom we will call Lothario as he was then married to one cast member and dating another, which added a certain frisson to their performances. They were staying in the guesthouse adjacent to ours, a government-owned cinderblock house that looked very much like a chicken coop. It lacked beds, running water, and a generator, and it was more abundant in rats than our guesthouse. It did, however, have the benefit of being perched atop a seawall overlooking the lagoon. On Butaritari the hours between dusk and dawn pass slowly and quietly, unless, of course, you are traveling with both your wife and your mistress, and so on most evenings we attached ourselves to the troupe. Around sunset, a fish would be cleaned and a bottle that once contained soy sauce but now brimmed with sour toddy was passed around. A guitar was strummed and they would sing under the expanding white light of a rounding moon and a million stars. Bright is the moonlight on an equatorial atoll.

"O.K.," Tawita said, finishing a sweet tune and turning to me and Sylvia. "Now it's your turn. You must sing."

I dreaded this. It often happened that we were asked to sing. The I-Kiribati are unselfconscious about singing. This is because they have the voices of angels. When I sing, however, small children begin to cry, dogs whimper, and rats scurry to the water and drown themselves. Sylvia, who is ravishingly beautiful, possesses a formidable intellect, and whose very existence illuminates my life, sings like a distressed cow. Entire villages scatter into the bush when we sing together. I tried to explain this to Tawita, but she was having none of it. "You must sing. Do not be shy."

And so we did. We sang Bob Dylan's "Tambourine Man." We sang it just like Bob, with raspy, nasally voices and a peculiar sense of harmony. *Heeey Mr. Tambourine Man/ Play aaa song fer me/ I'm nooot sleepy and there is no place I'm goiiiiing tooo.*

The theater troupe drowned themselves in the lagoon before we could finish. Actually, they didn't do that. Rather, they drowned in tears of laughter. It began with a snicker that turned into a titter which led to guffaws and soon the group was convulsing in hysterical laughter.

"Stop!" Tawita cried. "That was very bad."

"Yes," I said. "We are aware of that."

"You must never sing again," she said.

"That is how we prefer it."

During the days, *Te Iitibwerere* guided us through the formalities of the *maneaba*, which functions essentially like a town hall, a community center, a church, a Motel 6, and the U.S. Senate, but with more dignity. A *maneaba*, typically built with coconut wood, thatch, and coconut fiber rope, can be upwards of a hundred feet long and sixty feet high, and it is here that just about everything of consequence occurs. Kiribati is a deeply conservative country, and inside the *maneaba* etiquette is important. As an *I-Matang* accustomed to a culture that no longer has much place for formality and tradition, I paid attention. There were rules, Tawita explained. Women, for instance, must never reveal their thighs. Breasts, fine. Thighs, no. Shoes must be taken off before entering a *maneaba*, and it is considered bad form to sit with legs outstretched, pointing your blackened soles at those across. Sitting cross-legged is best, but since you can be sure that once inside a *maneaba* you will not be leaving for at least a couple of hours, you soon find yourself quietly stretching and unknotting, here and there daring an outstretched foot. A hat must never be worn inside a *maneaba*, and on some islands hats must be removed even if you are simply walking past a *maneaba*. If biking, you should dismount and walk. "Also," Tawita continued, "what is it called when you make a stinky from your backside?"

"A fart," I offered.

"Yes. You must never fart inside a *maneaba*."

We absorbed this, and as we entered the *maneaba* in the village of Kuma we rehearsed our speeches. We would have to introduce ourselves in I-Kiribati, and we were determined to get it right. Since I-Kiribati has no relationship to the languages we spoke, learning it could only be done by rote memorization, which gives a teacher an opportunity to create mischief. Sylvia's staff enjoyed recounting the time when one of her predecessors, a particularly humorless woman, asked them to help her with a speech she needed to make welcoming the Minister of Environment to a workshop. Instead of bland niceties, they had her say, "I would like to see your penis." She felt encouraged by the laughter and continued on with ever more lurid statements. "I think it is very big," she said. I respect I-Kiribati humor. I like its bawdiness.

As we settled in the corner of the *maneaba* reserved for visitors, a woman offered us young coconuts, which are refreshing and nutritious and impossible to drink without slurping loudly. The entire village was soon congregated inside the *maneaba*, and after an *unimane* welcomed us to Kuma, we were asked to introduce ourselves. Following custom, which requires that you share your name, your father's name and his home island, I stood up and said, in I-Kiribati: "Greetings. I am Maarten, son of Herman of Holland."

"Aiyah, aiyah," the village responded. "We welcome Maarten, son of Herman of Holland."

I liked the sound of that. Maarten, son of Herman of Holland, had a medieval ring. True, it wasn't as evocative as say Vlad the Impaler, but still, Maarten, son of Herman of Holland, suggested trouble.

After a few more words, Sylvia followed: "Greetings. I am Sylvia, daughter of Joe of California."

"Aiyah. Aiyah. We welcome Sylvia, daughter of Joe of California."

"You know, darling," I said, "California is part of the United States now."

"Yes," she said. "For the time being."

One by one, the theater troupe followed. Now that we all knew each other, the play could begin. One would think that childhood diarrhea and respiratory infections would be difficult subjects for a play, but *Te Iitibwerere* carried it off

———☽———

By the time my bowels start to move I realize that here in the center of Szeged there is no bog in sight. I discover a cemetery and squat behind a gravestone. A small dog appears. Where is its owner? I'm still squatting. I don't want to put my head above the gravestone until I'm all done. Inspiration! I rummage for the sausage I'd intended for supper. The dog wags its tail enthusiastically. I launch the sausage into the air and it lands twenty meters away. The dog rushes after it and I squeeze out the last of the toxic waste. Quick wipe with a few leaves and some grass, zip up, pull on my rucksack, and emerge to see a rotund woman in her fifties trying to disengage the sausage from her dog's mouth. Perhaps her husband will get sausage for supper.

◆

—Jim Kavala, from *How to Shit Around the World* by Dr. Jane Wilson-Howarth

brilliantly, possibly because diarrhea and respiratory infections are the stuff of everyday drama in Kiribati, but perhaps also because storytelling and songs are still the primary transmitters of knowledge in Kiribati. There are no I-Kiribati writers. Although the people of Kiribati are fairly literate, there is nothing to read beyond what their church provides, which means that nearly all knowledge of themselves is transmitted orally. Thus the plays about the runs. In New York, plays examine the ennui of contemporary life; in Kiribati, plays explore the art of rehydration. The audience laughed knowingly and nodded thoughtfully, and Sylvia was very pleased. It is one thing to sit in an air-conditioned office in Washington, poring over thousands of pages of buzzword drivel—"disseminating knowledge over the internet"—and it is another thing all together to be in a village on the far side of the world, watching people get the health care information they need in a clever, effective, low-tech, real-world kind of way. If this had been a World Bank health program, a gazillion dollars would have been spent on consultants and first-class air travel, culminating in a report issued four years later recommending that Kiribati build a dam.

While the actors and the elders traded another round of speeches, lunch was brought to the center of the *maneaba*, where it remained for a very long time. There were flies, big flies, and they swarmed around the food. A half-dozen women languorously swept their hands back and forth over the assorted plastic plates, which elsewhere are called disposable, but here will be used to the end of time. There were more speeches. Sylvia was thanked for her $20 contribution to the preparation of the meal. There were songs sung heartily. There were garlands placed upon our heads, crowns of flowers. Talcum powder was sprinkled on our necks, Impulse deodorant sprayed under our arms. And finally we could partake of the meal. Ah…one last speech. An elder, a gentle moon-faced man, explained that we hadn't been expected until the following day—it happens, there is but one radio-phone on Butaritari—and so would we please excuse the humbleness of the meal. No worries, we said. It would no doubt be delicious. It was not.

Have you ever wondered what an eel the size of a python tastes like? No? Well, I can attest that it is the most wretchedly foul-tasting victual ever consumed by a human being. Slimy, boiled fish fat that could only be swallowed because, as was the custom, the entire village was silently watching us consume this meal, and they would likely be offended if we let the gag reflex do its work. For ten long minutes, the village did nothing else but silently watch us eat. A few of the men were shaving. With machetes. These are tough people. It's very *kang-kang*, we said, as another dozen flies settled on the sliver of eel we held in our hands. And then finally, the village elders, the men, the children, and the women, in that order, partook of the meal, and with the center of attention elsewhere, I began to quietly place the contents of my plate behind me, donating it to the mangy dogs that circled the *maneaba*.

And then we danced. The exuberance of the I-Kiribati for dancing cannot be overstated, as we had already witnessed with the Inter-Ministerial Song and Dance Competition. But it is *te twist* that inspires a certain madness in the I-Kiribati. No matter what time of day or night a *maneaba* function occurs, there comes a moment when the village generator is brought to life, feeding energy to a Japanese boombox, and with startling rapidity all the old ways recede, replaced instead with the throbbing atmosphere of an outdoor disco devoted not to the nurturing of sexual tension, but rather to the propagation of shameless silliness. It is the pinnacle of bad form to refuse an offer to dance *te twist*, and as the most exotic guests, we were often asked to dance, Sylvia by good-looking young men, and me by the village aunties. To the sounds of Pacific pop and the ubiquitous *La Macarena*, we twisted, flailed, bumped, and grinded. As we danced, someone thoughtfully sprayed us with Impulse deodorant and showered our necks in talcum powder. My dancing aunt goaded me into ever greater displays of silliness, and just as I settled into a series of moves that closely resembled the movements of a chicken surprised to have lost its head, women from every corner of the *maneaba* rushed at me like linebackers, grasping onto me with ferocious bear hugs. These were strong women. Though I was not quite as substantial as I once was, I was by no means a small man, and yet they flung me around like a rag doll. Later, outside the *maneaba*, members of the theater troupe told Sylvia that this was a fairly risky, though not unheard of, method used by women to display their partiality toward someone.

"You should have hit them," Tawita said to her. "Some women would have bit off their noses if they had done that. You should at least demand mats and bananas."

"Are you kidding?" Sylvia replied. "Did you see how they threw him around? I'm not getting involved. They can do what they want with him."

J. Maarten Troost's essays have appeared in The Atlantic Monthly, Washington Post, *and* Prague Post. *The two years he spent in Kiribati inspired his book,* The Sex Lives of Cannibals: Adrift in the Equatorial Pacific, *from which this story was excerpted. After living in Fiji for several years, he now resides with his wife and son in Northern California.*

✳

Imagine our relief to find smooth sailing across the Pacific, and, even on our return, only a few thunderstorms interrupted sunny weather. Then, as we began to pack preparatory to arriving in Philadelphia, the line storm hit just north of Cape Hatteras.

Right afterward we retired to our cabin. Harry slept in a regular-size bed, but mine was a Murphy sofa that converted at night into my bed. Two pins were used to keep it in place, but early on we noticed that only one pin was holding the bed down and asked our steward to replace the missing one. He had not done so.

Worn out by the shaking and shuddering of our ship, and too worried to read, we turned off our lights and finally went to sleep. In the middle of the night, the ship shook so that I awoke. Then I heard Harry cry out. I snapped on my light and saw him carried across the cabin on his mattress as if it were a flying carpet. Finally he landed with a thump and let out a howl.

"Are you all right?" I asked. He responded with a groan. "I've bandaged my right toe." He went back to sleep on his mattress that now lay on the floor.

Later on there was a terrible crash. Had our ship snapped in two? Half awake, I found my bed rising. My pin had slipped out, and I was going up into the wall. Just as the bed was about to close, I stuck my finger in the crack in order to have air to breathe. I've always had a fear of suffocating.

I then called Harry, but from where I lay at the base of the sofa, my voice wouldn't project enough for him to hear me. After many attempts to wake him, I grew desperate. Then when I had almost given up, I heard him say, "June, where are you?" What a relief! Then he yelled, "My God, the bed's closed!" and I heard him open the door and call Jim in the next cabin.

I tried to keep calm, recalling an old Lucille Ball movie when she had disappeared into the wall just as I had. I even giggled.

—June Lyman, "Adventure by Freighter"

SEAN PRESANT

* * *

Little Fish that Eat You

Not everything that sucks is bad.

I'VE ALWAYS LOVED THE STRANGE.

Don't know what it is, but presented with a choice between one of the Seven Wonders of the World and a place where people live with bats, I'd be torn.

Thus when I read about the thermal baths of Balikli Kaplica near Kangal, in north-central Turkey, a health spa where people go to have little fish eat off their dead skin, I knew I had found my new Giza.

The problem was how to get there.

"Bus" was my first thought. That's the way most people travel through Turkey—on immaculate buses with TVs that play important cultural films like *Anaconda* as odd male drive attendants circulate with a refreshing lemon hand cleaner that keeps humanity smelling like it just went through the rinse cycle with the forks.

Unfortunately I was in Sanli Urfa, not far from the Syrian border, and there were no buses from Sanli Urfa to Balikli Kaplika.

I had to think, for as much as I love the strange, I don't love it if it's going to cost me $200 in cab fare—which is why you don't want to be a traveler anywhere in my immediate vicinity when I hear about something like this.

As it happened, I had already assembled a small posse over the past couple days. We had shared a minivan from Malatya, the dried apricot capital of the world, to Nemrut Dagi, the inspiring giant-head-laden burial spot of King Antiochus. We had eaten together. We had watched the sunrise. We had pointed at a large insect swimming in the hotel toilet and said, "We shall call him Kevin." Now we were friends for life…or at least three or four days.

Fortunately for me, they were the kind of people who I knew, based on their radical itineraries, were not afraid of the unknown. Their interest was easily piqued when I mentioned the natural hot springs and the miraculous healing fish that live in their 95-degree waters.

We propositioned the guy who drove us to Nemrut Dagi and bartered him down to $20 a head. Quite a deal.

And so we set off on our adventure, en route stopping to pick up a hitchhiking soldier who jumped in the front seat, thanked the driver, and set his gun casually down so it aimed straight back into the cab. The six of us subtly leaned out of the line of fire and sat back for the two-and-a-half-hour drive.

The spa announced itself quite subtly. The area was shrubby and not particularly attractive. Lots of dry brush. Rolling yellow hills. Thunder. A sign for the place, roughly translated, read, "Kangal Hot Springs with Fish." Sounded like a menu item.

Our driver parked in the road and wandered off to get the lay of the land.

The springs are really nothing more than a number of

cement and marble compounds nestled on either side of a small stream. A blocky five-story hotel and cafeteria provide the only visible amenities. Calling it inspiring would be like calling a cinderblock exotic, but we weren't there for an architectural tour.

As the one responsible for dragging everyone to this remote hole, I insisted that we go straight to the pool with the most fish. We had traveled a long distance and we needed to be eaten immediately. Spare us the little pools where perhaps one fish would nibble. We wanted to look like those freaks on TV who made beards out of live bees.

Our driver disappeared to make the arrangements as we poured out of the van, excited for the opportunity to enjoy some quality time at the other end of the food chain.

I thought about what these "doctor fish" might do for me. I was a little tired lately. Maybe the fish would wake me up. Maybe they'd be the new alternative to coffee. Maybe I could market them to Starbucks.

"I'll have a venti non-fat macchiato."

"Room for cream?"

"No thanks."

"Cinnamon?"

"Nope."

"Carnivorous fish?"

"Please."

I was lost somewhere in this reverie when the bad news arrived.

"There's a problem," the driver told us.

We looked behind him at a stone-faced guard.

"The full fish pools are reserved for people who are really sick."

"Did you mention some of us are American?" I thought. "Many nations now consider that to be an illness."

I could feel the spines curling. We drove two hours and we weren't going to be eaten?

"What sort of sick?" a British woman demanded, all business.

"Skin illness," the driver said, waving his hand over his arms as if to suggest some kind of leprosy would suffice.

"What if you just *tell* him we're sick?" I asked.

The driver considered it.

"O.K.," he said. "But please, try to look not healthy."

We could do that.

He went back to the guard, while we did some gold medal slouching. Some of us coughed. Others scratched. A few were legitimately still bent to the side from two hours of trying to lean away from where the bullets come out of the gun.

It was a losing battle. We were all generally healthy, mostly in our twenties and thirties. We looked more like a sports team than a medical outing from the house of psoriasis.

The driver returned with some surprising news.

"He said O.K., but men and women have to separate."

No problem. We quietly split into two groups, each of us looking at the ground and assuming a sort of druid gait.

The women entered easily enough, but when we approached, the guard stopped us, mumbling something to the driver.

"He says you do not look sick and can only go to the big pool," he told us.

We don't look sick? Was he serious? Didn't he see how we were bent over? Didn't he see our clearly not-fake limping? Didn't he see how focused we all were on the pain of our…diseases that can only be cured by man-eating, half-boiled fish?

Apparently not.

We walked through the compound to "the big pool," a large, murky body of water with a flat cement deck. Twenty or so kids frolicked in the dark green bilge as their disinterested parents slept on plastic chairs.

We had found the Turkish equivalent of a trailer park pool.

I dipped a toe in the water. It was lukewarm. No fish would be living here.

We decided to get something to eat.

En route to the cafeteria, we met back up with the girls, whose wet hair indicated that they had in fact been dipped in something.

"Well?" we said anxiously, looking for bleeding, missing limbs, or, on the other side, evidence of some great healing, like the ability to fly or maybe ESP.

"I think it was not so clean," a young French woman said in a sort of "I just saw things I didn't want to see" sort of way. She wrung the water out of her hair, wiping her hands on a towel as if she'd just dipped them in a big bowl of rancid evil.

"What about the fish?!" I asked.

They said there were a few pools, sort of like big jacuzzis, and if you looked in the water you could see dozens of fish swimming around.

"Did any of them have a hand in their mouth?" I asked.

The women ignored me and walked on as if to signal that no more details would be forthcoming.

Naturally it started to rain.

As we crossed the little bridge to the cafeteria—cold, marble-floored, and institutional—I thought what a failure this trip had been.

No fish would be seen. No me eaten.

As the rest of the group sat, consuming whatever was sealed and prepackaged, I wandered outside and down the small bank to the little trickling stream. It ran from somewhere up the hill, down under the bridge, and into a gulley, where it disappeared into a shallow, tree-lined ravine.

A few people sat here and there looking at it, enjoying the quiet woods and the gentle tapping of the rain as it hit the shallow canopy of leaves above.

And that's when I noticed it.

Steam.

There was steam rising up from the water. White, airy, "hot water below" kind of steam.

My heart leapt.

If this came from the spring, that had to mean…could it be…might there be…

Fish.

Yes. There they were.

The little guys were about two inches long, brown and gray, and not immediately visible. In fact, they seemed to be nowhere until you gave them a reason to be.

On closer examination, that's what these people were doing.

A few paces upstream, a man with what can only be described as a super-disgusting ginormous club foot (actual medical term) looked down at the red flesh of his extremity, kindly being attended to by four or five of these fish. He had a content look on his face, like his long lost dog had at last come home to rest by his side.

Further upstream, a woman stood mid-water, still, smiling slightly, looking down as she, too, was attended to by these little workers.

I took off a shoe, sat on the bank, and put a foot in the hot water. I only had to wait a minute or two before they came.

They were small and thin, looking a little like the sucker

fish you find pressed against aquarium glass everywhere. They circled a dry patch of skin atop my big toe, taking it in, considering it, working up an estimate maybe. (For the record, I have extremely handsome feet, but we're all prone to a little dry skin here and there.)

There was a slight tickling as they touched down and set to work. Though I imagine there was biting, I couldn't feel it. All I noticed was the gentle rubbing of the fins as the current moved them back and forth.

Now it should be noted that there are actually two species of fish in the springs—*cyprinion macrostomus* (strikers) and *garra rufa obtusa* (lickers). The strikers bite off the skin. The lickers…well I guess they lick the wound. Fortunately for the human part of the equation, they're able to discern dead, flaky skin from live, healthy tissue—thus minimizing the number of "wait, where's my arm?" incidents.

I let the fish continue for a few minutes, fascinated by this strangely beautiful act of animal-human cooperation. Then I had a disturbing thought.

Where has this fish been?

Seriously. People have dry skin all over their bodies. *All over* their bodies. And I don't think the lickers stop and go, "No way man. Not going there."

I looked at the others in the stream and thought about how many people visit this place every day, sticking their ginormous…parts…in the water, smiling as the same fish that was nibbling on me nibbled on them. As far as I could tell no one came out at night to disinfect the little suckers. What if sharing fish with sick people was like going to the doctor for a flu shot and having him say, "Used this needle on the last guy, but what the hell? There's still some left!" For all I knew the fish carried blood-borne illnesses like ebola, Spanish ebola, or super deluxe German Luftwaffe ebola. I could catch plague, legionnaires disease, or, worse, disgusting ginormous club-foot syndrome.

I quickly pulled my leg out of the water.

The fish slipped off and hovered a moment, as if checking to make sure there was no other work to be done.

And then they disappeared into the current, leaving me alone on the bank.

An hour later I was still counting potentially transmittable diseases as we headed back to Sanli Urfa. But the rain was falling, the yellow hills were rolling by in the window, and my new neuroses proved no match for the comforting numbness of the road.

I looked at my fellow travelers and smiled.

Tomorrow I would drag them to a place where the only hotel accommodations were in trees.

Sean Presant has crossed the globe writing for the Let's Go series, making the world safe for adventurous travelers seeking relics of the ancient world and all-you-can-eat pizza. When not questioning the air supply in crowded Egyptian pyramids, tripping over confused iguanas in the Galapagos, or biking with chickens through Asia, Sean is a Los Angeles-based director and screenwriter.

GARY BUSLIK

. * * .

El Max

Revenge, it is sweet.

I KNEW THE BUS DRIVER WAS GOING TO BE TROUBLE.
He evidently had no first name, but his last name was Lopez,
and he was small and angular, and his eyes were round and
black like a rat's. He never looked at you but stared out the
windshield, even though the bus was still parked and it was
the middle of the night. He didn't respond when you said
holá, just tapped his gnarly fingers on the steering wheel,
gazed out at the dim lot, and occasionally picked gook out
of his eyes. He refused to budge.

We had landed after midnight, but some of the group
were coming in on a separate plane, and there was no telling
when they'd get to Havana. But our bus driver refused to
take the first part of the group to our hotel and return for
the others. We had been traveling for almost twenty-four
hours. After delays in Chicago, Toronto, and Montreal, we
had finally taken off in a blinding ice storm, terrorized by
the paroxysms of a 1950s Aeroflot Soviet jetliner with
chewing gum for hors d'oeuvres and rivets. We were too

exhausted even to cheer when we finally touched down, and now the son of a bitch wanted us to sit on the bus and wait for the other plane. He wouldn't budge.

We knew his name was Lopez because our HavanaTur guide, a handsome, affable young man in his early twenties, whose name was Roberto Baez but who asked us to call him Bob, kept yelling at him in Spanish to take us to the hotel. Most of us did not speak Spanish, but we got the gist of it, and every once in a while Bob would sprinkle his exhortations with the name *Lopez*, so that's how we knew. One of us who did speak a little Spanish said Bob called the driver a "dog's anus," but Lopez only replied by staring at his reflection in the windshield and scratching his butt.

After each vain appeal, Bob turned to us with a forced smile and, in pretty good English, said, "We assure you, your friends are almost here, and we will be on our way extremely shortly. We know it has been an extremely long day, and extremely shortly you will be asleep on your extremely soft pillow in your hotel. We welcome you extremely much to our extremely beautiful city, which you cannot see now, but you will surely see in the daytime."

Then he turned again to the driver and—for our benefit—pretended to engage in good-natured banter but was really calling him combinations of names that included animals and orifices. But Lopez still wouldn't budge.

So right away I knew he was going to be trouble.

I'm cranky when I'm tired. Also when I'm hungry, thirsty, have missed any episodes of *The Apprentice*, or am visiting any country that doesn't have Starbucks or macaroni and cheese. Long about one-thirty, after another of Bob's futile go-rounds with Lopez, I had had enough. I had been a courteous American for an hour and a half—way longer than average. Being a man of action, I got up to offer Lopez a bribe, when the long arm of the law, my wife, pulled me back by my elbow skin. "Sit," she said. When I looked down, my glance was met by the same malevolent gaze as Christ's detractors in Mel Gibson's *Passion*. I did not actually see the movie, but I saw enough excerpts on TV to guess the main idea. When they showed Jesus with deep, bloody lacerations all over his face and body, I thought: *cat owner*. Oh, great, so in addition to killing Christ, Jews were also responsible for not declawing their pets. That's what I thought. Sue me.

Five hours in an ice storm with Force 5 hurricane winds on a Soviet airplane with a beaded curtain for a toilet door and krill for meal service cannot compare with the terror-inducing of my wife's gaze, usually reserved for when I say something mean but truthful about her nephew, the thirty-year-old Nintendo wiz. I sat back down.

"You're not going to spend two weeks in a Havana jail," she hissed.

"How come?"

"It might distract me."

Our companion plane arrived from Canada at four-thirty in the morning, and by the time that group was interrogated and frisked, it was dawn over Cuba, but we were at last on our way. Havana is lovely in the morning, assuming your underpants haven't risen into your small intestine.

On the plus side, our hotel, the Parque Central in La Habana Vieja, was clean and luxurious. The Dutch always run first-rate accommodations, to make up for the fact that you have to dig up tulip bulbs in the fall and replant them every spring. They probably also felt guilty because in Cuba you can't eat without involving pig parts, although this is not the fault of Dutch people but of Fidel Castro, who, every time the Americans talk about lifting the embargo, opens his big yap. Not a pork lover myself, I had to remind myself that Hemingway would not only have eaten the oinkers, he would have shot them. In that order.

At eleven-thirty, a knock woke us up. "It is I, Bob."

For a moment, I forgot who Bob was. Havana does not yet have peep holes or other basic security devices, probably because they do not have many lawyers. Shirtless, I cracked the door and peeked at our guide's grinning kisser. "Bob," he repeated. "Might I come in?"

"My wife's still sleeping."

"I'm awake," Janice said behind me. She dashed into the bathroom with her clothes, afraid she might miss an excursion that involved purchasing carved coconut heads. "Don't let them leave without us."

Bob glanced up and down the hallway, then

Safety has seldom been a priority on Aeroflot or its spin-offs. My wife interrupted three stewardesses on their break to report exposed wires sparking and popping in a gaping hole in the restroom wall. "Is normal," one replied, the others giggling appreciatively at the time-honored Russian disavowal of responsibility for anything gone wrong. On another flight I followed a trail of smoke to the galley to find attendants hacking up chicken with cleavers and cooking it over an open flame. During a refueling stop on the runway in Mineralny Vody, the dizzying aroma of jet fuel wafted up the lowered aft stairway while dozens of passengers, seated around me, puffed away on their cigarettes.

◆

—Lee Forsythe, "Aeroflotsam and Jetsam"

stepped in. "It's an extremely beautiful hotel, don't you think? They are holding breakfast until noon today, in honor of your extremely late arrival. Excellent pork." The front of his guayabera shirt bulged weirdly, as if his own breakfast had consisted of a cinder block.

"What can I do for you?"

"Lopez is a scoundrel. A worm's earhole. Complete turtle excretion…if I understand the term correctly."

"You're doing fine."

"My brother Alberto, a police *capitano*, would like to arrest him for being such a goat's ass." He raised an eyebrow. "He would take care of him extremely firmly, I assure you. No further visitors would be so inconvenienced."

I motioned to the chair. He pulled it out and sat, the bulge under his shirt rising to his chest.

"Unfortunately, my brother's hands are tied. Do I use the phrase correctly?" He lowered his voice. "Lopez is a good communist. Head of his CDR—Committee for the Defense of the Revolution." He lowered his voice even more, and his forehead furled. "He has broken bread with El Maximo. I myself am not political. I stay out of it. But Lopez is a pig's nostril. I am here to give you advice. Be careful what you and your friends say on the bus. The villain reports everything."

"I don't have any friends."

"Ah, I see. Extremely wise. Your wife, then."

Janice popped out of the bathroom. "His wife what?"

"Don't talk in front of Lopez."

"And, good heavens, never offer him a bribe!"

She glanced at me and whistled soundlessly.

Bob grimaced, the cinder block digging into his spleen.

"I think Bob brought us a box lunch. Pork, I'll bet."

"Oh," our guide said, pretending he had just remembered

the hidden package. "Oh, yes, this." He motioned to the bulge. "Do you mind?" He slipped the bundle out of his guayabera. He plopped a filthy, fat manila envelope onto his lap and took a breath. "Your visa says you are a writer."

"A bad one," I assured him.

He patted the grease-spotted envelope. "I am wondering if you would read my novel. Not here, of course. Take it home and read it when you are relaxed."

"You want me to smuggle your manuscript out of Cuba?"

"I thought perhaps, and only if you like it, you might show it to a publisher—"

"We'll get into trouble."

Bob flicked a finger. "My brother would not allow that. Do not worry." His glance fell on my Star of David necklace. "We have a secret weapon." He whispered, "We, too, are of Hebrew persuasion."

Janice's toes did a little conga. "You? Jewish?"

"And Alberto, naturally." He chortled. "Fidel thinks he is, too." He paused and looked around. "Not that we want him. But it comes in extremely handy. My brother is teaching him Yiddish. Alberto doesn't speak a word of it. He makes it all up. You should hear the Bearded One trying to talk like a Jew. Extremely amusing."

"Of course we'll take your novel," Janice piped. "And my husband is a *very good* writer." Always there when I need her.

"Wonderful! Wonderful!" He handed her the package. "You can tell no one it is mine, naturally," he whispered. "I left my name off it entirely."

I took it from Janice and handed it back. "Sorry. Out of the question. Anyhow, I'm disliked in the trade."

She took it back and buried it at the bottom of my suit-case. "It's in good hands."

"Written entirely in English," Bob puffed. "Printed for ease of reading."

"*Longhand?*" Janice exclaimed.

"I will be glad to divide any money with you fifty-fifty, if I'm phrasing that correctly?" He got up and offered me his hand.

Janice took it. "Not necessary, we assure you. We're glad to help an oppressed artist."

"You will have a glorious ten days in Cuba, with me as your guide."

"I have no doubt."

"Well, *I* have a doubt," I said, reaching for the manuscript. But before I could shove it back into his shirt, he was out the door.

I turned to Janice. "I thought you said my being in jail would be a distraction."

"This is different. He's probably a literary genius. A Cuban J. D. Salinger. Think of his determination and hardship, writing it out longhand. He's *Jewish.*"

"So is Ed Asner, but I wouldn't trust him with my pork chop."

"All right, if they make a fuss—which I highly doubt—*I'll* go to jail. How's that?"

"It doesn't work that way. Do the names Julius and Ethel Rosenberg ring a bell?"

"You're on vacation. Relax." She kissed my chin. "Who knows, maybe he'll dedicate it to you. That would be something, wouldn't it? Anyhow, they shoot you here, they don't electrocute you."

"It must be nice being married to a love-sick imbecile."

"It comes in extremely handy. Now get dressed and let's go for breakfast. Then I want to buy something shiny." She suddenly looked worried. "Communists sell shiny things, don't they?"

After lunch the bus was waiting. Bob had held the front seats for Janice and me. The other people in the group drilled us a look. One woman in particular, a manicurist from Detroit with six-inch fingernails painted to depict important events in the life of black leaders—one pinky being Marcus Garvey's parade down Lenox Avenue, and a thumb Martin Luther King's "I Have A Dream" speech on the Washington mall—cut me a snarl, possibly sensing race-related shenanigans. I knew that unless I got on her good side, I would never leave Cuba with both eyes. Nevertheless, I sat. May as well enjoy the scenery while you still have depth perception.

"Today we are going to Veradero Beach," Bob reminded us, as Lopez swung the bus onto the Malecón. "We will have lunch and enjoy the sun." He sliced me a wink. "Cubans themselves are not permitted on the beach." He glanced at Lopez accusatorially. "Only tourists." I did not wink back.

Twenty minutes later I told Janice I had to go to the bathroom.

"So go. What do you want from me?"

"I have to pass that woman."

"Protect your eyes."

"What if she goes for the family jewels?"

"One hand on your face, one on your crotch. This is not brain surgery."

"It'll look like I'm afraid of her."

"You are afraid of her."

"People will think I'm weak and eat off my plate."

"Think pork."

"Point taken."

"Besides," she whispered, "we've got Roberto's brother."

I smiled at Bob and, yes, winked. I got up and walked gingerly to the back, whistling "Candy Man" by Sammy Davis Jr. Other than her staring at my hand covering my crotch, there were no incidents.

Until I tried to leave the bathroom. The door stuck. I mean, S-T-U-C-K. I wiggled the sliding latch and jammed it back hard. *Nada.* I pulled it back and got my knee up and pushed my other leg against the commode and heaved, but the door didn't budge. It occurred to me that the Detroit woman was leaning on it from the other side. Perhaps she had recruited the other members of our group, many of whom had wanted to sit in the front seat. Perhaps some of them were familiar with my writing. Meanwhile, the bus was barreling down the coastal road, picking up speed, jouncing me like an asymmetrical Cuban-lottery ball, and the windowless three-by-three cubical, which was directly over the diesel engine, was getting ten degrees hotter every minute. And guess what? I'm claustrophobic.

Sometimes I get panic attacks when my sheets are tucked in too tight, even when I'm not in bed. If you've ever had a claustrophobia attack, you know they are terrifying, degrading, and make you regret all those times you promised to write something nice about a hotel or restaurant just to get a free room or food, knowing full well you were going to stiff them, review-wise. You're sure you're going to pass out and poop in your pants, and that strangers will rifle through your wallet and find a picture of your parakeet. You're also sure that no one else on the bus will have to go to the bathroom all the way to Veradero, and that your wife will fall asleep, which she likes to do, and that you'll pass out with your head in the potty, and that it will get so hot in there that by the time anyone notices you're missing, your skull will have shrunk to the size and consistency of a nutmeg.

It was time to pound.

With the engine roaring like an F-16 or my lawn mower after Janice's nephew borrowed it and forgot to put in oil, I wasn't sure if anyone could hear me. I took no chances. I pounded and yelled, yelled and pounded, my panic attack in full shock and awe. The louder I screamed and whacked the door, the more spiritedly Lopez revved the engine. The bus was going faster and faster, and the bathroom was getting hotter and hotter, and my breaths were harder and harder, and my temples percussed like 10,000-pound bunker-busters.

The son of a bitch must have known I had Bob's novel.

"Help! I'm stuck!"

Bob yelled back at me. "Pull the latch back!"

Janice shouted, "Take deep breaths and slow down your alpha waves, like Dr. Luce taught you."

"It's hot! I can't breathe!"

"Close your eyes and imagine yourself lying in a lovely meadow next to a country lake!"

"Tell Lopez to stop the bus! I'm going to pass out from the fumes!"

"I'll be right back!" Roberto hollered.

"Hurry!"

The bus went faster.

"You still there, honey?!" Janice shouted.

"Kill Lopez!"

"Roberto's talking to him! Close your eyes and pretend you're listening to Handel's *Water Music*."

"Kill the commie motherfucker!"

Finally, finally, Bob ran back. "He won't stop! He said the nation depends on him to arrive on time! It is a matter of prestige! But don't worry, we will get you out!"

He shoved something into the door jam. "I have a pen. If only it will go—"

But, writing instruments being useless when you really need them, it was too fat to reach the lock tongue.

"Do you have a tire iron?!" I shouted.

No answer. Janice might have been interpreting.

"A tire iron!" Roberto confirmed. "To fix flat tires! Of course!"

"*Pry* me the hell out of here!"

"It's with the spare tire! Under the bus! We would have to stop!"

Lopez went faster.

"I love you, honey!"

I felt woozy. The rumble of the diesel receded, approached, receded again. Janice's voice sounded tinny and far away—even more than usual. My vision blurred. I could feel my carotid artery in my toes. My tongue was the size and consistency of a Vienna salami, my flesh cold and lifeless. I lost sense of time. The walls began to swirl. My knees gave way. I remembered being born.

Then, as if in a dream, I saw Martin Luther King slip through the door crack.

A moment later, the latch slammed back, the door jolted open, and the manicurist from Detroit filled the doorway. "You all right now, sweet baby!" she trumpeted, fanning me with her nails. Fresh air whooshed over my bloodless mug. "Charmaine set you free!"

She hefted me to my feet and hauled me down the aisle,

pushing Bob and Janice aside, shouting, "Get outta the way, we marching to freedom!" She deposited me in my front-row seat, warning Janice, "Take care of him. Men with good nails don't grow on trees." Then she turned to Lopez and bared her teeth, but he was too busy picking gook out of his eye to notice.

The day we left Cuba I noticed my Star of David pendant missing. It was a stamped, fourteen-karat gold–plated cheapy, but my Aunt Rose had bought it for me in Israel, so I liked it. Anyhow, my taste tends to run toward the cheap—not in the Donald Trump sense of the word, but in the inexpensive sense of the word. I lose things a lot when traveling, and this time it was my necklace. Still, after breakfast I offhandedly asked Roberto if anyone had turned it in. He said no and even though I assured him it was junk jewelry, he seemed extremely concerned and checked with the concierge. Shaking his head solemnly, he took me aside and whispered, "Do you think you lost it on the bus?"

"It's possible, I guess."

He pursed his lips. "I see."

"You do?"

"Lopez must have found it and kept it, that thieving sheep rectum. Well, we'll see about that." He lowered his voice even more. "You still have my…merchandise?"

I nodded.

"I await your verdict with pines and noodles. You can reach me through my brother."

When, a few weeks later, I finished reading Bob's manuscript, I handed it to my wife. Janice is always trying to sign over our home and other assets to foreign people who say they love America. Our Polish cleaning lady, for example, is an indefatigable young woman who hunts down dirt like Purvis hunted down Dillinger. Believe me, I like her, too. But I still don't see why I should marry her to make her a citizen. I also like our gardener, Raoul, even though he formed an offshore corporation to launder the money we pay him. Or Viktor, our Croatian painter, whose rehab treatments Janice offered to subsidize, forcing us to cash in the savings bonds I got at my bar mitzvah, and who's only on Step Two.

So I knew she really, really wanted to like Bob's novel. She had been watching me from the corner of her eye as I leafed through the manuscript, stone-faced. Finally, it was hers.

A couple of days later, she handed it back. "It's horrible."

"What? Not worth rotting in a tropical prison for?"

"As near as I can figure it, it's *Fiddler on the Roof*—without a fiddler or a roof."

"Or a shred of talent. In itself not enough to keep it off the *Times*' bestseller list, mind you."

Her eyes lit up. "You're not saying there's actually hope for—"

I hefted the manuscript. "Cat litter."

She deflated. "What are you going to tell Bob?"

"*Me?*"

"Technically, he gave it to you, not me. Let him down easy. Promise?"

I had her. She had lurched unwittingly into my trap. What she didn't know was that, at that very moment, hunkered in my desk drawer was a letter I had plucked from the mailbox yesterday, while she had been out shopping for something nice for herself.

My Dear Señor Gary,

We are knowing about your stoling star and we

opened a file on your theft. We will not rest, we will
never rest, until we solve this badly crime. Our
nation depends on us. It is a matter of prestige.

Yours truly,
Cpt. Alberto Paul Baez (Captain)
District Centro
La Habana, Cuba

Postscript: We have now a suspect into custody, your
bus driver.

"O.K.," I agreed, promising Janice I'd let Bob down gently. Then, trying to appear depressed, I shuffled to my office,
where I typed:

Dear Roberto,

My wife and I read *Castanets on the Bus*, and we
agree that it [I dug deeply for the right phrase that
did not include the words *total dreck*] elicits great
promise. I will keep you informed. Meanwhile, please
tell your brother to keep the pressure on regarding
my precious stoling star. Tell him I am *extremely*
happy he has a suspect and that I will do everything I
can to make you a famous author. I promise.

Sincerely (I really mean it!),
Gary

P.S. If enough pressure is applied, sooner or later the
suspect will confess.

I lobbed Roberto's masterpiece onto my desk, next to my
framed eight-by-ten of Charmaine hugging the Reverend Al
Sharpton, and admired my nails. Every month or so I'd write
Bob another letter to keep his and, especially, his brother's

hopes up. He wants to be a writer? Fine. Why should he suffer any less extremely than the rest of us?

Besides, the thought of Capitano Baez pistol-whipping Lopez *clack-clacked* off the rooftop of my brain like happy little concave shells.

Gary Buslik teaches creative writing at the University of Illinois, Chicago. He writes short stories, essays, and novels, and his work appears in many commercial and literary magazines. His most recent novel is The Missionary's Position. *The selection here is from his book-in-progress,* A Rotten Person Travels the West Indies. *He windsurfs and plays softball. He does not play golf. Please do not call him to play golf.*

*

Albanian leaders felt guilty after forty years of an ultra-communist police state that locked up 35 percent of the population for political crimes. So the government instituted a restitution program that gave ex-political prisoners some kind of facility to manage or work in—a hospital, hotel, or restaurant. You might think that the hotel service is really bad and the place is run like a prison. This is actually true! The workers are all former prisoners who learned their hotel management and culinary skills from watching how efficiently Albanian prisons were operated. That explains why our manager at the State Hotel in Skhoder would stand in dark corners smoking and chatting with his staff. The rooms that were left (part of the cement structure gave way in the back and fell into the vacant lot) were like caves. Mine had a toilet with no seat, one small forty-watt light bulb, and a broken shower. Only the electricity worked and this powered my portable heater which I brought with me on all trips. The catch was the heater only worked when there was power.

My partner on this mission was in a better room but it faced the street. The location became problematic one night when rocks were flung through his window, breaking the glass and creating a major racket. While it was probably a random event (i.e., drunks heading home), he was frightened to death that someone was in his room, and proceeded to unload his portable mace gun in the emptiness. Naturally this burned his own face and made it difficult for him to get back to sleep. So we all looked like shit each morning, exchanging incredible tales of the night before.

—George M. Guess, "World-Class Hotels"

SCOTT TURNER

* * *

The Most Tenacious Turd in Nairobi

What comes up must go down. Eventually.

UNLIKE AMERICANS, KENYANS BELIEVE IN FATE. THEY know they're not in charge of their destiny. It explains their nonchalant attitude toward the near-total absence of car seatbelts. Even when you can find a taxi that has them installed, they're usually buried so deep in the crack that by the time you dig them out you've already arrived at your destination. According to one of my students, "If Death has your name on his list, a little strap across your waist won't stand in his way."

My Masai friend Nicholas Sironka insisted that nothing is accidental, and he began every sentence about the future with the prayer, "God willing." "God willing, I will see you tomorrow at noon." "God willing, we will have a new calf by spring." "God willing, the mechanic will fix my car by Tuesday."

Likewise, my students at the university were baffled by the concept of insurance. "How can you insure against something that's going to happen anyway?" I suppose if I had hopped a hazardous *matatu* to work each day, I would have adopted a similarly fatalistic attitude. But Cathy and I tenaciously clung to the need for control, no matter how inconvenient it became.

During our nine-month sojourn in University of Nairobi housing, we replaced our toilet seat a total of seven times. Even when we sprang for the most expensive units at Nakumatt, the plastic screws only held for a couple of months. Reliable bathroom fixtures were clearly not a priority in the Kenyan economy.

Cathy wondered what the security guard could have been thinking as we continued to lug our broken seats to the trash bin. *Just what are those Americans doing in there?* Perhaps he concluded that the astonishing amounts of food we carried in from our grocery runs produced violent convulsions down the line that ordinary Kenyan toilet seats could not withstand.

Cathy became quite the handyman, jerry-rigging the seat back together for a day or two at a time. Eventually we resolved that a perpetually broken seat was preferable to the heartache of constantly buying new ones only to have them break again. I started to empathize with the middle-aged waitress who sticks out her third marriage to an abusive alcoholic because life has taught her that she just isn't likely to do any better. Is there a country music song about broken toilet seats? Like the no-good cheatin' husband, at least we knew what we had, and it helped us to develop better balance. I will never have to worry about falling off a chair again, at least not while sober. It also helped us to empathize with our daughter Rebecca's potty training, a similarly distressing culture shock. We were all learning how to shit with greater finesse.

The broken seat was not the worst of our toilet conundrums, however. During the frequent occasions when the water went out for days on end, we had to try to flush the toilet manually with the water we kept stored in jerry cans. In the interest of conservation, we only flushed the solids, and Cathy tried to control the odor with a rim-hook sanitizer that she bought at Uchumi. I suspected she was coming unhinged when she asked if I had noticed the beautiful shade of green that was produced by the mix of blue base cleaning solution and yellow urine. The surviving strands of toilet paper added lovely streaks of white, and once I caught her pouring in milk to accentuate it. It was true art—a breathtaking kaleidoscope of filth.

Eventually the whole system became clogged, and we were unable to dispose of the more substantial effluvia with a simple flush, even when the water returned. Consequently, I acquired the thankless responsibility of carving the biggies into more manageable tasks with a wire coat hanger. In India I would have been marked as an untouchable. After a series of flushes that could take up to half an hour, I would finally manage to pack away most of our business to the common trust. But there was one stubborn bugger who just kept popping back up no matter how many times I flushed him down. It wasn't the size, but seemingly, pure spite that kept him afloat. It was as though a decision had been made deep within the bowels of the Nairobi sewer system to keep sending him back just to taunt me. Urban infrastructure was a serious problem, as the ubiquitous trash on the walkways demonstrated. But why did this single little golf ball possess a unique capacity to survive all my attempts to dispose of him? I would slice him and dice him and send him on his way, only to discover thirty minutes later that he had been bodily resurrected, peering up contemptuously from the narrow drain basin at the bottom of the bowl.

I eventually resolved simply to fish him out and remove him to the outdoor garbage bin in a plastic bag, or maybe just fling him from the balcony like the notorious flying toilets in Kibera slum. But as though sensing my change of strategy, whenever I entered the bathroom and hunkered over the bowl with a net crafted from a pencil and Ziploc bag, he was nowhere to be found. Only later when my commitment to victory had waned, would he reappear. I never knew just which of us was originally responsible for the wily deposit, or what dietary anomaly could have accounted for his strange tenacity. Surviving all my determined efforts, he managed to stick around like an unwanted house guest for nearly a month. But then one day when I finally resolved simply to surrender to the distressful fate he had imposed upon our lives, he simply vanished of his own accord, never to be seen again.

God willing.

In addition to teaching political science at the University of Montevallo in Alabama, Scott Turner has gone Nashville honky-tonking with a Masai warrior, grocery shopping with a Tibetan monk, and jet skiing with the Kuwaiti royal family. He taught at the University of Nairobi on a Fulbright scholarship in 2002-03, and has completed an unpublished manuscript entitled Nine Months in Nairobi. *He and his high school sweetheart Cathy have two children, Gareth and Rebecca, and they all travel with him as often as possible.*

★

Many years ago I took a bus trip through Greece with some college classmates. Toward the end of the journey, I felt that I might be having an attack of appendicitis. I had severe abdominal pain, so severe I confided in a wise, old priest who was acting as a guide.

He suggested a suppository. "What for?" I asked. "I'm not consti-pated." But as the words tumbled out of my mouth a ray of hope presented itself. What if I was only constipated, and not dying of an unknown illness?

As soon as we got to Athens, I hastened to the pharmacy. Returning to my room, I gazed with loathing at the enormous ob-ject that I was supposed to insert into my backside. Reluctantly, yet with haste, as the abdominal pains surged, I bent to my task. Soon I was squatting over a hole in the marble floor of the bathroom, giving birth to an enormous pile of excrement that, like a mad ter-mite colony or a volcano, could hardly be contained by the space in which it grew. Gazing with wonder at this ziggurat of colonic filth, I rose a new man, knowing with renewed clarity the mean-ing of resurrection.

—Sean O'Reilly, from *How to Shit Around the World* by Dr. Jane Wilson-Howarth

* ✳ *

Ecstasy at the Altar

Maybe that's why they call it stained glass.

"WE'RE NOT EVEN CHRISTIAN," WAILED DANNY AS I dragged my family to Chartres Cathedral on the train from Gare Montparnasse. "Why do we have to go to so many churches?"

For my kids, Europe's vast, vaulted cathedrals weren't glorious icons of medieval society, but creepy, dark places full of dead people. Being hecka-old didn't make them less boring. Both Danny, eleven, and Becca, fourteen, had seen enough cathedrals on this trip. But I remembered Chartres fondly from a trip to Europe many years before. And my wife Susan, who had studied for a year in France, was eager to go.

The tour guide led our group to the North Porch of the cathedral to read the sculptures, which told the stories of Adam and Eve and Paradise Lost: "…Third down, on this side, Adam is standing naked in the garden, he's sleeping naked, when God created Eve at the top. Next down, Eve is naked, by an apple tree…

"As they are expelled from Paradise, they're still hiding

their nudity; at the bottom, they've left Paradise, and my gosh, they're wearing clothes. Adam is digging, and Eve is spinning, and God on the outside is blessing them... Paradise lost..."

We followed him into the cathedral through the Royal Portal, the main entrance, and the temperature seemed to drop twenty degrees. We walked around the stone labyrinth in the floor and sat on pews in the nave.

With his back to the altar, the guide told us that Chartres Cathedral was built on the ruins of three or four burned-out churches dating back to the days of Charlemagne, and that the pictures in the stained glass had enabled illiterate medieval churchgoers to read Bible stories. I peeked at my family. Becca was paying attention, but Danny was getting that "creepy old church" look. Susan smiled at me, enraptured by the cathedral and the lecture.

I followed her eyes as she took in the grand upward sweep of the interior lines of the building. Gothic architecture had seemed old and stuffy and outmoded when I studied it in college. No, we weren't Christians, but the magnificent verticality of the architecture drew me inward and upward. Surely God was up there somewhere in the play of light streaming in through the bright clerestory windows and shafting down the stone walls.

We examined the Incarnation Window, one of the oldest in Chartres: "Bottom left, Gabriel announces to Mary that she will be the mother of God, and she jumps from her seat in surprise, with a raised hand...Wouldn't you?" The group tittered. "Second row, on the left, the Annunciation to the shepherds..." I heard a gasp and a stirring among the hundreds of tourists in the building.

I shifted my heavenward glance down to the guide, who stumbled, paused, ruffled his hair, and stopped his presentation.

Still with his back to the altar, he peered around at our group, trying to find the source of distraction. He turned and looked over his shoulder, and I followed his gaze. There on the white altar, standing in a shard of bright light from above, a pretty young blonde woman in a bright red dress faced upward. Her arms outstretched to the sides, her eyes closed, she leaned back, legs spread, undulating to some ecstatic internal musical beat. As I watched, she made a peculiar shrugging motion, and the dress fell at her feet.

She was naked and voluptuous. Her hair shining white in the light, she rotated her hips in a slow, suggestive manner. We all stared, frozen in silence for a long moment. Then activity picked up around us. The cathedral was filled with pilgrims and tourists from all over the world, and dozens of cameras started to click and flash. Asian businessmen and Danish schoolboys jockeyed for camera positions. A group of Belgian nuns stared, but took no snapshots. "What's going on here?" I wondered aloud.

"Can I have the video camera, Daddy?" asked Danny, in an odd voice.

"No, I don't want any shots of naked bodies on our summer travel movie."

"I won't shoot, I'll just look."

"No bodies."

The guide's reaction was less than dramatic. "How unusual," he muttered, then slipped through a small side door. Five long minutes later he returned with an elderly security guard, who was soon joined by another. They approached the woman gingerly. Seemingly in a trance, she was startled by their approach, but she put up no resistance. One guard covered her with his jacket, and they gently started to lead her away. She stopped, looked around, went back to the altar, and picked up her crumpled red dress from the floor. The guards and the dazed blonde lady disappeared through the same side door.

Our cathedral mentor took up his place in front of the tour group and muttered a comment about occasional disruptions by troubled souls. "She'll be treated kindly," he said.

"Will she go to jail?" someone asked.

"Probably not."

I wondered if the cathedral, a holy and enthrallingly beautiful place, tended to attract odd behavior. Sometimes people reacted in unusual ways to iconic landmarks.

As a San Franciscan, I knew that the Golden Gate Bridge had, tragically, lured many troubled souls to commit suicide over the years. I wondered if Chartres Cathedral had a history of bizarre expressions of spirituality—or whatever it was we had seen.

We theorized excitedly on the walk to the station.

"That woman looked like a model," I said with grave authority, as we boarded our train back to Paris. "Maybe she was posing for a photo spread in a girlie magazine, and it was all a setup for her photographer to take pictures." Certainly there had been plenty of time to shoot a whole roll, before they led her away to be treated kindly. Some Japanese tourists had shot a lot more than that. I fantasized a headline on the cover of a tawdry skin mag called something like *Bone Appetite*—"Charlotte does Chartres!"

The mild reaction from the authorities had impressed Susan, and she wondered if that kind of thing had happened often, or even if the guards knew the woman.

The kids had various theories. The blonde was crazy, they contended, or sick, or high on drugs. "You should have let me look through the video camera," said Danny. "I might have found some clues."

Right. If she wasn't a porn queen, she could have been a tourist overcome by a holy ecstasy, inspired by the imagery around her. The excitement of the day ebbed. The rhythm of the train lulled me to drowsiness, and the words of the guide echoed in my brain: "As they are expelled from Paradise they're still hiding their nudity. Paradise lost…"

Bill Zarchy (www.billzarchy.com) is a free-lance director of photography, writer, and teacher based in San Francisco. Over the past thirty years, he has shot film, video, and HDTV projects in two dozen countries and three dozen states. Recently he filmed interviews with three former presidents for the Emmy-winning West Wing Documentary Special, *and he was Director of Photography/Virtual Sets for the feature film* Conceiving Ada. *He has a B.A. in Government from Dartmouth and an M.A. in Film from Stanford, and he teaches Advanced Cinematography at San Francisco State University. His personal essays, tales from the road, and technical articles have appeared in newspapers and literary and trade magazines, and he is working on* Roving Camera, *a book about his work and travels.*

✦ ✳ ✦

Fawlty Towers, Tibet-Style

He could run a perfectly good hotel if it weren't
for the bloody guests.

CROSSING THE LOBBY OF THE LHASA HOLIDAY INN WAS
becoming increasingly hazardous. Since I was wearing a suit,
I was an obvious target—it became impossible to get
through without being bombarded with question after question from irate guests. Barba avoided them by stepping
through the windows across the back corridors of the hotel.
Somehow, Chef was never approached by the angry guests
but instead attracted the stupid ones. They would see him
dressed in his blue-chequered trousers, chef's jacket and hat
and ask, "Do you work here?"

"No. I am at a chefs' convention," he would reply and the
guests wouldn't bother him again.

I was a glutton for punishment and headed through the
lobby to reach the Hard Yak Café and my room. A guest
handed me a torn rag which he pointed out had been a perfectly good sock when he had given it to the Housekeeping
Department.

"So the other one is O.K. then?" I asked him. "And you
expect a *full* refund?"

The Bank of China ran out of small bank notes, so we had no change to give guests. The post office ran out of stamps and resorted to selling philatelic sets. These were very beautiful stamps, but they were in such small denominations that once you had stuck the required eighteen stamps, each five centimeters by four centimeters, on the back of a postcard, there was no room to write the address, let alone a message.

I had a call from the town of Shigatse. There was no direct line and the call had been passed to the Lhasa Holiday Inn via the Beijing operator. It was an English tour operator and through the crackles I could just make out her distraught voice.

"Is that Mr. Alec? I was told to contact you. One of our group has died. Peacefully. In her sleep. Heart attack. There is no telex here. No fax. No phone to the outside world. The group has gone on to Kathmandu. None of the drivers will touch the body. Can you pass a message on to my travel agency in England?"

I placed the call to London and passed on the sad news. As Lhasa was the only point of communication, I became the messenger between the tour guide stuck in Shigatse, the British Embassy in Beijing, and the travel agency and insurance company in London.

I broke the news to Barba.

"One of our guests has died."

"Oh no. Where?"

"In Shigatse."

"Thank God for that! Alec, there is nothing worse than a stiff in the hotel."

The insurance company called with the news that the relatives wanted a cremation and would come out to Tibet to witness it. I asked Tashi for the number of the Shigatse

Hotel so that I could place the call with our hotel operator, who in turn would call the Beijing operator, who would relay the call to Shigatse.

"I don't know the Shigatse Hotel telephone number Mr. Alec."

He picked the receiver up, dialed 2222 for our operator and asked her. She didn't know either. One of our staff had a bright idea; "Mr. Alec, you could call the Shigatse Hotel and ask them for their number—they must know."

It was painful process but we eventually managed to find the number and place the call. The connection was weak and I had to shout, "The relatives want to come out to see the body. They want a cremation."

There was silence down the other end of the phone. Then I heard the faint voice back. "Listen, there is no fridge here. You can smell the body from the lobby—there is no time for family visits."

I placed a call back to the insurance company. The call came through as I was crossing the lobby. I fought away a guest who was complaining about the toilet paper being too stiff. He wanted his money back and was going to write to Holiday Inn head office.

"If you will excuse me, I shall have to attend to your stiff toilet paper in a while," I said politely to him.

The receptionist passed me the receiver across the counter. It was another bad connection and I had to shout, *"You can smell the body in the lobby. We strongly recommend cremation on the spot!"*

I looked around me. The crowd in the Holiday Inn lobby had gone silent. The man with the stiff toilet paper was running away down the corridor. "Not here. Not here," I called out to the stunned guests. "But if you go to Shigatse tonight, don't ask for room 238."

"No," the voice came back down the line, "the family insists that the deceased's son comes out to attend the proceedings."

The local travel agency involved had managed to find a truck driver willing to transport the body back to Lhasa. It had taken several cartons of cigarettes and promises of Johnnie Walker Black Label. The tour leader had sat in the passenger seat of the truck as the driver raced through the night back to Lhasa.

They arrived early in the morning and went straight to the hospital. The doctors refused to take the body—there was no point—and in despair the driver came to the hotel and demanded that the body be stored in the hotel's walk-in refrigerator.

Chef would have had a heart attack—going in to take out the Spam for breakfast and finding Mrs. Simkins laid out on the floor. We declined their request. We had enough trouble from live guests.

There are no morgues in Tibet as bodies are not stored as they are in the West. Under the Tibetan system of sky burials, where the corpses are taken out at dawn and fed to friendly vultures, morgues are a waste of time. After much persuasion, the hospital admitted that they had a freezer but they would only keep the body for a few days. There was not long to wait, as the Chinese had cut through the normal red tape and allowed a permit to be issued immediately to the son, who was already on his way to Lhasa. He would be arriving the following morning and the local travel agency had arranged a cremation for the same day.

I had a stiff drink with the tour leader. It had been a harrowing experience for her—stuck in Shigatse with a body and then a ten-hour Tibetan truck drive through the night with Mrs. Simkins bouncing around in the back. But the worst was yet to come. What kind of cremation did the relatives expect? A few kind words from the vicar in a little village church? Organ music, a coffin on the conveyor belt, and the parting of velvet drapes?

The son arrived, somewhat dazed—knocked out from the altitude and emotions. The tour leader and I accompanied him in the hotel Land Cruiser, and we pulled out of the courtyard at the head of a long cavalcade of cars toward the hills near Drepung monastery. We stopped for a while by the side of the road and when a lorry overtook us we started off again.

The tour leader suddenly started to strike up stupid conversation with the son. "Look a tree!" she said pointing out of the window. "What glorious weather today. Look! A cloud in the sky over there!" I knew we had to

———— ☽ ————

At the Savior-Transfiguration Cathedral in St. Petersburg I wandered through the multi-tiered chapel past simultaneous weddings, baptisms, and other rites, mesmerized by the ornate interior, soft music, burning incense, and the cadences of the Russian services. As I walked, my eyes were drawn upward to small candle-lit platforms suspended from the ceiling. Suddenly I plunged headlong down a short flight of steps and through a circle of mourners to slam against an open casket. The coffin and its occupant, an old lady, shuddered at the impact as did I when the bereaved turned their shocked, angry looks on me. I retreated apologizing profusely and actually feeling relieved in the knowledge that with only slightly more momentum I would have fallen into the casket on top of her.

◆

—Lee Forsythe, "How I Got My Diplomatic License Revoked"

make polite conversation to keep his mind busy but this was ridiculous. Then I saw what she had seen—the lorry in front of us was loaded with a loose pile of firewood and on top of the wood was something wrapped in a white sheet, bouncing up and down as we sped over the bumps. Mrs. Simkins!

"Look!" I said to the son, "There is a yak over there and if you look behind us you can see some more trees."

We turned off the main road and along a narrow dusty track up the foothills to the east of Drepung. The track became progressively steeper and at the sharpest gradient, by a vertical drop into a quarry, the lorry in front of us spluttered to a halt. The wood for the funeral pyre and Mrs. Simkins shot back towards us and the body balanced on the lorry's tailboard above our windscreen. Fortunately they could start the engine again and the body swung back onto the lorry-side of the tailboard. We carried up another few meters and arrived at the base of small mound which was to be the cremation site.

We waited by the car while the preparations were carried out. There were dozens of people about, many in uniform, including a Chinaman who seemed to be the official photographer of the event, who zoomed in on all of us with a video camera. We were called up when everything was ready and the son was able to pay his last respects. The tour leader had cut a bouquet of flowers from the hotel greenhouse. A monk sat cross-legged by the pile of wood, reading aloud prayers from the Tibetan *Book of the Dead*.

A very cheerful Tibetan then arrived wearing overalls spotted with brown flecks. The Chinese travel agent motioned for us to go back to the car.

"No. No. You don't understand," said the son. "I have come all this way just to be here for this moment."

The Chinaman became anxious. "You really must go now. Please!" He looked at me. "Please go now!"

My mind clicked into action. Of course there are no cremations in Tibet as we know them in the West! I suggested that we could go down to the car and return when the fire was going. Reluctantly the son agreed with me. As I hurried him down the slope, we could hear the sound of steel—the Tibetan was sharpening his knives. I glanced around and caught the glint of sunlight on the sharpened edge of his rusty sky burial daggers. "Just some preparations they have to make before they can start," I said quietly.

"Look out there! Some trees," the tour leader pointed out to the valley, continuing our inane conversation from the car. The minutes seemed like hours. At long last we heard the crackle of the fire and saw smoke rising from the hill above us. We returned up the path to the cremation site. A Chinese policeman was urinating over the track from on top of the mound as we waited for him to finish before we could pass. They were pleased that everything was going so well and had already started on the beers.

The funeral pyre was in a spectacular setting—with the view of the surrounding hills, the town of Lhasa far below and the Potala Palace framed at the bottom of the valley. It is going to happen to all of us one day and as I watched the flames lick the sky I thought that there can be no better ending than this. To pass away peacefully in the night and then go up in smoke with the Potala in the background and a Tibetan monk chanting prayers for your soul. It was a moving experience for all of us.

Our profound thoughts were interrupted by the Tibetan in the splattered overalls who approached the fire carrying a bucket. He flung the contents on to the fire and a gigantic fireball engulfed the sky. The son and I dived for cover, but the monk sitting cross-legged could not get out of the way quick enough and had his eyebrows singed. The Tibetan came up to us with his empty petrol bucket, grinning from ear to ear. His gold tooth flashed at us in the sunlight and he gave us the thumbs up sign as if to say, "It's a good one!"

We shared a gritty bottle of Lhasa Beer and returned to the hotel in a daze. It had been quite a day for all of us and I was not in the mood to face the pack of guests who were shouting in the lobby. They had been down to the airport two days in a row and had returned again to the hotel, having been refused boarding passes for the aircraft. Some of them were at the CAAC office, staging a sit-in—the first demonstration by foreigners in Tibet. Our Holiday Inn tour groups had also been victims of the overbooking and we were doing our best with cartons of cigarettes and invitations to dinner to try and get them seats. CAAC were in a bit of a sticky situation. Their plane to Kathmandu had 123 seats and they had sold 420 tickets.

That evening I had a call from Mrs. Simkins's son. He had been given a black metal box to take the ashes in back to England but there was a problem. They rattled. He was right, he couldn't go back with his mother rattling under the seat. I suppose a few twigs and a bucket of petrol does not match the fierce heat of a Western crematorium.

"Do you have a cloth to wrap them in? And a piece of string?" he asked. I promised I would find some. I managed to persuade Charlie to open up the Housekeeping store and I found an old bath mat and a piece of telephone wire. This would have to do.

I returned to room 3101 to give them to the son. He thanked me for them and said, "There's just one more thing. Do you think you could wrap them up for me?"

He did have a point. To me they were just pieces of bone but I could understand his feelings.

"Of course."

He went off into the bathroom. I spread out the bath mat on the luggage stand in the room, opened up the metal box and tipped out the bones. I had expected there to be a small pile of ash and a few larger pieces but no, the box had been full. Splinters and bone fragments went everywhere—rolling off the luggage stand on to the carpet and across the floor.

"Just a minute!" I called out, frantically picking up pieces and stuffing them into the rolled up mat. "Just a minute! Nearly ready!"

Happy that I had collected everything I gave him the all clear. Just as I was leaving I saw one more piece—right down by the bedside, precisely where he would step with his bare feet when he got into bed. I started the same ridiculous conversation that the tour leader had struck up in the car. "Oh lovely weather today wasn't it? Look! Have you seen that picture over there?"

As he turned, I dived for the floor, scooped up the fragment and put it in my pocket. After bidding him farewell and wishing him a safe trip home I emptied my pocket into the rose bed of the Holiday Inn Lhasa. Whether in heaven, nirvana, or back as a reincarnation, I hope that Mrs. Simkins approves.

Ever since, I was known by the expats as "Alec the Undertaker." Fortunately, I never had to deal with any more cases. The only other fatality that year had taken place in the no-man's land between the borders at Zhangmu. A Frenchman had died on the slope. The rest of the group traveling with him just thought he wasn't feeling very well and carried him up the three-hour hike to the Chinese customs post. The Chinese pointed out that he was dead and refused to accept him. The group had to carry him down to the Nepalese customs again who also refused to accept the body. "He was definitely alive when he left here. The Chinese must deal with it."

I never did find out the end of the story—perhaps he is still there.

Alec Le Sueur graduated with a degree in hotel management and worked for several of the world's top hotels before making the strangest decision of his career—to work as sales manager for the Holiday Inn in Lhasa, Tibet. He spent five years there, working and traveling and spawning the book, Running a Hotel on the Roof of the World: Five Years in Tibet, *from which this story was excerpted. He has since moved back to his native Jersey in the U.K. and now works as the marketing manager for Jersey Tourism.*

ROLF POTTS

* * *

Signs of Confusion

*As the world gets smaller, written English
pops up in a variety of new flavors.*

ONE AFTERNOON LATE LAST YEAR, I WENT OUT FOR lunch at a restaurant not far from the south Thailand guesthouse where I'd been staying. My landlady ran the place, and on this day she seemed particularly pleased to see me. "We have new English menu!" she exclaimed, presenting me with a glossy list of entrees.

I took a seat and scanned the menu, which listed the kinds of dishes I'd always eaten there—red curry, *pad thai*, *tom yum*. Then, amidst the standard delicacies (and in cheery capital letters) I noticed a dish I'd never before sampled in this part of the world: FRIED RICE WITH CRAP.

Concerned, I took the menu over to my landlady. "I think this dish is a mistake," I told her.

"Oh, no!" she replied brightly. "We make seafood for you! Fresh from water!"

I gave my landlady a skeptical look. "But surely 'crap' is not what you meant to write."

"Yes, crap! Very delicious!"

I considered this. "Do you by chance mean 'carp'?"

"No!" she laughed. "Crap!" She splayed her hands and mimicked the scuttling movement of a crustacean.

"Oh, you mean crab. C–R–A–B. Not C–R–A–P."

"Yes!" she said, handing the menu back to me. "Crab. Both sound same to me."

Then, almost as an afterthought, she asked: "What means 'crap'?"

This was not the first time I'd chanced into such an awkwardly comical situation in Thailand. At the central market in Ranong, one could buy packets of "COCK CONDITIONING PILLS" (which I very much hope are for roosters), and the local supermarket did fast trade in a brand of toilet paper called "Sit and Smile." Perhaps most notably, however, a toy vendor along the main street sold packs of tiny plastic animals that came with a sober warning for parents: "BE CARE-FUL OF BEING EATEN BY SMALL CHILDREN."

To be sure, Thailand holds no monopoly on poorly trans-lated English. Some years ago, a series of forwarded emails made the rounds, describing bizarre signs posted in Kenyan restaurants ("Customers who find our waitresses rude ought to see the manager"), Norwegian cocktail lounges ("Ladies are requested not to have children in the bar"), and Russian monasteries ("You are welcome to visit the cemetery where famous Russian artists and writers are buried daily except Thursday"). A similar round of emails celebrated the lin-guistic gaffes that resulted when American corporations in-troduced new slogans into foreign markets. In Mexico, for example, "Got Milk?" translated into the decidedly un-hip slogan, "Are You Lactating?"

No doubt this tradition of global mistranslation goes back to the days when Greek and Roman tourists fre-quented the sights of Anatolia and Egypt (one can imagine shaky Latin letters scrawled onto papyrus outside an Alex-andria dry cleaner: "Let us put happiness in your toga!"), but the modern practice of publicly butchering English can be traced back to the American occupation of post-war Japan in the '40s and '50s. There, amidst the sudden rush to emulate all things Western, G.I.s were able to buy tubes of "Snot" brand toothpaste, and the Japanese brass band that played at General MacArthur's election reputedly commis-sioned a banner that read: "We pray for General Mac-Arthur's erection." To this day, Japan still leads the world in mistranslated English (see www.engrish.com for a splendid collection).

Other societies are rapidly catching up to the Japanese example, however, mainly in proportion to how fast they modernize. Korea, where I lived for two years as an English teacher in the late '90s ("Praise the Load!" read posters for my school's Bible club), boasts a fine tradition of mangling the English language.

If there is a growth market in dodgy English, however, look no further than China, where 1 billion increasingly globalized citizens have begun translating area signage into English in anticipation of the 2008 Olympics. Brian Baker, a fellow Kansas émigré who spent a year teaching English in China, once found the following tourist information posted in a Wuhan statue park:

1. The tourists must care for the statues, consciously avoid carving, writing, climbing, and damnification. Trying to be a civilized citizen.
2. The tourists climbing the statues must be fined from 5-50 yuan.
3. The tourists carving or scratching the statues must be fined from 50-500 yuan.

4. The tourists making a breakage for the statues' instruments must be fined 1,000–5,000 yuan.

5. The tourists making a breakage for the second half of the statue must be fined 2,000–8,000 yuan.

6. The tourists making a breakage for the first half of the statue (without the face) must be charged 3,000–10,000 yuan.

One can imagine tourists sizing up such vandalism options with the kind of anticipation usually reserved for fine wine lists ("Ooh look, honey, let's make a breakage for the statues' instruments—it's totally within our price range!").

Brian's most vivid experience with Chinese English, however, came in a provincial grocery store. "There," he reports, "between the natural powdered jellyfish and the yak ham, I saw what looked, to my hungry eyes, to be a package of sliced turkey. Imagine my surprise when, upon closer inspection, the label clearly read: CHOICE AROMATIC LION BUTT. I still can't imagine what Chinese-English dictionary yielded that monstrosity of translation."

The potential flip side to all this, of course, lies in the recent Western vogue for Chinese characters on clothing and skin art. As a case in point, I once bought a t-shirt that, according to the vendor, featured the Chinese symbol for "Lucky." It wasn't until months later that a Hong Kong friend informed me that it wasn't even close to "Lucky"— that it really meant "Super." Had it read "Dork," or "Kick Me," I would have been none the wiser. Similarly, all the hipsters who went out and got Chinese ideogram tattoos over the past decade could be in for a nasty surprise if they ever travel to China. After all, a "Crouching Tiger" buttock tattoo purchased in good faith in Seattle might eventually be revealed as provincial slang for "Impotent," and a Melbourne tattoo artist who designs stylized "Freedom" ideograms might accidentally miss a stroke and send his clients off with a symbol that means, say, "Adult Diapers."

Beneath the dangers of dabbling in other languages, of course, lies an optimistic truth: that, regardless of syntactic differences, the basic human meanings behind our languages remain the same. After all, "Sit and Smile" is indeed a desirable activity after having used toilet paper, and even the most diabolical of restaurateurs wouldn't literally serve you fried rice with crap.

To be on the safe side, however, I think I'll stick to the red curry and *tom yum*.

Rolf Potts is the author of Vagabonding: An Uncommon Guide to the Art of Long-Term World Travel. *The former Salon.com columnist is best known for promoting the ethic of vagabonding—a way of living that makes extended, personally meaningful travel possible. His work has appeared in* National Geographic Adventure, National Geographic Traveler, The Best American Travel Writing, *and on* National Public Radio. *Visit his website at www.rolfpotts.com.*

*

After a couple of fun weeks in Moscow, I decided I wanted to see something else, so I booked flights to Yekaterinburg in the Ural Mountains, where the last Russian Tsar family was executed in 1918. I boarded the early morning flight feeling somewhat reduced, as my host family had given me one too many vodka shots the night before in celebration of this exciting journey. All I could do was wear sunglasses and a bandanna to cover up the strain excessive alcohol consumption had had on my eighteen-year-old physique. As soon as I boarded the plane and started looking for my economy-class seat, the crew looked at me strangely. Finally, a flight attendant grabbed my arm and said:

"You! You mest come vit me!"

Uh-oh, I thought, am I gonna get kicked off a plane in Russia, the land of excessive drinking, for having had one too many? Man, what a story to tell.

The flight attendant, however, briskly marched me up to the empty first-class section of the plane and told me to sit there. Then she did the weirdest thing a Russian can possibly do to a stranger—she smiled. I was dumbfounded, but happy. First class was sectioned off, and I remember thinking—yeah!

"Here, champagne for you." Moët & Chandon. Wow, Aeroflot was really going to town today. I sipped the bubbly, and watched the monotonous landscape below.

"Here, ashtray for you."

"Uh, isn't this a non-smoking flight?" I asked, my nicotine-addicted body eyeing salvation in the distance.

"Oh, of course not," said the flight attendant, "not for you."

Umm, yeah. O.K. Now that's really weird. I lit a cigarette, self-consciously looking around, but the flight attendant just contorted her face into what I assume was a smile and returned to the galley.

A few minutes later, I saw the curtain twisting and a couple of other flight attendants were craning their heads, staring at me. When they noticed me looking back at them, they dissolved in fits of giggles and hid behind the curtain. Finally, just before we landed, a tall, serious-looking girl around my age came out from behind the curtain and asked in a trembling voice:

"Britney, please you sign autograph for me. I would very appreciate."

Oh, shit. So, that's who I'm supposed to be. That's how, in a flurry of letters on a napkin, I became a pop star for a day.

"Dear Natasha, thank you for taking such good care of me on this flight. Love, Britney."

—Alexandra Bockfelt, "Who Me?"

TOMMY KERR

* * *

When in Rome, Cross-Dress for Success!

Don't underestimate your mother.

"THE VATICAN IS NOT IN ROME" MY BAPTIST-BORN mother (who once said she thought she was really meant to be Jewish) insisted. "The Vatican is actually a completely sovereign state, recognized as separate from any other government. The Catholics and the Pope have their own country, and as soon as we go through these gates—look, see, they even have their own flag—we will no longer be in Rome or even in Italy, but in the Vatican, the smallest nation in the world. They have their own soldiers and everything. You gotta love those Catholics. And the incense, I love the incense and all that Latin they chant."

At seventy years of age, she was a walking encyclopedia of culture, religion, history, and her all-time favorite—art. She was taking me to see the great works of Botticelli, Roselli, and Michelangelo, painted and frescoed against the vaulted ceilings of the Sistine Chapel. "I have been waiting forever to bring you here," she said, as we mounted the steep marble steps and prepared to step across the threshold of the grand entrance, which was crowded with worshippers and tourists. Suddenly a tall, powerful-looking man in uniform—a Vatican secret service agent, for all I knew—put his body between me and art history, or me and God, or both.

"You cannot go in there!" he glared. "This is a place of worship!" He pointed at my hiking shorts. "You must cover your knees." He was disgusted. I felt like a wimp and wished I had worn my macho carpenter jeans instead.

I tried to negotiate, but it was hopeless. The guy was totally rigid and stern. Plus, he had a sovereign government to back him up and wasn't about to budge for some wussy thirty-something American in goofy-looking shorts.

"Sorry about that, Mama. But it's cool. We didn't know there was a dress code. We'll just come back tomorrow, and I'll wear long pants." Satisfied, I turned to leave.

"But we're already here," she protested. "Hey, wait!" she exclaimed. "I have an idea! You can wear this!"

I turned around to see my silver-haired mother standing in broad daylight in the doorway of one of the biggest and busiest churches on earth, surrounded by hundreds of people. She skillfully slipped off her black skirt and stepped out of it. As she held it aloft between her thumb and forefinger and dangled it like a Vegas stripper, she grew impatient with excitement.

"Hurry up, Tommy. Put it on over your pants. It's long enough to cover your knees and I'll just wear what I have on now." She stood there in a slinky black half-slip, looking at me through her bifocals.

The guard watched, almost as shocked as I was, but could not intervene because her knees were still covered by a hemline of sexy satin lace.

"Let's just come back tomorrow, Mama."

"But I planned the whole day around this, Tommy. Just put on my skirt and let's get inside and look at some art. What's the matter, you're not self-conscious are you?"

I didn't think I was, until then, when I was faced with the opportunity to cross-dress in my mother's skirt and accompany her—while she wore lingerie—into the Sistine Chapel during Sunday Mass.

Tommy Kerr is a freelance writer and editor from Asheville, North Carolina. He wrote the story you just read while wearing long pants. Sometimes he lives in Guatemala where he once picked wildflowers for his girlfriend before learning from locals that "those blossoms make you insane." He is currently working on two new travel guides entitled How to French Kiss without an American Accent *and* Russian to Finnish Packing before Czech-Out Time. *He is also looking for a sane girlfriend with a crazy foreign accent, who has a working knowledge of dangerous flora.*

✳

As someone who was born and raised in Hollywood, I was awestruck as I strolled through the bustling thoroughfares of glorious Rome. So taken by the ancient architecture, I was the first in my group to congratulate the Romans on their accurate portrayal of the Universal Studios back lot. For an L.A. boy who thinks an historical building is the local Café 50's, this was amazing.

A glorious Monday started with a harrowing taxi ride right to the doorstep of the Vatican Museum where we gazed upon a tidy row of tourists, stretching to infinity. "They must have some awesome rides in there," I thought.

Undaunted, we zipped to St. Peters Square and toured the "my thesaurus isn't good enough to describe" St. Peters Basilica. As we left the cathedral, my shutter finger aching, we noticed a commotion at the end of the square. A small crowd was forming and my fellow tourists began sprinting toward the gathering. When in Rome...

As we traversed the massive plaza, the clatter of cheers grew louder, flags were waving, passing double-decker tour buses became moving grandstands. I'm no Einstein but I can add. The Vatican + insane crowd = Pope-Time! Now I know this new guy is no John Paul but hey, a Pope is a Pope. Even as a card-carrying Jew (we should have cards, that would be neat) seeing the actual Pope at the actual Vatican would be pretty damn cool.

I reached the edge of the throng, held my camera high and blindly fired away. *Click*…my viewfinder showed nothing! *Click* again…no luck! Is it O.K. to say "shit" at the Vatican? Then suddenly, there it was…a white cap! A white robe! Excellent! Smile…*CLICK!* Got it! The crowd now going wild, I looked down at my camera to admire my masterpiece when the comfort of an American accent blaring from a bullhorn stopped me short. "People please, no video cameras! This is supposed to be 1980!!!" I glimpsed my camera and marveled at a brilliant snapshot of an actor who kinda looked like John Paul.

You can take the boy out of Hollywood, but…

—Don Priess, "6600 Miles for This?"

* ✱ *

Guns and Frivolity in Cambodia

Boys will be boys.

I STOOD IN THE SHADOW OF THE BUS AND WATCHED the spray of my urine rise off the parched, dirt road onto the tire, and slowly drip down in tears of salt and dust. I wondered if the bus driver would notice—or even care. Cambodia is among the world's most heavily contaminated by landmines and unexploded ordinance. The seriousness of the danger is somewhat apparent when our bus infrequently pulls over to allow the passengers to relieve themselves. It is ill advised to step off the main roads, so we stick pretty close to the bus.

I ended up in Southeast Asia somewhat abruptly after getting laid off from my job. I had known my job was in danger and expected to lose it, but was still stunned when they told me to pack up my stuff.

I obviously had some decisions to make. The job market couldn't get much worse. And my savings account lacked "security" by about two zeroes. My sensible side said, "Suck it up and a get a new job." My frivolous side said, "Buy a plane ticket to somewhere far from here."

I soon decided that frivolity was sexier than sensibility, and that I needed to take full advantage of my new freedom. I knew there may not be many more times in my life when I'm the only person depending on me. So I paid off my credit cards, gave away my plant, stuffed my backpack, and got on a plane. I picked Cambodia because it's about as far out of my element as I could get. What I hoped to take away when I resurfaced was the kind of learning you can't get from books.

I had already spent a week in northern Cambodia exploring the ancient temples of Angkor Wat before catching the bus heading south to the capital city, Phnom Penh. This bus (well, junk heap van) was noisy, cramped, and had rust spreading like cancer. It looked like something donated to a high-school auto body class. Plus, at over 100 degrees, it was rather disappointing that the AC appeared to have been ripped out of the dashboard. We were forced to keep the windows open to avoid heat stroke, despite the heavy clouds of dust streaming into our faces. Everyone wrapped t-shirts or bandannas around their faces "outlaw style" to keep from gagging, and wore sunglasses to prevent eyelids from caking up. I thought the bus was hot and crowded when it left Siem Reap with seven or eight of us foreigners—but it soon became unbearable as the driver kept picking up locals to make a little extra money under the table. I wanted to scream every time he pulled over but chose to bite my tongue. We gained another half dozen passengers before he was satisfied. The roads only exacerbated the situation, resembling nothing more than neglected hiking trails. The conditions kept the bus under 40 mph but more than once we hit potholes that sent us out of our seats, and into the ceiling. Occasionally, we would disappear into whale-sized craters before emerging again from the other side.

The only comforting part of the journey was that I still had water left when the bus broke down in the desolate mid-section of Cambodia. We sat without shade on the side of the road in pools of our own sweat, when we weren't pushing the bus up and down the road to try to jump-start it. We quietly read pirated, photocopies of classic novels and travel books. We played magnetic backgammon and tic-tac-toe in the dirt. And we watched the bus driver with his head buried under the hood, tinkering with the engine and swearing in his native Khmer. At one point I relinquished some of my water to the driver for the bus's radiator. I'm no mechanic, but when it poured out of the bottom onto the ground, I figured we would be there for a while.

Every ten minutes or so, a small procession of humble, inquisitive faces would slowly drive by in a plume of dust: peasant, migrant workers on makeshift tractors; a family of four packed onto a decrepit, Chinese-made moped; a rusty, diesel cattle truck loaded with farmers-turned-minesweepers. We traded gentle stares with equal curiosity. Most passersby would offer innocent waves as if to make us feel welcome. Our return waves brought shy smiles and giggles at the idea of simply communicating with such unusual visitors.

About two hours had gone by when we noticed a car racing towards us from the direction we had come. It was traveling much faster than any other vehicle we had seen, swerving violently, and appeared to be catching air over some of the larger mounds in the road. It reached us quickly and rocketed past in an enormous whirlwind of dust like the cartoon Tasmanian Devil. About twenty yards down the road it slammed on its breaks and skidded dangerously to a stop. The car's wheels then spun in reverse, it backed fiercely through its own trail of smoke, and locked its breaks across from where we were sitting.

The old car was badly dented and rusty, and so covered in dirt you couldn't see through the windows or even discern its original color. I strained to look through the haze as the dust slowly dissipated and noticed the window nearest to us slowly winding down. Then suddenly, a young, grinning Khmer face popped out through the window and said, "Taxi?"

The other bus passengers and I exchanged looks of disbelief. No one said a word. The taxi driver glanced back and forth along the line of stranded foreigners and gestured towards his car with amused bewilderment, "Taxi!" No one moved. I began weighing my options and tried to recall if there was an entry in my *Lonely Planet Cambodia* guidebook about taxi murders or kidnappings. I was tired, hot, and restless and wondered how long it would be before another bus showed up. "Taxi!" beckoned the driver as he thumped the outside of the door with his palm. I wavered for another moment and then slowly clambered to my feet, hefting my backpack onto my shoulders. My fellow bus passengers stared up at me with wide eyes. I contemplated my actions hesitantly as the taxi driver waved me over with encouragement. I turned to the bus driver who simply shrugged as if to say, "It's your call buddy." I shrugged back, and climbed into the cab.

We sped along the grueling, prehistoric road at teeth-rattling speed. I was amazed the car held up under such conditions. The driver worked the steering wheel with a frenzied mastery, constantly correcting our path as we bounded over rocks and around potholes. The shoelaces on my hiking boots would have come untied if I hadn't doubled the knots. I was both impressed and horrified. About twenty minutes passed before I offered "Phnom Penh" as my destination. The driver nodded vigorously in the rearview mirror as if there was no other plausible option. I sat silently, gripping the door handle and gazing intently out the window. About thirty minutes later, the driver abruptly turned to me and said, "Guns. You like?" I was dumbfounded. "You like guns? I take you shoot guns. You shoot guns. Many guns."

I responded tentatively, "I, aah, don't really need to be shooting any guns. I really just want to get to…"

He interrupted, "You American, yes?"

"Yes, but I…"

"All American like guns. You like. No problem."

I replied, "Yeah, that's cool but I really don't…" He suddenly jammed on the breaks and sent the car sliding to a stop in the middle of the road. He turned to me with a look of firm sincerity and said, "It's O.K. I good friend. You shoot guns. Very good guns. No problem. You like." He then turned around and jerked the car back into motion, our Tasmanian cloud of dust trailing behind.

Q. What if a foreign person points a gun at me and tells me to get into the trunk of his car?

A. The State Department takes no position on this. In some countries, it is considered impolite to refuse to get into someone's car trunk. If you choose to get in, you may spend the next five years chained to a radiator while enduring lectures about the evils of America. In that event, you may be visited by State Department representatives. They are authorized to make mild protests to your captors and to offer you Tylenol and moist towelettes. They are not authorized to risk derailing the "peace process" by threatening your captors with extinction-level air strikes by B-52 bombers. Rest assured that high-level diplomatic personnel are expressing "concern" over your situation, or even "serious concern."

◆

—Anonymous

Forty-five minutes later we pulled off the main road onto an unfathomably worse side road. We had to slow down significantly in order to navigate the holes and gaps in our path. We passed through villages dotted with primitive huts and small patchwork houses, all stained brown with dirt kicked up by passing vehicles. We drove by gaunt, tireless men in conical hats digging in rice paddies. We passed women shouldering wooden buckets of water and families hiding from the sun under shelters made from palm fronds.

Cambodia is the poorest country in Southeast Asia and the roadside images brought to life the descriptions of poverty we skim past in *The New York Times*. Village streets are lined with litter, stray dogs, and naked children playing in the dirt. You also can't help noticing the extraordinary number of amputees—1 out of every 236 people in Cambodia. Some bound along masterfully with makeshift crutches. Other less fortunate victims drag legless midsections along the road using their bare hands.

We left the villages behind and drove for another thirty minutes or so before entering an endless web of back roads bordered with rusted barbed-wire fences. I was beginning to wonder if I would ever be heard from again. Eventually, we came upon a tall, narrow, whitewashed shack that resembled an outhouse. The shack stood next to a small side road blocked by a manual barricade like something you might imagine at a rural Russian border crossing. We pulled up to find a middle-aged Khmer man sitting on a stool wearing a grubby t-shirt, camouflage pants, and a sidearm. He got up slowly, fanning himself with a tattered newspaper, and walked out to the cab. The driver muttered a few words in Khmer and motioned toward me in the back. The guard glanced at me indifferently, nodded slowly to the driver, and walked casually over to the barricade. He leaned down on the weighted end, raising the opposite side of the pole just high enough to clear the top of the cab, and waved us through. We followed the road for over a mile to an uninviting building pieced together with cinderblocks, corrugated steel, and bamboo. We pulled up next to a couple of rickety pickup trucks and climbed out of the taxi. The driver put his hand on my shoulder, smiled enthusiastically, and said, "Time to shoot guns."

It was a little unsettling when we were greeted by a toothless, Khmer soldier holding an M-16 assault rifle. He was wearing an American t-shirt with a skull and crossbones that said, "Mess with the best, die like the rest." I said hello the politest way I knew how. The soldier sized me up for a moment and then pointed to an impressive selection of guns hanging from small wooden dowels hammered into a bamboo wall. There were small caliber handguns, hunting rifles, shotguns, and intimidating automatic machine guns. I have a rudimentary knowledge of guns but identified a German Luger, a Colt .45, an Uzi, several M-16s, and even what looked like an old Tommy gun straight out of a mobster movie. As I examined the weapons, I did my best to appear composed and knowledgeable as if choosing an album at a hip record store. But in actuality, I was severely intimidated and wishing I was back on the side of the road next to the broken-down bus.

My demeanor changed pretty quickly after firing off thirty rounds with an AK-47 assault rifle. It was kick-ass and I was having trouble holding back the drool. I was a kid again, the star of my own war movie. I wanted to pull the trigger on everything he had. I wanted to blow shit up. I was a dangerous man. There was certainly still a degree of fear when I put down the smoking gun but it was overcome by exhilaration and adrenaline. The soldier had dealt with people like me before. He could sense my pathetic, juvenile fascination and complete lack of will power. He walked over and handed me a laminated menu with a list of handguns, shotguns, and machine guns, and asked me what was next. A gun menu!? I couldn't believe it. I scanned the list greedily like a fat chick at a buffet. I didn't want to have to choose. Then, with a burst of courage, I peered up at the soldier and asked if he had anything with a little more kick. He smiled sadistically, flipped the menu over, and revealed some seriously heavy artillery.

It was a tough decision, but I had to go with the fully automatic Russian-made K57, armor-piercing machine gun. It's the kind of weapon that's mounted to the side of a helicopter, and similar in size to the American M60 that Stallone shouldered in *Rambo*. The Khmer soldier didn't have much trouble talking me into buying 150 rounds of ammo, which took two guys to feed into the gun from the side. Three-inch bullet shells spat out of the gun in bursts of flame as it recoiled, showering around me like a copper hailstorm. It was like holding a jackhammer, only louder. But I could still hear the perverse laughing of the taxi driver who stood behind me, thumping me on the back as I fired, and hollering with approval. I was sweating by the time I ran out of ammo and had a few shell burns on my forearms. I was hoping they'd scar.

Before the gun even stopped smoking, the soldier held the evil menu in front of me again and pointed to the bottom of the list: "B-40 Anti-armor, Rocket Propelled Grenade Launcher." I was at a loss for words. I had already spent $30 bucks on the AK-47 and $150 on the K57 (a buck a bullet). The B-40 would set me back another $250 and the soldier said I would have to take a forty-five-minute drive in his truck to get to a safe place in the mountains to fire it. My week's travel budget was already blown and I really didn't want to get into a truck with this guy. But we were talking

bazooka. I would be the envy of all my sick friends. As I wres-
tled with a decision, the soldier, with a heartless grin, informed
me that for an extra $100 he would throw in a water buffalo
for a target. It was clearly time to exit the shooting range.

I was headed for the cab when another Khmer soldier
strolled up with a hand grenade dangling precariously by the
pin from his index finger (probably not the safest way to
carry it). I stood, somewhat in shock, staring at the live
grenade. The cab driver patted me on the back, smiled, and
nodded slowly with approval. A little over the top, but I figured, what's another $20. I followed the two soldiers, with
cab driver in tow, through a barbed-wire fence behind the
shooting range. We walked about a quarter-mile through a
barren, dirt field until we got to a small, muddy pond. The
grenade-throwing lesson took about fifteen seconds. One of
the soldiers picked up a rock, put it in my hand, and made
an underhand throwing motion toward the water. I managed
to land the rock near the center of the pond and he gave me
a thumbs-up with approval. He then put on a Kevlar helmet,
handed me the grenade and took a step back. It was a little
shocking to be standing in the middle of Cambodia holding
a live hand grenade.

I hesitated for a moment and then pointed to the helmet
the soldier was wearing and the baseball hat on my head. He
reassured me in broken English that the Kevlar helmet was
far too hot and that I was much better off with my baseball
hat. So I posed for a quick picture for the taxi driver who was
serving as my official photographer, pulled out the pin and
tossed the grenade into the pond. We were only standing
about twenty yards from where the grenade landed. The cab
driver ducked behind the second soldier but my friend with
the helmet stood firm. He calmly indicated with hand sig-
nals that there was no need to run. I still wished I were

wearing Adidas instead of Tevas when the thing exploded and emptied half the pond into a mushroom cloud of water.

It was pretty cool, to say the least.

I sat quietly in the cab gazing through the window as we slowly made our way out of the compound, past the meager villages, and back to the main road. I was physically exhausted but my mind was racing. Sadly, my thoughts weren't occupied with the thrill or gravity of what I just experienced. Instead, I was sweating my unemployment and the job I had lost in San Francisco. I guess I was suffering from the backlash of indulgence. It was like the anxiety or guilt felt after spending money on something extravagant, sleeping with someone you shouldn't, or devouring a half bucket of Kentucky Fried Chicken. After all, I should be walking out of an interview, not off a shooting range in Cambodia. It was the worst job market in decades and I didn't have a lead. My money was literally going up in smoke and I had no income. I sat thinking about the phone call when my boss laid me off. I thought about the strained silence when I told my father the news. I thought about my ex-coworkers and friends and the client relationships I tried so hard to build. I thought about my paltry 401-K plan. I thought about my career. I thought about my future.

"Tomorrow in morning, ten o'clock," announced the cab driver from the front seat.

"Excuse me?" I asked.

The driver twisted around to face me, "I pick you up hotel ten o'clock. We go back gun range."

I was perplexed. "Go back? What for?"

He smiled widely, "B-40 shoulder grenade launcher." It took me a moment to comprehend his reply. I stared at him feebly. I took a few long, contemplative breaths.

"Make it eleven."

*Eben Strousse hails from Manhattan where he recently returned after
a nomadic decade. He's lived in Ohio, Atlanta, Colorado and San
Francisco but claims his best anecdotes come from his third world tra-
vails in such places as Central America, South America and Southeast
Asia. He's finally settled down to begin working his way through shoe-
boxes full of journals and dictaphone tapes but some of his more memorable follies can be found lurking on popular travel web sites.*

*

The urinal spoke to me. This had never happened before. True,
there had been occasions when toilet bowls had spoken to me.
Don't do shots, they said. Particularly tequila shots. I listened, and no
toilet bowl has ever spoken to me again. But this was the first time
a urinal had spoken to me. It made some comments about my
manhood. "Ha-ha," it continued, "just kidding." The urinal called
himself Norm. Norm had a television show. Norm wanted me to
watch his television show. It aired weekly on the ABC network.
When I finished, Norm quieted. Then someone else approached
the urinal. Norm the Urinal began to talk again.

I returned to the seat next to my wife Sylvia at a bar in
Washington D.C.

"The urinal spoke to me," I told her.

"What did it say?"

"It said its name was Norm. It asked me to watch his television
show on the ABC network."

"What did you say?"

"I said, 'Norm, I piss on you.'"

Sylvia looked at me oddly. "You're not adjusting very well, are
you?"

"I am, too."

"You have to accept that bathrooms are an acceptable place to
advertise television shows. That's how it's done here. The U.S. is our
home again and we have to adjust."

—J. Maarten Troost, *The Sex Lives of Cannibals*

RACHEL THURSTON

* * *

Mama Chihuahua, World's Fiercest Travel Partner

An aggressive lap dog of a mother attacks a mob
of taxi drivers in Nepal.

IF MY MOTHER WERE A DOG, SHE'D BE A CHIHUAHUA. Physically she looks nothing like her hair-challenged, anorexic, eye-bulging canine counterpart: she's blessed with a Medusa-like mane of curly black hair, a curvaceous figure, and sapphire eyes. It's her behavior while traveling which makes her most like a small fighting dog: she's impetuous, fierce, and compelled to physically assault anyone bigger than her if our personal space is invaded.

Over the years of our travels she's frightened off a team of armed muggers determined to procure our money belts in San Jose, Costa Rica, shamed a hash dealer out of his business in a village in the Himalayas, bluffed a charging yak in Tibet, and thwarted the advances of a smarmy Croatian policeman intent on kidnapping me and dragging me off to an uninhabited island for who knows what sort of domestic Adriatic tortures.

As a young child, and before we began traveling together, I feared my mother. She once hurled a 200-pound dresser down the stairwell at my father in a rage over a vacation dispute. And I still remember how—during my high school years—she would embarrass me at dinner in front of dates I'd bring home. If I teased her one too many times, as teenagers are prone to do, she'd get that evil twinkle in her eye. Before I had time to escape, she would catch me, tackle me, and grind her sharp elbows into my chest until I conceded defeat.

She would cackle her alpha she-male laugh as I wriggled helplessly on the linoleum floor, winking at my potential suitor as if to say, "This is what will happen to *you* if you don't treat my daughter well."

I know from years of various public embarrassments that there's nothing more humiliating than drooling on yourself on a linoleum floor beneath the weight of your mother in front of a date.

I used to fantasize that one day I'd have my own sweet revenge against "Mommy Dearest." She'd be old and crippled and confined to a hand-pushed wheelchair and if she ever got out of line with me, then I'd let her go flying down a long steep wheelchair ramp, heading disastrously for a hedge. Something which wouldn't kill her but would at least scratch her up a little and make her think twice about being such a smartass to me.

I never expected she would become the best travel partner I've ever had.

After my parents' divorce, we began traveling together as mother and daughter. We discovered that we are interested in going to the same countries, places which usually involve a lack of flushing toilets, respect for women, and reliable hospitals. Her rage, instead of being directed at me, is now asserted on sexist taxi drivers, stingy hotel owners, unrelenting sticky-fingered children, and the random yak that wanders too close to us on trails. I no longer have to carry pepper spray or stun guns. I just wait for her to do her thing. Anyone intent on hurting either of us has to pass through the Mama Chihuahua Shield of Terror. Occasionally, however, her temper gets out of hand and people get hurt; my job then becomes that of a peacekeeper and not that of a daughter.

Like that messy altercation in a Nepali parking lot.

On our first trip to Asia as nascent travelers, we weren't yet accustomed to the close physical proximity that Nepalis have with one another. After a day's nauseating and winding journey to the large town of Pokhara, we tumbled out of the bus with several locals into the overpowering heat of the afternoon. A gang of aggressive young taxi drivers in sweat-soaked t-shirts pushed into my mother and me like a mass of screaming locusts.

"Come with me, yes Miss, Miss! Let me take that for you!" A short-haired guy wearing a Michael Jordan t-shirt, jeans, and flip-flops tried to grab my backpack from my shoulders.

Another young man on my left elbowed him away and pressed in between us. It was so hot I could taste the rice I had for lunch gurgling back up from my stomach. "Over here, Miss. I give you verrry good deal." The second driver—who smelled like burnt garlic and onions—demanded, "Where do you and Mom want to go?" I just wanted *shade*. Shade and fresh air.

The sun beat down mercilessly on our heads of dark hair. Our nerves were shot. We kept telling them to back off, to give us more space. Mom snapped "NO!" over and over as if they were Boston terriers nipping at our heels. All the other locals had left for town and the mob had pushed us up against the side of the bus. The driver was nowhere to be seen. We were the only women in sight. And the only ones with money.

More young men gathered around us. A few had brought their lunch plates of lentils and rice to eat while they watched the spectacle. They pointed and laughed, amused that we were so feisty and that we insisted on carrying our own mammoth-size backpacks. They especially enjoyed taunting my mother, whose anger confounded them. Not being taken seriously only fueled her building rage.

"Miss? Miss! Where you want to go?" pressed one of the drivers wearing '70s-style sunglasses, a black button-down shirt, and slicked-back hair that made him look like an extra from *Grease*. "I have a very nice taxi! See?" he gestured proudly across the dirt parking lot to what looked like a large metal box with broken windows and a headlight that was duct-taped back in place. Mushy tires protruded from beneath each of its corners like smashed black boots.

I stifled a laugh. Another taxi driver laughed, too.

Mom wasn't laughing, however.

"You guys should back up. You're a little too close to my mother." I pleaded with them, becoming increasingly nervous that someone was going to get knocked out. *And I knew it wouldn't be one of us.*

Just then, two of the youngest guys had the bright idea of trying to remove my mother's backpack from her shoulders.

She bristled with their advances.

"Listen up!" I tried to push the young men back, to warn them. There were fathers, sons, and brothers here. For god's sakes, they had families to think of. "Get back, she has a temper. She gets very, *very* angry."

But it was too late.

Mama Chihuahua was transforming into The Urban Hulk. The physiological signs of change were unmistakable:

her tightly set jaw, the posturing of a fighting stance, and the narrowing of her eyes into a hateful glare cold enough to chill the sweetest grandmother's heart. It all added up to one thing: the all-consuming impulse to punch, gouge, and dismember anything in her way.

Mama Chihuahua had been unleashed and hell hath no fury like a fearful lap dog or a protective mother.

Suddenly, she let out a blood-curdling war shriek and threw all 126 pounds of her petite but muscular frame with a full backpack into the mob of hapless young men. Her arms exploded like propellers across their chests making hollow THUMPTHUMPTHUMP thuds as she made contact with their sternums. There were gasps, cries for help, and a general sense of shock.

When the dust-choked air had cleared, it looked like a war zone. A few of the Nepalis had run for the safety of their cars but five of the young men were strewn across the ground in a tangle of twisted arms and legs covered in dirt and dusty bits of lentils and rice. The Nepali men weren't especially big men but it was an incredible feat for a middle-aged, five-foot-four woman.

My mother stood up and brushed her skirt off. Silently, she stepped over the bodies and began walking across the dirt parking lot.

I looked down at them, riddled with guilt. "I'm so sorry, I think we'll just walk to our hotel." I put my palms together in upright prayer and bowed towards each of them as if to bless their injuries. This was a familiar sight to me. I had flashbacks of myself sprawled across the linoleum floor. "Thank you. *Namaste*. Thank you. *Namaste*. I'm so sorry," I told each of them with sympathy.

The *Grease* extra groaned, his broken sunglasses dangled from his face.

Up ahead and across the parking lot, the "thing" inhabiting my mother's body turned back to me and asked in a distinctly familiar voice, "Are you coming or what, sweetheart?"

The look on her face reminded me of something. And then I remembered what. It was the same look that would flash across her face after she'd just pummeled me on the kitchen floor and right before she would apologize for having embarrassed me in front of company, in front of a boy I was trying to impress.

The look was at once wickedly joyful and unapologetic.

I fear sometimes, that my mother will end up in a third-world jail one day for assaulting the wrong guy, perhaps an undercover policeman having an especially bad day. I even admit that I plan on leaving her incarcerated for a few days until she cools off and learns a thing or two about self-control, anger management, and ruining a perfectly good vacation.

But that, I've decided, would be unconscionably cruel.

To her cellmate, that is.

Rachel Thurston is a freelance writer, recovering river guide, and the unabashed lead singer of a retro rock 'n' roll band based in Santa Barbara, California. She's currently writing an adventure fem-moir book about her travel adventures working as a commitment-phobic river guide. Her feature articles have appeared in Santa Barbara Magazine, Food and Home Magazine, *and* The Independent. *She's a graduate student in the Masters of Writing Program at the University of Southern California. Rachel and her beloved mother, Mama Chihuahua, are planning their next adventure to northern India where they are assured of more rude taxi drivers, bad bus trips, and disastrous encounters with aggressive men who have no idea what they're getting into. You can follow her adventures at www.rsthurston.com.*

*

Stan's car was getting a 10,000-kilometer sacrifice in his front garden in Kathmandu. It had been washed and polished and the bonnet was open so flowers could be scattered across the engine. The brown goat had been quietly munching on the flowerbed by the garden wall. Now it was dragged over to the front of the car, the wicked-looking but prettily garlanded kukri knife was grabbed off the table and, with one swift chop, goat head was detached from goat body. The two men picked up the still twitching carcass and quickly moved around the car so fresh blood would spill on all four wheels. There were more ceremonies to complete, but soon Stan could be assured of not just reliable but safe motoring until the festival of Dasain rolled around next year.

"What else needs a sacrifice?" I asked Stan as we sipped our coffee and looked down on the carnage from the upstairs veranda.

"Well, motorcycles require a chicken or duck," Stan mused. "Everybody from the office brings theirs around so it gets done at company expense. Fortunately we don't have to sacrifice anything for computers anymore. But the sewing machine also needs a sacrifice every year—I think another chicken will do."

—Tony Wheeler, "High Times," *The Age*

BILL FINK

* * *

The Hostile Hostel

Escaping your host sometimes requires a little ingenuity.

I RAN THE TWO MILES FROM SIENNA TO THE HOSTEL, backpack bouncing on my shoulders at every stride. The manager had told me on the phone they only had one space remaining.

When I arrived, panting, at the doors of the three-story brick-and-steel building, I was dismayed to see a mob of backpackers crowded around the front desk. Two surly male staff members shouted in Italian at the visitors. As I made my way to the counter, I heard one of the men answer the phone.

"No! No reservations! One space only. You come now. Immediately!" He slammed down the phone.

The clerks grabbed crumpled piles of money and registration papers from backpackers, stuffing each form into one of the 100 cubbie holes in the wall behind them. Each of the nooks denoted one of the bed spots. The wall was still filled with at least two dozen empty spaces.

As I exchanged my money for bed #42, the clerk pointed an accusing finger at me, and spouted the rules in heavily accented English: "No drinking! No food! No noise at night! Lights out at midnight! Curfew 11:30—absolutely no entry after then, doors locked! Doors locked ten in morning to three in afternoon. Everyone must go. Doors locked at night until seven in morning. No entry, no exit."

I thought this a rather rigid set of commands, particularly since I had just left the famously uptight countries of Switzerland and Germany. Italy was supposed to be the home of sun-drenched, relaxed Mediterranean attitude. So I requested the rules to be altered a bit.

"*Signore, por favore*, I have to catch a bus at seven in the morning, so I need to leave a little earlier, maybe 6:30. Hope it's not a problem."

"Impossible!!"

Perhaps he meant it would be impossible for me, if I left at 6:30, to walk the two miles back to town in time to make the Rome bus. It was nice of him to be concerned.

"No, no, 6:30 O.K.," I made a running motion with my arms. He looked at me with what looked like pure hatred.

"Maybe 6:15?"

"IMMM-POSSIBLE!" He waved his raised hands back and forth vigorously, as if he was trying to keep an airplane from landing in the room.

"No, really," I tried to explain myself slowly in as simple English as I could. "I must catch bus. Only one morning bus. Seven in the morning. I must get to Rome tomorrow afternoon. So I must leave hostel by 6:30."

"No. Impossible. Im-possible." He waved his hand to the side, dismissing me like a serf.

Still stupefied, I stood there for a moment until anxious backpackers jostling for the hostel's "one last space" bumped me away from the counter.

I hoped it was just a linguistic misunderstanding. He must have meant the doors were locked to keep people from entering before the desk was open. They couldn't possibly lock people *inside* the hostel, could they?

At six the next morning I crept down the stairs to the lobby, figuring if I was quiet enough, I could unlock the front door, and nobody would be the wiser.

But I couldn't even get to the front door. Another set of interior glass doors divided the stairwell from the entrance way. Not only were these doors locked, but a couch had been moved behind them as a barricade. And on the couch slept a guard dog. It raised its head, starting to snarl before its eyes were even open. I fled up the stairs, hoping the dog wouldn't bark and awaken the manager. If things continued to form, they'd probably throw me into some Medici-inspired torture chamber hidden in a dungeon beneath the building.

I returned to my room, where eight backpackers lay half awake on rickety iron bunk beds.

"What, doors locked, really?" asked one German teen to whom I had told my problem, "It is like prison, ya?"

"Ya. And now I need to escape." I opened our second story window to look down to the asphalt below.

"No jumping. This I think is bad." A pimply Danish high-schooler sat up in his cot. I had teased him the night before about the high suicide rate in Denmark, and I believe he still felt obligated to point out living solutions in our daily lives.

I started to strip the sheets off my bed, and knot them into a rope of sorts. The German and Dane jumped out of bed to do the same, waking their friends amid laughter.

We formed three sets of sheets into a twenty-foot strand with which I could lower my backpack, full of breakable

—— ☽ ——

One of the very few moments when a long-term backpacker feels almost human and respectable is when they triumphantly pack away all of their newly clean clothes and ball up the empty dirty clothes bag and stuff it into a small side pocket of their backpack. When you have a backpack full of clean clothes, the difference in your appearance, odor, confidence, and general outlook on life is astounding. For a precious few days, your spirits are as boundless and unsullied as your choice of underwear. Yes, you detest the moment of knuckling down and washing your clothes like you used to loathe cleaning out the gerbil cage when you were a kid, but the end result is the same swollen feeling of accomplishment.

◆

—Leif Pettersen, "Clean Underwear: The Secret to Backpacker Ecstasy"

souvenirs and my camera, down to the pavement.

Then, despite the protests of the Dane, I held the knotted end of another sheet and stepped out the window onto a small ledge. My backpacking escape team held the other end, anchoring themselves against one of the bed frames.

I inched along the ledge until I could grasp a drain pipe bolted onto the side of the building. It was large enough so I was able to shimmy down the side of the building without incident.

The worried faces poking out my window burst into cheers until I quickly silenced them with a finger to my lips. I glanced toward the front doors, expecting them to fly open any moment, the desk clerks and their dog sent to drag me back inside. I unknotted the sheets from my backpack and after a couple tries, tossed them back through my window.

It was already 6:40. I strapped on my backpack and started my jog into town, worried despite my best efforts I might still miss the bus. As I hustled up the road, a few people working early in the fields looked at me with alarm. In my paranoia I imagined their thoughts: the only people who ran in Italy were thieves and soccer players, and I wasn't wearing a jersey.

I arrived in the bus terminal, drenched in sweat, at 7:05. There wasn't a single person in the waiting area. The bus must have left! I gnashed my teeth and cursed the hostel loudly. A sleepy head poked out from behind the ticket window. "Che?"

"The bus, the seven o'clock Rome bus, is it gone? Can I still catch it at another station in town?"

The ticket clerk first recoiled at my wide-eyed, sweaty face. Then he laughed.

"No, no, no, seven o'clock bus, she never come at seven." He wagged his finger. "Seven o'clock bus always come after nine." He slammed the shutter locked behind the window.

Reflexively, I looked for an exit, worried they had locked me inside again.

Bill Fink made his bus, and eventually returned to San Francisco where he wrote the Tuscany and Umbria chapters for the upcoming Frommer's guidebook: Pauline Frommer's Italy 2006. *This hostel didn't make the guide. Bill is a regular contributor to the* San Francisco Chronicle *and one of his stories was selected for Travelers' Tales* The Best Travel Writing 2006. *For more tales of foolishness, see www.geocities.com/billfink2004.*

❋

In bad situations, it's always useful to find someone worse off than yourself. It provides perspective and calms you down. I ran into a Chilean several times in Santo Domingo, Dominican Republic,

who was there for a conference of Latin American health minis-
ters. He was quietly recounting to a staff member in the elevator
how nothing at all worked in his room. Not even the phone. I
asked him about it and he told me a few more things that were
broken. Clearly, he was used to this and didn't get excited or make
threats. So I was impressed and always greeted the guy when I
could. To this he would smile weakly and shrug, as if to say, "My
sentence here will never end!"

On my last morning, I was in the breakfast room having whatever was available that day—a few pieces of old bread and sugared-
up orange juice. The tea was O.K. Suddenly, the ceiling collapsed
right in front of me and a huge wave of water sloshed over two to
three tables. Water was everywhere—it could have been from
someone's toilet, shower, or both. Fortunately, no one was sitting
at the tables. Behind them was my Chilean friend with his colleagues at another table. He was watching the event, smoking,
contemplating the whole mess quietly. Didn't even shrug this time
as if to say, "So what else is new?" No question about it, the place
was a dangerous dump.

—George M. Guess, "World-Class Hotels"

* * *

Anything with Two Legs and a Pulse

…and now, let me introduce you to my friend.

AT TWENTY-FOUR, I IMPULSIVELY THREW AWAY A respectable but boring life in suburban California for a stint as a London-based flight attendant. A whirlwind of parties, clubs, and pubs had me yearning for something real, and a down-to-earth connection proved ever harder to find in my fashionable fast-lane crowd. Enter Jimmy, the owner of a new Chinese restaurant adjacent to my flat. He seemed to be flirting, as he more and more frequently forked over a free won-ton here and a side of jasmine rice there. A few months into this valuable courtship, I agreed to go out with him.

Yes, I could probably do better than a thirty-three-year-old man who still went by "Jimmy," but consider my most recent dates:

An over-hyped blind date with an Italian named Barney who turned out to have a voice an octave higher than mine and sopping yellow stains that expanded by the minute under the arms of his thin white oxford shirt.

A pilot who boldly informed me that to be with him, I'd have to enjoy frequenting strip clubs.

And a gorgeous French attorney with land and a title who turned out to be gay.

Through all this, I had remained a fairly timid and polite young thing. It seemed rude to just get up and walk out, so I'd suffer through tedious or even revolting conversations until the date naturally ended. Jimmy Lay would change all this.

Normally I would think meeting a date at 11 P.M. was a bit late, but he had to close up the restaurant, and I was willing to make allowances. I'd been eating at his shop for the past month or two and had never been poisoned. He'd been patiently flirting for months. How much more do you usually have to go on for a first date? Not to mention that, at 5'4", he didn't seem too threatening.

We went for a walk along the Thames where I quickly realized I wasn't attracted to him. Maybe it was when we stood side-by-side for the first time and I truly noticed his diminutive height. Or maybe it was when he grabbed for my hand and I felt his own disproportionately tiny and disturbingly rough palms. But the pleasant conversation turned to how much I missed living on the ocean, and when he said, "Let's go nice place on coast. You love it." I found myself agreeing. I lived for adventure, and I lived for the ocean. Chemistry be damned, this would be a great night.

His car, a small Volkswagen Polo, was clean and well-maintained. Nothing seemed out of the ordinary except his poor taste in music. I wasn't sure if he was trying to conjure a time fifteen years earlier when perhaps he'd been cool, or if he was trying to seduce me when he put in a cassette tape, obviously a homemade compilation with its telltale clicks and abrupt stops, that featured love songs from the likes of Luther Vandross, Richard Marx, and Stevie Wonder. "They're my favorite songs for karaoke," he said. I rolled my eyes, and psyched myself up for the beach.

The drive was longer than he'd let on, and after about forty-five minutes we pulled off the motorway when I asked to find a toilet. We found a run-of-the-mill chip shop and queued up for the loo. When Jimmy finally took his turn, I thought someone else was already in the men's room, but wasn't sure as I'd been distracted by an attractive leather-clad guy in the line for fish. Maybe he was just waiting in the small washroom outside the toilet stall. I went back to looking at the guy in line. Damn, he had a girlfriend.

When Jimmy and I walked out to the car to continue our journey, a burly gray-haired Scotsman lunged forward, towering above us, and began shouting. Through a drunken slur of mostly indiscernible cursing, I deciphered this much:

"You f'ing Chinaman bastard....blah blah blah.....you peed in the sink!"

What!? My date did not just pee in the sink. It just did not happen.

Although stunned, Jimmy ignored the man and got in the car without confirming or denying the allegations. I convinced myself this man was just a drunk with a grudge against innocent Asian immigrants. What a Nazi.

I refused to consider this new side of Jimmy, but a little voice kept reminding me that he had after all gone in and out of the washroom while I believed the toilet to be occupied.

We finally reached the town of Southend on Sea, which wasn't much more than a dilapidated boardwalk lined with slot machines and cheap bars. It must have been at least 1 A.M., and the streets were full of trashy young locals stumbling away from second-rate clubs.

We walked along the "sea," which was more of a bay, with empty beer cans and fast-food wrappers in the place of cresting waves. He reached out to me, but I lightly batted his rough little hands away. He leaned in for a kiss, and I turned away, hoping he'd taken the hint. Now tired and disappointed both in the ocean and this pathetic date (who may or may not have just soiled a bathroom sink) I yawned and turned back for the car.

I looked to my right, where he sat in the driver's seat, and wondered why he hadn't started the car yet. He quickly leaned over and with a very impressive and fluid, probably well-rehearsed motion, my seat was instantly lowered to a full recline. Just as my head jerked back against the headrest, I felt his lips on mine. I shoved him away, brought my seat back to its full upright position, and had to restrain myself from slapping him. I'd found that in London although it was harder to get a first date than in the States, once you did, it wasn't unusual for things to move rapidly. Considering this, I opted for a little tact.

"Jimmy. You're a great guy. I'm having a wonderful time, but things are just moving too fast for me."

He backed off, saying, "Sorry. I'm so sorry." So he wasn't exactly smooth, but when I asked him to cool it, he did. I put the angry Scotsman out of my mind and looked forward to going home.

Now remember I was young and stupid, so when he pulled up to his new house on the outskirts of London, I foolishly agreed to take a quick tour before heading home.

The moment I walked in, I knew something was wrong. I had this sick feeling like when you're watching a murder flick and you see the unsuspecting heroine calmly heading to her doom and you just want to shout run, Run, RUN. I should have run. I couldn't point to one thing that led me to this feeling, but immediately upon entering his lair, the hairs on my neck, honest to God, stood up of their own volition.

I reached for the lights. Jimmy whispered, "Don't turn on lights."

"Why?" I asked loudly in defiance of his intimidating whisper.

He didn't answer. Instead he offered me a drink. Which I refused. He insisted. Again, I refused. I was ready to go.

"Jimmy, I'm really tired. It's just so late. I'd like to go home now."

He finally turned on a lamp, revealing a meticulously stocked wet bar. Although he was a restaurateur, this elaborate bar still seemed peculiar with hundreds of bottles ranging from Chambord and Drambuie to at least six different whiskeys and perhaps ten tequilas. All of them unopened and all together a little fishy for a single man who lived alone.

He opened the door to the living room, and as I rounded the corner from the hallway, huge brown eyes glared back at me from the center of the room. I froze. Perched on the sofa and angled toward the door as if to welcome each foolish young girl who happened through this nightmarish household, was an enormous doll. It wasn't a blow-up, sex-fetish-type thing, that would have somehow seemed more acceptable. This was a four-foot-tall baby doll in a pink silken pantsuit, which except for its extraordinary height and black plastic bowl cut, had frighteningly realistic features.

He went on about his liquor collection making absolutely no reference to this large stranger in front of me.

I blurted out with an accusing rather than curious tone, "Why do you have a doll?"

I hoped the answer would have to do with a rather tall young niece staying for the weekend, which would also explain why we had to whisper and keep the lights out. I stood aghast, nearly shaking from the chills sprinting up and down my body when he calmly walked over to the couch, and in all seriousness picked up the plastic child, brought her over and said nonchalantly, "Tiffany, I want you to meet my doll, Betsy," and held out her hand presumably for me to shake.

That was it. I'd had enough. I darted for the door, but he was right behind me, overgrown dolly in hand. He then released poor Betsy and grabbed me, sat down on a chair and pulled me onto his lap where he started trying to kiss my ears as he mumbled, "You driving me crazy baby."

Once again, I pushed this strange little man away and this time shouted, "Back off."

I grabbed the door handle, but in England most doors lock from both sides, and without a key, you can't get out. I pushed and pulled frantically but the door wouldn't open. Jimmy was at my side laughing quietly.

"What? D'you think I'm going to kidnap you?" he whispered only inches from my face.

"Yes," I replied in all honesty.

Then as calmly as ever, he opened the front door and let me out. He apologized for being too aggressive, "So so sorry," and seemed like a normal responsible man once again. It was past two in the morning, and having no idea where we were, I saw no choice but to assume he was weird but safe and let him drive me home.

During the drive he broke down.

Although he barely knew me, and we certainly hadn't made a love connection that night, he cried and whimpered saying, "I'm afraid I move too fast and scare you away. I feel like I know you my whole life. I'm so afraid you won't contact me." Tears poured down his face as he shook uncontrollably.

As we neared my building, I feared for my life with this psychotic chef behind the wheel. To keep him calm, I reassured him that I'd had a wonderful time but was just so tired I needed to go home. We'd definitely do it again.

He bought it and let me peacefully leave the car. As I strolled away, I turned back to smile and wave. Then as soon as I rounded the corner and was out of sight, I broke out into a wild sprint. I pushed the security door closed behind me, ran four flights of stairs up to my flat, slammed the door, clicked all three locks behind me for the first time since I'd moved in and pushed a chair under the knob for good measure.

For months, I walked a block out of my way to keep from passing his restaurant on the way to my tube stop. Finally nearly six months later, after I had avoided dozens of his calls, he was right in front of me at the station. We'd made eye contact and there was no way for me to pretend I hadn't seen him. He wasn't angry, or whimpering, or strange, just polite and happy to run into me. He was surprised he hadn't seen me in so long and wondered if I'd been away. After a moment of polite conversation, I moved to board the train, and he nervously asked, "Can I ring you sometime? Maybe we can go out." I guess he still hadn't found the right girl. Shocker.

"No," I said bluntly, as I no longer left room for politeness in my dating search.

As I made my escape, he called after me, "Why not? I thought we had brilliant time?"

I remembered his friend Betsy and could clearly see why a pulse wasn't high on this man's dating wish list.

Tiffany Hawk, a former London-based flight attendant, now lives in Newport Beach, where she nervously eats Chinese food whenever her writer's budget allows it. She has traveled throughout Asia, India, Europe, North and Central America.

JENNIFER R. CARLISLE

* * *

As the Worm Turns

...so does her stomach.

"THIS IS WHAT WE CALL THE JUSTICE TREE," explained Victor, my guide for the Amazon Basin trek, as he pointed to a harmless looking tree.

He explained that in this area of Peru, if a person committed a crime, he would be bound to the Justice Tree and left overnight. By daybreak only a skeleton would remain. All the flesh would be devoured.

"But what, you ask, would devour a man?" Victor said with a magician's flourish. He tapped the tree bark with his machete. Thousands of fire ants covered the bark, prepared to fight and devour. "This is why tomorrow, when we trek through the jungle of Monkey Island you must cover all of your skin. You don't want to get bit by a fire ant or mosquito or something else."

I had no desire to find out what "something else" meant. The next morning I was careful to leave no flesh exposed. I looked like the bundled up kid from *A Christmas Story*, despite the fact it was 95 degrees, sunny, and humid. I had no desire to be a snack for an insect.

Victor brandished a machete and hacked a way for us through the brush. He pointed out tarantulas, which were as large as my hand, and monkeys that swooped down from the ceiling of trees and allowed us to hand feed them bananas. In the evening, our group returned to the lodge. The lodge consisted of quaint screened-in wooden cabins offering two beds, two hammocks, a rocking chair, and a shower. The cabins were not equipped with electricity. Which, although annoying at first, was probably good as I'm sure in the night all the creepy crawly insects populated the cabin floor. Some things are just better left unseen.

I know that aside from my roommate, there were indeed, other creatures living in the room. One night, I woke sitting upright in bed scratching my ankle with such ferocity as to remove skin. Mercifully, I fell back to sleep and in the morning examined the red welt on the inside of my left ankle.

I looked closely at the bump. At first I thought it was a spider bite. I once had a spider bite and the bump was visible and hardened in the same manner. The only difference was at the summit of the bump, only one opening was visible, while usually with a spider bite there are two small incisions. As I layered up for the day's hike, I made a mental note to watch the bite to make sure an infection would not grow.

For the next several days the bite itched periodically but the redness remained in a localized area. I flew back to New Jersey and began treating the wound by drowning it in hydrogen peroxide and rubbing alcohol. By now I had irritated the wound so badly it resembled a small volcano. The red bump was a half-inch in height and in the center of the wound there was an opening. I affectionately referred to the bump as my second ankle. I kept waiting for the opening to scab up and heal. For the next several days, I poured peroxide directly into the hole and covered it with a Band-Aid.

Several boxes of Band-Aids later, the opening in my flesh still was not closing. So, I did the next logical step. I ignored it. I thought by constantly flooding the cut with peroxide, I was not allowing the chance for it to heal and dry up on its own. Yes, ignoring the wound seemed the next best course.

Four weeks after being bitten in the Amazon, the wound was still not better. I finally decided to go to a doctor. I went to the most convenient place, a walk-in medical center. The doctor prescribed me a topical antibiotic, a white cream called Bactroban, which I think, is a turbocharged form of Neosporin, and an oral antibiotic of Amoxicillin and Clavulanate Potassium tablets. The pills were so large, it was possible to throw them in spiral fashion like a football. Since I dislike taking pills, I decided to only use the topical antibiotic.

I eagerly filled the prescription and went home to do battle with my flesh wound. I slathered on the ointment and spackled up the hole in my leg. I noticed after a minute of filling the hole up with the cream, the hole blew out the cream like a valve. I thought to myself, "Hmmm. It looks like my second ankle is breathing." I pushed some more cream into the hole and firmly secured it with a Band-Aid.

I followed this regimen for several days. I noticed my second ankle was no longer as red, but it was still very hard and the hole was as big as ever. Also, every two hours I experienced a stabbing sensation, as if someone was taking a needle and shoving it directly into the hole in my leg. I discovered that draining the wound, like squeezing a giant pimple with my thumbs, helped alleviate the pain.

Now I had a new step to my regimen. About four times a day I would drain my volcano, then spackle it shut with the cream. I would wait for the stabbing sensation to return and then repeat the procedure.

One day at work, exactly six weeks since the time of the original bite, I had enough. I was doing computer work when the acute stabbing feeling returned. I went to an empty room, propped my leg on a table and vowed to finally drain this wound for good. I grabbed a ream of paper towels and went to work. The more I pressed, the more transparent orange-yellow liquid oozed. I mopped up the exudate with a paper towel. I changed the position of my thumbs and pressed on the wound from different angles. More liquid poured from the hole. I pressed harder. Tears welled in my eyes. I was really hurting myself.

As I continued pressing, I could see a white substance surface at the hole. I thought it was pus and believed that was the cause of my hardened lump on my leg. I hoped I could simply squeeze the pus capsule out. Now I had a goal. I attacked my leg with a vengeance. I pressed on it again and saw the white thing surface once more. I resolutely gave my wound the mother of all squeezes, and suddenly a half-inch-long white thing that looked like a piece of uncooked spaghetti, shot out from my wound.

I grabbed the thing, still thinking it was a large column of pus between my thumb and forefinger. It stood firm and erect and was still anchored in the wound. It was not squishy. It was hard and it was wiggling and it was trying to get back into my leg!

"Oh my God!" I shouted to no one. "It's not pus! It's a worm!!!!" I sat at the desk hyperventilating holding half a maggot that's been living in me for six weeks. If I had let the worm go, it would have retreated back into my leg. If I had pulled on it, the worm would have ripped in half. The larva was not letting go of my ankle. I felt my stomach do a back flip and I began to gag. "Get a hold of yourself!" I thought. "Focus! Get the worm out of your leg, *now*!"

I continued to hold the worm between my thumb and index finger to prevent it from retreating back into my leg. Using my other hand, I dug my fingernails into the skin around the hole in my ankle from which the worm was protruding. I gave the worm a good pull. It snapped in half. I put that half on the paper towel and popped the other half from my ankle. I sealed the worm in a baggie as proof of what I had endured. I hysterically told a few colleagues my struggle and rushed to the doctor clutching my baggie full of worm.

In the doctor's office, I was seated upon the upholstered, paper-covered patient table. The doctor entered and calmly asked what brought me here today. I proudly held up my baggie and exclaimed, "I just popped this out of my leg!"

This is the first time I have seen a doctor visibly pale.

He brought in another doctor to help him, as he admits this is the strangest thing he has had to deal with. I asked him to imagine how I felt.

The three of us poured over a volume of Clinical Dermatology, and discovered that the parasite I played host to for six weeks was *Dermatobia hominis*, better known as the Human Botfly. My understanding of what happened was the botfly landed on me while I was sleeping, bit me, and quickly deposited an egg in my skin. The egg hatched and the larva grew and fed and tunneled about in my ankle happy to be living in a warm nutrient-filled home. I guess the worm did not know it would be journeying to New Jersey.

The inflamed cyst on my leg was properly called a warble, not a mini volcano. The maggot is called a bot. Flies that do this type of torture to people are called botflies. While living in the warble, the larva needs to poke its head out and surface for air once a minute. This explained why the layer of cream I used to cover the hole continued to flap open.

There are three ways to remove a botfly larva from the skin. The first is by manual pressure, squeezing the wound like a pimple. The second is by flushing out the maggot by injecting a solution of lidocaine hydrochloride, like removing the gopher in *Caddyshack*. The third is the Bacon method. I thought this procedure was named after a doctor distantly related to Kevin Bacon, but it is aptly named as the procedure requires the patient to place a fatty piece of bacon atop the hole of the wound. Within three hours, the maggot chooses to eat bacon rather than human flesh. (Mmmmmmmm, bacon!) Needless to say, I was relieved not to have to go food shopping for my larva.

My life has been changed forever by this experience. The mere fact I gave birth to an entity through a hole in my ankle has rendered me minor celebrity status. Many people curiously want to know who is the father and some are trying to help me get time off from work, since I did give birth. My friends have yet to organize a baby shower on my behalf, but certainly, bacon would be an appropriate gift.

Jennifer R. Carlisle is passionate about writing, travel, and eating food prepared for her. As a member of the Hysterical Society, she has written numerous articles for the Uncle John's Bathroom Readers' book series, in addition to on-line travel articles. She currently resides in New Jersey and works as a teacher and writer while planning her next journey.

PETER MANDEL

⋆ ⋆ ⋆

The Importance of
Being Patrick

*The inner life of a starfish isn't what
it's cracked up to be.*

IT IS SUMMER AT PARAMOUNT'S KINGS DOMINION
theme park near Richmond, Virginia. And as Patrick the
Starfish, SpongeBob SquarePants' best cartoon friend, I am
the goofy hero of the afternoon.

Kids are lining up to shake my pink fleece flippers and—
hey, watch out there—one keeps snapping the stretchy fabric of my Nickelodeon pantaloons.

I'm not allowed to talk in here, so I can't tell this six-year-
old to lay off. I scan around for help, but inside my suit it's
dark and hot. I check my key-chain thermometer: 102 degrees. My plastic starfish eyes are fogged.

Suddenly, I feel lightheaded. It feels as if someone—
maybe SpongeBob, who is gyrating next to me—has sucked
the oxygen out of my suit.

Stand back, I think. I am going down.

My day as SpongeBob's TV series sidekick, Patrick the
Starfish, gets started because I am nosy. I'm one of those who
can't just relax and enjoy the magic of theme parks. I need

to know what is really going on. How do the rides work? What's behind the fences and landscaped sets? And, in particular, what's it feel like to be one of those friendly, furry characters who hugs everyone and dances around? Is it fun inside the suits, or a nightmare of bad jokes, pushy parents and screaming kids?

One way to find out is to see if someone will let me be one. After I'm turned down by a string of parks, Kings Dominion, which is owned by Paramount and features Nickelodeon characters, comes through.

When I suit up, I'll be joining a small but important part of the amusement park industry. According to Sarah Lovejoy, Kings Dominion's manager of public relations operations, the park's costumed characters can end up hugging and high-fiving as many as 7,500 park visitors on an average summer day. Multiply that by 137 (the number of days the park is open this season) and you're talking more than one million guest contacts per summer.

Pay varies depending on experience, but starts at $7 an hour. "Entertainment associates" must be at least sixteen. No worries there: I have just turned forty-eight.

At five-feet ten-inches tall and 170 pounds, I'm too big to try out for SpongeBob, who's such a squat character that he demands an actor of about five feet. But if I agree to go through training and follow "character integrity" guidelines, I can spend one day in the role of SpongeBob's relaxed-fit companion. Patrick is big and dorky, and even though I don't have kids, I've seen his mug on coloring books and lunchboxes. Blundering along with Bob in series after series of deep-sea adventures, he is co-star of what Nickelodeon says is the most popular show in its history.

10:15 A.M. I report for duty. "Character actors punch a time clock," Lovejoy tells me sternly—I am fifteen minutes late—"and then head on to one of the costume areas to suit up."

10:42 A.M. Lovejoy gives me a tour of the park. Highlights include the two areas for kids—Nickelodeon Central and Kidzville—where actors gear up daily for four to six half-hour-long "meet and greets" or "walks" in their suits.

"I'm ready," I announce.

Lovejoy glares. "It's going to take time to train you," she notes. "Not to mention fitting you in the suit."

"Do we get lunch?" I ask.

"Forty-five minutes," says Lovejoy. "But then it's back on the clock."

11:30 A.M. New-character boot camp. But today I'm the only inductee. Before learning the ropes, I limber up with some shin-touching and as many push-ups as I can do: nearly five. "A lot of this job has to do with endurance," says Amy Vest, who's in charge of characters and training and eyes me skeptically. "So we get mostly high school kids. It's tough. You'll have to crouch, you'll do a lot of hugging, and you'll dance, sometimes for as long as a mile. One time, during our parade, Patrick had an asthma issue and had to be brought back in."

> A man called, furious about a Florida package we offered. I asked him what was wrong with the vacation in Orlando. He said he was expecting an ocean-view room. I tried to explain that is not possible, since Orlando is in the middle of the state. He replied, "Don't lie to me. I looked on the map and Florida is a very thin state."
>
> ◆
>
> —Anonymous travel agent

12:10 P.M. After assuring Vest I don't need an inhaler, I am introduced to my gear in one of the park's top-secret suiting-up shacks. Vest refers to it as the Green Room. Visitors are strictly prohibited, and I can see why. It is crammed with disembodied character heads and hanging torsos.

"They just got washed," says Vest about the torsos. "That's why they don't have arms yet."

A sign on the wall says:

IS IT LAUNDRY DAY? THEN MAKE SURE YOU LEAVE THESE THINGS IN THE SHACK:

    SCOOBY'S HEAD
    SCOOBY'S BELT
    SCOOBY'S TAIL
    SCOOBY'S FEET PODS

I'm not worried about Scooby-Doo's feet pods. I'm concerned with the pieces of Patrick.

12:30 P.M. Lunch. Starfish or not, I down a fried shrimp sandwich from one of the park's fast-food joints. It's decent shrimp, but I feel like a cannibal.

1:04 P.M. Time to suit up. My costume is the color of Pepto-Bismol. Only it's a brighter pink.

Since we performers are responsible for our suits, I spray down all the places that will touch my skin with a hospital-grade disinfectant known as TOR.

1:35 P.M. I step into giant fuzzy leg pods and pull up my mesh-style underwear and suspenders. Next come a pair of massive pea-green pantaloons.

Patrick's head and body unit is heavy—under the pink fuzz there's a structural shell. I need help from Vest and an assistant to hoist it over my head and get my arms through the knapsack-style harness inside.

SpongeBob's suit, I'm told, is equipped with a personal fan. Nothing fancy like that in mine. It's like a tropical evening in here: dim, roughly the color of sunset, scraps of thread and duct tape hanging limp in the humid air.

As a final touch, I attach some Velcro straps and slide my arms into the arm pods, which I try to flap using subway-style fabric straps. Voila.

2:25 P.M. Vest and her assistant explain the rules. No talking in the suit. No food. No gum. No running. No signing autographs (how could you grip a pen with a flipper?). And no embellishing the costume.

"Once SpongeBob came out with a bracelet on," explains Vest, "that's supposed to go with Dino from the Flintstones. Someone was like, 'Hey, look, SpongeBob has bling-bling!' I had him back in the shack in two seconds."

The bracelet story reminds me of the controversy over whether SpongeBob is gay, whatever that means in the world of cartoons. The founder of a conservative Christian group had addressed members of Congress at a Washington dinner, warning that SpongeBob was the star of a "pro-homosexual" video that was to be mailed to elementary schools across the country. The video turned out to encourage kids to be "tolerant" of a wide range of differences, but since it touched off a national debate, I decide to get an opinion on it from the actor who, at this exact moment, is struggling to squeeze into the bottom part of SpongeBob's suit.

She is Tiffany Vowell, eighteen, of Milford, Virginia, a short and cute person about to be topped off by a rectangular cube of pockmarked, airbrushed foam.

"Gay?" says Vowell. "I really don't think so. SpongeBob and Patrick are just friends."

2:56 P.M. We make the final preparations for our first

meet-and-greet at Nickelodeon Central. We'll have to wave, shuffle to the music that seems to be blasting everywhere and, of course, pose for pictures.

But because it's started to rain, we're going to have to do this under a canopy. And though trussed up in our suits, we're going to have to break the rules and run for shelter.

How come? I say. What's wrong with a sponge and a starfish getting wet?

"Your paint will run," says Vest impatiently. "And SpongeBob turns black."

3:00 P.M. It's time to exit the shack. Vowell offers some last-minute advice. "Don't be nervous," she says. "It's easy to stiffen up in there. But you don't want your movements to look forced." Fact is, when I try to move in the suit, I find myself wobbling, not walking. I am top-heavy.

Suddenly there's a loud crack. It could be thunder. It could be part of my costume snapping as I accidentally bump into a wall. I can't really tell.

3:05 P.M. The rain is coming down in torrents. Our walk is aborted, says Vest. "It's just too wet. But stand by."

3:48 P.M. Due to the haze in my suit and the delay, I realize I've been dozing. How much time has gone by? I slip my hand out of one of my arm pods to check my watch— probably only a couple of minutes, I think.

SpongeBob and a friend are playing Monopoly to pass the time. Vest is checking the weather. No one has noticed my nap.

3:55 P.M. It's drizzling now, dry enough to make another try. I jiggle and shake my pods to wake up. My plastic eye-holes are small and scratched.

Vest and SpongeBob look like the art on an Etch-a-Sketch, but I can tell from sudden squeals that Bob is on the move, out of the Green Room and in public view.

"SpongeBob!"

"Look, it's SpongeyBob!"

"Over here, Bob!"

"Where's Patrick?"

4:06 P.M. Fans are screaming for me! The only problem is that at the moment, I happen to be wedged into the doorway of the shack.

"Duck your head," says Vest. "Come on. This is ridiculous. Twist sideways." She and her assistant give me a shove, and I am loose and stumbling into a crowd of what must be children. "Patrick! Patrick! Can I hold your flipper?" I am grasped by larger shapes, who must be teenagers or parents.

I hear the raindrops plopping onto my hollow head. We get hustled toward the canopy and, surrounded by fans, I try to sway from side to side like SpongeBob. Dancing is impossible. Standing up and not looking desperate are my goals.

4:35 P.M. I feel like a Beatle. There are screams and bursting flashbulbs.

At the height of my fame, inside an enormous knot of kids, my pantaloons get pulled. Two of my Velcro straps are loose. I try to hike things up, but it's difficult with flippers.

I attempt the "help" sign I was taught—a pantomime of snapping a pencil—but there are too many bodies against me, crowded around. I am like an astronaut in space. My suit is leaking air. And the hour in here has changed: It's no longer sunset. It is tropical night.

4:50 P.M. I'm bending forward dizzily—now I'm tipping, thanks to my giant head. I land temporarily on a padded knee.

There are little noises of surprise: Patrick never does this on TV!

SpongeBob is holding out his delicate hand, but I am going over, until I'm stopped by something firm but small.

It is a hug.

My head is being held by a little girl. She is hugging so hard I can't fall forward. I can't even move.

"Goodbye, Patrick," she says. "I love you."

I know the rules. I know I'm not allowed to talk. But I am Patrick the Starfish and it's clear what I must do.

I reach out one flipper, then another.

I hug back.

"Goodbye," I hear Patrick say. "I love you, too."

Peter Mandel is a writer of books for children, including Say Hey! A Song of Willie Mays.

JENNIFER COLVIN

* * *

Office *"Cou"* in France

She learns her way around "le water cooler."

MY NEW BOSS HELD THE DOOR OPEN FOR ME, AND AS
soon as I walked into the room housing the marketing department, I realized I had made a horrible mistake. I had come
to France for a summer internship with an e-commerce company, expecting to simultaneously sharpen my dot-com skills
that had lain dormant since the bubble bust in 2001, dazzle
my co-workers with my newfound MBA knowledge, and let
the sophisticated inner French businesswoman that I knew
was inside me shine for six wonderful weeks.

To be certain, I was already shining. But it had nothing to
do with my brilliance, and everything to do with perspiration from the muggy, early morning heat. I quickly glanced
around the open room. Desks were grouped in fours, and at
those desks sat six beautiful twenty-something girls wearing
form-fitting halter dresses, skimpy tank tops, or black lace.

This looked like dot-com circa 1999, with a French accent. And I was dressed like a thirty-something librarian.
Or, more accurately, I was wearing what a thirty-something

librarian imagined a sophisticated French businesswoman might wear: pinstripe skirt and jacket, and an argyle top that had looked a lot more trendy in the J. Crew catalog than it did now. My boss introduced me to the six girls in the office and the one token cute guy.

"I am in a meeting, so I must go," my boss told me. "This is your computer." He pointed to a computer screen on a desk that was now partially blocking the aisle. "We will talk later. O.K.?"

Everyone else in the room went back to typing. I looked at my new desk, and the space where a chair should have been. No problem. I could get my own chair. I walked over to a chair in the corner, my sensible heels clicking loudly on the wood floor, but when I grabbed the arm, the chair leaned drunkenly to one side. A wheel was missing.

"Excuse me, is there a chair I can use?" I asked the pretty, dark-haired girl sitting closest to the door.

"You can sit in this chair," she said, and gestured languorously to the broken chair.

"But it's broken," I said, foolishly pointing out the obvious. She shrugged. Deciding to make the best of it, I started to drag the chair to my desk.

"No, no, no, no, no, no, no," the cute guy said as he rushed over. "This chair is no good—it is broken," he explained, worried that I had somehow not seen the missing wheel. "I will get you a chair."

I stood awkwardly by my desk as he dashed out of the room, and came back with not only a chair, but also a tech guy to set up my e-mail account. So much for the leadership and resourcefulness I had learned in business school. But one of the reasons why I was here was to learn about doing business in France, which apparently meant letting the cute guy take care of the details.

"I will take you on a tour," he said, and led me to the door. One of the girls said something, and the rest of them erupted in laughter. I didn't blame them, really. I was the new girl, and the cute guy clearly had a crush on me. Still, it was not a very good start.

The next day, I arrived at the office *sans* business suit, wearing the skimpiest shirt I had brought with me. I smiled at my boss and the few girls already at work, and sat at my desk. Without any actual work yet to do, I made myself look busy by alternately clicking on web sites and writing serious-looking notes in my legal pad, until the next girl arrived at the office and appeared at my elbow.

"*Bonjour*," she said. I looked up, and the girl who had wanted me to sit in the broken chair the day before leaned down to kiss me hello on both cheeks. Maybe she felt bad about the chair incident. I decided to forgive her.

The cute guy arrived next, and kissed all the other girls in the room, including me. Maybe, as the token cute guy, it was his job to kiss all of the women. Surely we weren't all supposed to kiss everyone hello? Then he leaned over to kiss the boss. Interesting. Perhaps the awkwardness of the previous day hadn't really been caused by the cute guy's infatuation with me (as it turned out, he had a live-in girlfriend and a son, anyway). The fact that I had snubbed everyone when I arrived, though, would certainly help explain my rocky start.

The relief of figuring out this office ritual didn't last long, as I hadn't yet cleared all of the social hurdles the day would bring. Before long, it was time for the scheduled mid-morning smoke break.

I followed everyone outside to the small, cobblestone courtyard and briefly considered taking up smoking, but I figured the hacking and coughing would probably doom my already damaged reputation. Conversation was ruled out, since my French vocabulary was limited to three topics: the weather (it's hot), where I'm from (California), or sports (Lance Armstrong).

Instead, I stood on the edge of the group and smiled, pretending like I understood what everyone was saying. Secretly, though, I was trying to decode who was sleeping with whom. I suspected it was the cute guy, with the youngest intern, in the mornings before work—but with all of the kissing going on, I couldn't confirm it.

My third day of work, I resolved to get things right. When I arrived at the office, I kissed everyone hello as though I'd been kissing all my life. The young intern I suspected of sleeping with the cute guy offered me a *pan au chocolate* from a bag.

"*Non, merci,*" I said, thinking that if I had to wear formfitting tank tops for the rest of my stay in France, there was no way I could afford to eat pastries.

She looked at me, the confusion on her face turning to disbelief. "*Non?*" she asked, as though she had simply misunderstood what I had said.

"I've already eaten."

"But you must have one," she insisted.

I was suspicious of her motives. Although I had always considered myself athletically-shaped, compared to the rest of the girls in the office who couldn't have weighed more than 108 pounds, I was just this side of fat. Even my hair was fat in France, thanks to the non-stop humidity. My eyes pleaded *non*. Unfazed, she held out the bag.

"*Merci,*" I said grudgingly as I reached for a pastry, cursing her young, energetic metabolism. She had won that round, but I was unwilling to give in on my stance about the coffee.

It wasn't the coffee itself that I was afraid of, even though it came from a vending machine in the hall. It was the idea of payback that I feared. My office mates took turns getting coffee for everyone else, but I always declined the offer, figuring it was the safest way to avoid taking a turn as the vending-machine barista for the day. Plus, as an unpaid intern, I didn't want to shell out for everyone's caffeine fix.

Even though I wasn't getting a paycheck, I still felt like I had to earn my keep at the office. Having exhausted my web site clicking and note-taking routine, I decided to give myself an assignment and write a report in between the smoke breaks. Translating it into French would keep me busy for days.

Over the next few weeks, I expanded my French vocabulary, mastering web site-related words like "*le site web*" and "*le homepage*," and settled into the routine of a dot-commer in France. I caught up with all of that listening to the new Cypress Hill album that I'd been meaning to do, and I got over my anxiety about running into my boss in the communal bathroom, mostly because he left for vacation. When my chair disappeared one day, I tried not to take it personally.

"Perhaps it is a joke, you know?" the cute guy said. I found a chair without wheels, hoping that would discourage people from taking it.

Later, I considered it no small victory to confirm that the cute guy was really sleeping with the youngest intern. What gave it away was the punching. She kept hitting him, just like on school playgrounds everywhere. I was slightly shocked by the now obviousness of their affair, and the dismaying realization that I had outgrown the hitting stage of flirting and was simply too old for the cute guy.

I knew I was really fitting in the day that one of the girls sang out "*cou cou!*" as I kissed her hello in the morning, since that was the cool way to say "*bonjour*" to your friends. But I wouldn't feel like one of the gang for very long. After lunch,

I walked into the office to find it strangely silent—no chatter, no rap music. I didn't think much of it, because before I had a chance to sit down, the oldest girl in the office, who had seniority now that the boss was gone on vacation, called me over to her desk.

"We have a little problem," she said.

Finally! I was pleased that she was asking for my help. My business skills had clearly won the respect of my colleagues.

"Oh," I said casually. "What is it? I'm happy to help."

"It is this, you see," she started. I leaned over her desk a little, trying to get a better look at her computer screen so that I could help solve whatever problem she was facing.

"You must not be late coming back from lunch."

Lunch? What did lunch have to do with the problem?

"It is not just you, it is everyone," she announced to the room. "It is very, very important that you not be late."

Oh. I see. The problem was me. I looked at my watch. I was fifteen minutes late for an unpaid job where no one really cared if I actually did any work.

"O.K.," I said, and sat down at my desk. I put aside my translation work for a new task: seething and plotting bitter, brilliant comebacks.

The next day, she arrived at the office after me (five minutes late, I noticed) and kissed me hello as usual. "*Bonjour,*" I said coolly.

"*Cou cou!*" I gushed to the girl who walked in after her. We giggled and kissed hello. Since my reserved, professional demeanor had failed to win over my co-workers, I thought I'd give the scheming teenager act a shot.

Later that day, I came back from lunch late again, and sat down at my desk, waiting for the lunch policewoman to say something. She walked over to my side.

"What is it that you are working on?" she asked.

"I have this report, and I am trying to translate it into French, but it is not very good," I told her.

"If you ever want some help, I can help you," she said. "Just let me know."

I didn't know if it was my blatant defiance of her authority, or the sting of the *cou cous* that I never said to her, but suddenly, she had become my friend. The one thing I was certain of was that it had nothing to do with my sophisticated inner French businesswoman.

A few days before I left, a chair with wheels mysteriously appeared at my desk. I didn't say anything, but I knew what it meant. I had survived the treacherous office politics of a dot-com company in France, and if frizzy hair, a few extra pounds, and a teenaged demeanor were the consequences, well, those sacrifices seemed worth it. I had earned my chair in the office.

Jennifer Colvin is a freelance writer based in the San Francisco Bay Area. Her stories have appeared in several books, including Sand in My Bra, The Thong Also Rises, *and* A Woman's Europe. *She considers her greatest accomplishment during her internship in France to be the fact that she walked to work in high heels on cobblestone streets, and didn't once twist her ankle or step in dog crap.*

SARA R. LEVINE

* * *

Hip-Hop Hustle,
Oaxaca-Style

She goes shopping in the transnational meat market.

THE FIRST TIME I SAW UNPAID NON-PROFESSIONALS
have sex in public I was twenty-three. I was in Airlie Beach,
Australia, halfway through a four month solo backpacking
trip. The crowd cleared a small circle around the couple, she
with her legs around his waist, he with his pants visibly un-
done, his upward thrusting motion unmistakable. They were
either exhibitionists or too drunk to care.

Peru or Malawi, Bangkok or Bombay, there is one universal truth of the backpacking circuit: few escape the lure
of sexual debauchery while traveling far from home.
Inhibitions are waylaid, consequences irrelevant and unim-
portant. When traveling, participating in unusual activities is
standard—riding elephants, climbing Mayan ruins, scaling
volcanoes—why not mount a local stud as well? My friend
Val, staying at an infamous hostel on the island of Corfu,
found herself participating in a game of "Who Can Do the
Most Risqué Body Shot." She thought she had it in the bag
letting some guy lick the top part of her boob until she

turned her head and saw an English girl giving a guy a blow job on the bar.

When I decided to move to Oaxaca, Mexico I thought I was resigning myself to a year of celibacy. Just one year, I thought. That's not so bad. One year of self-imposed chastity seemed a reasonable price to pay for relocation to another city—tells you how desperately I wanted out of where I was. I'm not sure where the idea came from, why I decided life in Oaxaca would be different from any other foreign destination where men and women from different cultures intermingle. I think I imagined Oaxaca in the flowery language of the guidebooks and articles that ranked it as one of the most beautiful cities in the world: a quaint colonial town where round-faced *señoras* would warmly call to me in the market and the bright colors of southern Mexico would seep into every facet of my heretofore sepia-toned life. It was hard to envision exactly where lust fit into this picture postcard world.

Approximately forty-seven hours after arriving, my chaste delusion was revealed. Maggie and Hillary, two brassy-haired college students from my Spanish class, took me under their peroxided wings. They had been in Oaxaca the summer before and knew exactly where lust lived and thrived in Oaxaca: La Tentación, The Temptation.

From the street, the rhythmic pumping of music reverberates in the night air, the words barely discernable. The men standing at the door look at us flatly, their eyes flick over our bodies in rapid assessment:

Gringas? Check.

Low-cut shirts and tight pants? Check Check.

Before 11 P.M., there isn't a wait. The music grows louder

as you walk toward the back, down the long corridor that grows progressively darker. The air grows thick with smoke, and the heat that rises off the closely packed bodies inside hits you like a tropical storm. The room has a sort of hacienda theme to it—faux exposed timber, rough stucco walls, a balcony that encircles the dance floor from above from which men spy their prey. The club is where local boys meet foreign girls and is, I'm convinced, single-handedly responsible for 90 percent of the sex being had by eighteen- to thirty-five-year-olds of any race or nationality in Oaxaca at any given time.

Tenta, as the locals call it, is predominantly a salsa club, though the owners recently introduced hip-hop music on Wednesday nights to cater to the growing population of foreign students and backpackers. Every other night of the week, salsa reigns. Many a gringa arrives in Oaxaca equipped with the whole kit and caboodle of salsa garb—tight red dress and stiletto heels seemingly the requisite outfit to flaunt one's salsa commitment and expertise. I think salsa dancing can be fun, especially in the more serious clubs, where the dance itself draws men to the dance floor, and not the opportunity to play a little grab-ass.

La Tentación is not one of those clubs. It's a younger crowd, a crowd that comes in search of partners rather than arriving with them. Every conversation is the same: *Where are you from? How long are you here? Could we go out sometime?* He'll show me the city. He diligently asks these questions in English, the exoticism of speaking a language that might bear sexual fruits. Dance one dance and you are likely to escape unscathed; dance two and you're likely to be followed for the rest of the night by a young man with gel-slicked hair, eager to confirm the date you never made for next Friday.

The only time I went for salsa night, my friends and I fell in with several young men celebrating the birth of the first child of one of their crowd. He was celebrating by picking up women in La Tentación while his wife spent the night in the hospital. He explained this all quite sincerely, expressing pride in his new son, while simultaneously trying to slide a hand up my friend Rebeccas's skirt. I think of myself as an immutably sensible person yet I found myself several hours later in the back seat of a car with the proud papa's younger brother, a gorgeous well-sculpted surfer several years my junior.

While we didn't frequent salsa nights at Tenta, we went religiously to hip-hop night. To hear music from home, we said, to dance to music we knew, though that was only an excuse. There was no better place to meet men than Wednesday nights at Tenta. Hip-hop culture is still relatively new to Mexico, or at the very least, new to Oaxaca. There are Mexican hip-hop groups, and the biggest stars from the U.S. are popular in the pirated disc market, but hip-hop dancing is a different story. By far the best dancers in the bar are the predominantly white backpackers and students on study abroad programs whose pathetic attempts to imitate hip-hop videos still exceed the apprehensive moves of the locals. It's like entering a parallel universe in which middle-class suburban white chicks have finally become the fly-girls they always knew they could be. It's not that the Mexicans can't dance—quite the contrary. Latin dances are all quite complicated and require a well-developed sense of rhythm. But they don't involve the same improvisation and overtly sexual moves of hip-hop, and the earnest simulation of the hedonistic booty-shaking culture of hip-hop videos has yet to take hold. So far, the only move that seems to have been fully adopted by the local male population is the simulated ass-slap, which I'm pretty sure was imported by some geeky fraternity brother from Nebraska.

And just who were these men we sought? We were intoxicated with the idea of learning the words you don't learn by looking in the dictionary. Over the two years that I lived in Oaxaca I noticed trends in the kind of Mexican men I met at La Tentación. I got the feeling that they cultivated these personas to cater to the *gringa* requirements for Mexican boyfriends. There were the artists and the sensitive revolutionaries, the younger men looking to learn from older, preferably blond, women, the nice boys eager to tell you how much they loved their mother as a way to prove their undying respect for women. My friends and I dabbled at will, some relationships lasting longer than others, our otherness providing the lure of mystery for them and a convenient excuse for ourselves. I liked to tell myself I was conducting an elaborate socio-anthropological experiment. That college student? That pierced and tattooed bartender? It was all in the name of research.

About six months into my time in Oaxaca I met Enrique. He caught my eye with his arrhythmic exuberance—he jumped when others swayed, rocked wildly from side to side when others bounced gently up and down. He sat down at a table by himself and I joined him. He looked at me myopically, the drunk struggling to change focus.

"Touch the walls," he said. "Feel their texture, how they pulse with life."

I looked skeptically at the faux adobe yellow walls of the hacienda-themed interior. He shifted his gaze to the wall, lurching slightly to the left as he smoothed his hand down the rough surface.

"I am an artist," he said. "I came to Oaxaca for this, for its texture, its beauty, its life."

He turned back to me. "You too pulse with life," he said, his eyes burning bright with lust. And then he lunged at me with his tongue stuck out, apparently ready to plumb the depths of my throat in the name of artistic pursuits.

We dated for six months, the plumber and I. I suppose I made allowances for the exoticism of having sex in a different language, for his coffee-colored eyes, and eagerness for public displays of affection. He had a degree in industrial design, but had come to Oaxaca from Monterrey to pursue a more bohemian lifestyle in which he could create freely and be inspired by the beauty of the unspoiled landscape. Mostly he took the money his parents sent him every month and bought enormous quantities of high quality marijuana. In the time that we were together he produced approximately three pieces of art: a ceramic lamp made out of the local black clay that got so hot when it was turned on that it seared a ring into whatever surface on which it sat, an installation piece that involved fetus-like lumps of gummy plastic inside plastic IV bags (a commentary on human cloning) and some white papier-mâché fish. In short, pure crap. I chalked it all up to intercultural exchange.

There were also the men who got the genre right, but didn't pull off the execution of the details. A compactly built man with a goatee and wire-rimmed glasses gave me a poem entitled "Desperation." I marveled both at his rather unique take on the boy meets girl ritual—poetry having, in general, fallen out of favor as the quick way to a woman's heart—as well as his choice of title. I would not have thought that advertising one's desperation was an effective strategy for getting a date, but then who am I to judge the artist? He signed his masterpiece "El Mago," or the magician, along with his email address. Unfortunately for Señor Copperfield he'd given the exact same poem to my roommate the weekend before.

The sensitive yet fiery armchair revolutionaries were also a popular boyfriend model amongst the *gringa* set. Myself, I never fell for the revolutionary types—dirty hair and berets don't do it for me. But my friend Miranda was always swayed by their impassioned indignation, their tattered Che Guevera t-shirts and broodiness. Miranda met Fernando at Tenta one night—he seethed in the corner, shooting her sizzling looks until she was compelled to approach him. Above the din of the music, he railed against free-trade and bemoaned the plight of the Mexican poor. She listened, enraptured, ready to forgo bathing in the name of social justice. Of course, it turned out Fernando, like most of his comrades in Oaxaca, was studying to be an accountant, which somehow took the magic out of Miranda's revolutionary fantasy.

The man-who-respects-women was the most elusive of men in our dating world, so we were all excited when Melissa met dorky bespectacled Diego one night at Tenta. Diego was a nice boy, the first nice boy any of us had met in Mexico. He brought her flowers and took her dancing, kissed her chastely at the front door and didn't ask to be let upstairs. He made piñatas by hand, and hoped one day to buy a piece of land in the country where his mother could live out her days in peace. Mama liked to have him home by 11 P.M., which meant that as their relationship progressed Melissa found herself in the position of scheduling their dinners earlier and earlier so they would have time to go home and have sex afterwards, and he could be home by curfew. Diego was even polite when it came to his sexual kinks. "May I ejaculate on your face?" he asked Melissa one night, which was about the time she decided she wasn't that into nice boys.

After Enrique and I broke up I'd see him at Tenta, always with a new *gringa*. That was the danger of *La Tentación*—you were likely to run into your past mistakes, no matter how big or small. I started spending more time at a bar a few blocks away, *La Divina*, where I discovered how the remaining 10 percent of sex in Oaxaca came to fruition. The men circled like sharks, the women drank away their inhibitions. My research continued.

Sara R. Levine lived in Oaxaca, Mexico for two years, working with non-profit organizations and dipping into the local dating pool. She now resides in Berkeley, California.

* * *

Let Me Tell You About My Trip

Don't try this at home.

I SWEAR I AM NEVER LETTING MY PARENTS GO TO Europe again. The last time they went, they came back with roughly nine hundred of the same pictures that everyone who just comes back from Europe has. We were on Photo 765 when my father leaned over the dining room table and pointed to one teeny-tiny minuscule window on the side of an enormous cruise ship.

"Now, that was where we stayed," my father said, tapping the photo with his finger. "See that window? That was the window to our room on the boat. Behind it was your mother, and I think this was Mallorca, so she stayed in the room and scratched at herself."

"It was a rash, but it was more than a rash," my mother spoke up from the other side of the table. "It was like a full-body scab. It would not surprise me at all if that cruise ship washed its sheets in sand, because when I woke up that first morning, I was nothing more than a tomato with a mouth."

"A tomato with a mouth who vomited every time we hit a wave, which, on a ship, is a little difficult to avoid," my father added.

"That is a lie," my mother replied. "I didn't get seasick until we got to France."

For the benefit of his children and for the trip to Europe, my father invested in an extra-fancy camera that can take wide-angle 180-degree shots, so we "could really get a feel of what it was like," although that feeling could have been reached far more successfully if he had bought us all round-trip tickets to Rome. In any case, my dad had a little trouble figuring out how to use the 180-degree feature, so he basically stood still and clicked, moved a quarter of an inch to the left and clicked, moved another quarter of an inch to the left and clicked, and so on and so on, until he was satisfied after forty minutes that he had captured the whole shot faithfully. That dedication, however, was nothing compared to the time it took to assemble the jigsaw puzzle of the Tyrrhenian Sea my father had thus created and had spread out on my mother's dining room table. For nearly five hours, my entire family was held hostage while my father color-coded specific quadrants of the scene with Post-It notes, unable to leave until we ooohed and aaaahhhed over the finished creation, and individually told him what a good investment the 180-degree camera was. The massive work turned out to be not another boring picture, but another very large boring picture that didn't quite match up in some areas (overexposure was my father's explanation for the gaping holes in the two-foot-by-three-foot image, or maybe it was just the times when he had to reload the camera and forgot in what quadrant he had last taken his quarter-inch picture), which created minor waves of nausea if you looked at it for too long, or as my mother experienced it, "Makes me feel like France."

"This is Italy," my father said, flipping to Photo 766. "Frankly, I didn't like Italy too much. It was very... odd-looking."

"At first, I thought the Italians were very friendly and touchy feely," my mother added. "I thought they could sense we were related, or at one time were one of them—"

"As documented in Photo 768," I nodded, pointing out a woman whose hand looked disturbingly close to my mom's ass as my mother's sandblasted face attempted to smile for my father's expensive camera but looked more like she had just stepped on a nail.

"'Oh, that one," my mother nodded. "I thought she liked me until your father realized she was reaching for my wallet."

"Here," my dad said proudly, "is the Vatican." That's the Pope's window.

)

After my surprise hospitalization I decided that Italy is the perfect place to recuperate. In fact, I suggested to the Touring Club of Italy that they run a campaign that features the slogan—"Come for the Wine, Stay for the Surgery"—I thought they could do a poster with the beautiful hills of Tuscany and Umbria in the background and superimposed over the scenery would be a woman in a hospital bed bandaged up but looking fantastic with an IV in one arm that leads up to an inverted bottle of Brunello di Montalcino (a super Tuscan red wine), and a Prada bag slung over the other arm. It could be a real boost to the tourist industry!

◆

—Marcy Gordon,
"Days of Our Lives"

He sleeps in there. If the light is on, it mean's he's home. See? The light is ON. You know what that means?"

"If Photo 769 is a shadow of the Pope getting undressed and cameoed by the mystical 'Pope is Home' light, I am freaking out," I said blankly.

"See this?" my father continued, flipping to another photo. "This is a place called Pompeii where a volcano erupted and covered the town in ash."

"And when they dug the ash out, they found the shells of people lying like this," my mother said as she covered both of her eyes, "like this," she said as she stretched her arm across the table and grimaced, "and like this," she continued, and as she looked up, her mouth fell open and she put her hand to her forehead. "Of course, by the time they were dug out, most of them were dead. Isn't that what the guide said?"

"Something like that," my father said with a nod.

"I think Pompeii was kind of a…seedy town," I ventured. "I saw a special on TV that showed some old brothels with dirty pictures on the walls. Did you see anything like that?"

"Pornography was not on my agenda," my mother snapped. "I did not go to Europe to see a peep show and look at filth. Show her more pictures of the Vatican. You wouldn't believe that place if you saw it. The size of that gift shop really is a miracle. It's enormous!"

"Did you bring me back a Pope doll?" I asked eagerly.

"You know who else thinks that's funny?" my mother replied. "People who are turning on rotisserie spits in Hell, that's who. Do you think the Pope's still funny, or do you want to spend eternity as a Boston chicken?"

"Come on, it's funny," I argued. "He could come with a couple of outfits with matching pointy hats, one of those smoky lanterns, and a little tiny lamp with a string you could pull to make it light up and the Pope could say, 'I'm home,' 'I'm not home.' 'I'm home,' 'I'm not home.'"

"Oh, oh, look," my father commanded excitedly and then held up a picture. "Here is France! Here's France!"

"I was glad to get out of Italy," my mother said. "On our second day there, they fed me a mad cow."

"No one fed you a mad cow, Mom," I said. "You probably just drank some bad water."

"Yeah?" my mother said, shooting me a dirty look. "Water doesn't keep you in the bathroom for seven days and seven nights on a cruise ship. From the likes of what happened to me next, that cow wasn't just mad, it was pissed."

"Wow, look at France," my sister said as she handed me the photo.

I expected to see the Eiffel Tower, Versailles, maybe even the Louvre, but there, in my hand, was a photo of what looked unmistakably like a CVS or a Duane Reade.

"Now, France, we liked," my father said as he looked at the picture with me. "This was the place in France where we got Mommy's Imodium A-D."

"Oh, I loved France," my mother added. "That was a good day, a very good day. When I was finally able to go on deck, other people on the cruise told me they thought your father had killed me and thrown me overboard. Some were very worried, even though no one said anything."

It was then that I noticed something odd. In essentially every single photo—with the exception of the one in which my grimacing mother is about to get mugged by a distant relative—the scene or image was framed by what appeared to be red curtains. Not ruling out the possibility that this was the only fancy-pants feature on the expensive camera that my father figured out how to operate, I decided to ask.

"Dad, what's the deal with the red curtains? They're in almost every shot," I asked.

"Oh, those were just the curtains on the tour bus," my father explained. "They're on all of the windows."

"So…all of these photos were taken…*on the bus?*" I asked. "The Colosseum, the aqueducts, the Pope's house? The Spanish Steps? You didn't get off the bus? It looks like you saw Europe through a peep show!"

"Sure, we got off," my mother interjected. "We had to get off the bus so we could get back on the boat! Oh, and in France we got off, too!"

"To get the Imodium A-D?" I suggested weakly.

"I loved France," my mother beamed. "It was a nice drugstore!"

The rest of my parents' pictures weren't any more exciting, to be honest, and frankly, they were just as boring as the pictures I had seen of eight other trips to Europe this year, except that most of my friends who had gone to Europe actually touched the ground. Still, Europe had been "educational" for my parents, as evidenced when my mother commented on an obelisk that "it must have taken a lot of time to make that phallus so big."

I was choking on my own spit when my sister stumbled across the secret stash that was tucked under a placemat.

Pornography, apparently, was written on *someone's* agenda.

O.K., so it wasn't really pornography, just more like ancient world smut from the part of Pompeii that wasn't rated for family viewing. My dad had apparently stashed them away under a placemat while he handed off photos of the Vatican and the Spanish Steps that made me more sleepy than the time I took eight Tylenol PMs when I was in a very dramatic mood. In any case, he was keeping all of the exciting pictures to himself, such as the statue of the Roman man with a dinky-doo the size of a car bumper, the frescoes of ladies dancing in the buff, and paintings of what looked like some naked guys wrestling.

"Oh my God," my sister and I giggled as my dad grinned from ear to ear and my mother cried, "What's the big deal? It's just anatomy! Every male has an obelisk! Your father simply took scientific pictures!"

There was an element of biology in them, I'll grant him that, but it was antique porn that I was looking at. My dad had obviously stumbled upon the old Guccione homestead.

I felt my psyche swirl as $3,000 of psychotherapy went right down the drain.

Well, that is, as soon as I got over the amazement that my dad finally figured out how to work the 180-degree feature.

"I thought the colors were pretty," my father insisted.

"Oh, they're colorful, all right," I said. "It's Pompeii's version of the Spice Channel, they'd have to invent the Dirt Channel just to broadcast it. Did you see this shell of a person Mom? I don't think he's reaching for his forehead."

"Put those away!" my mother said as my father giggled.

"Did you notice anything odd about those pictures?" he asked.

I nodded. "Yep," I said. "No curtains."

Laurie Notaro is currently unemployed and childless and enjoys spending her days searching for Bigfoot documentaries on the Discovery Channel, delights in a good peach cobbler, and has sadly discovered that compulsively lying on her headgear chart in the seventh grade has come around to bite her in the behind. Despite several escape attempts, she still lives in Phoenix, Arizona, where she is technologically unable to set up the voice mail on her cell phone, which she has never charged anyway. She is the author of I Love Everybody (and Other

Atrocious Lies) *and* We Thought You'd Be Prettier: True Tales of the Dorkiest Girl Alive, *from which this story was excerpted.*

*

When packing for a trip, we have to sneak around at our house—otherwise, our suitcases will get peed in by our cat, Athena, who editorializes when we threaten to change the status quo. Likewise, travelers visit us at their peril. We admonish them to keep their things out of her way, for after they've worn out their welcome in Athena's estimation, their luggage is subject to the same treatment as ours.

When our Canadian friends once visited, we warned them, "Close your bags, stand them up so she can't get purchase on them, don't leave anything out for her to defile!" After about ten days, Athena, a cat of spooky intelligence, had had enough of those interlopers from the north. I walked into the office, where their things were stashed and blanched at what I saw: she had taken a whiz on the small Canadian flag that lay on the desk.

I cupped the dripping standard and timidly approached them with it. "Does this constitute an international incident?" I asked.

Relations between the United States and Canada appear stable, but we agree: It's better to be pissed off than pissed on.

—Carol Penn-Romine, "A Visit from the Canadians"

JOSEPH C. DIEDRICH

* * *

Greep

*It was kind of like getting your hand
caught in the cookie jar.*

MOST PEOPLE LEARN FROM THEIR MISTAKES. SOMETIMES I can do that too, but never from the first one. I have to screw things up two or three times before I catch on. Even then, sometimes, I catch on only at the last minute.

I always thought that Panama City was a dump but I liked the El Panama Hotel a lot. This was because the top floors weren't air conditioned. Up there the big rooms ran from back to front all the way across the building. You could open the windows and close the big wooden shutters and there would be fresh air scented by the afternoon rain and you could listen to the frog chorus as you went to sleep.

During the rainy season, which is most of the time in Panama, the evening frog chorus around the El Panama Hotel was one of the world's unexplained mysteries. After sundown everything would be quiet for a few hours. Then, somewhere in the distance, a lonely frog would start up; *greep-greep-greep*—slowly, steadily, rhythmically. Then a few other frogs would chime in from here and there, picking up

the beat; *greep-greep-greep*. Then, all at once, as if the Great
Frog Conductor had brought his baton down with a slash,
thousands and thousands of frogs would sound off in perfect
unison. *GREEP-GREEP-GREEP-GREEP-GREEP.*

For a few minutes the night throbbed with frog song, and
then the mysterious thing happened—the thousands of frogs,
every last mother-loving one of them, all stopped at the same
instant.

Dead silence.

After a rest they would do it again—and again—and
again—until they got tired and knocked off for the night.

I never could figure it out. How did they all know exactly when to stop? Did they count greeps or something? I
used to lie awake and wait for one of them to screw up and
go greep after the stop order was flashed, but none of them
ever did. Anyway, this story isn't about frogs. At least not al-
together.

I was at the El Panama one evening with a flight crew that
I didn't like so I opted for a solitary drink and a solitary supper. Rather than going to the relentlessly air-conditioned
ground floor bar, which was like attending a cigar smokers'
convention in an ice cave, I headed for the little bar up on
the roof next to the open-air nightclub.

The nightclub wasn't due to open for hours. At first there
was no one but the bartender and me at the little bar. Then
a blond girl in a tight topless dress and spike-heeled shoes
came in and asked where she could find the nightclub manager. The bartender didn't know. This seemed to upset her.
She said a few swear words in Portuguese and turned to go.
Then she changed her mind, turned around, sat down on a
bar stool, lit a cigarette, and looked over at me, two whole
stools away.

"I'm supposed to be in the show here tomorrow night and I have to talk to the manager," she said in good English, correctly guessing my nationality. "I've been looking for him all afternoon."

"Well, this is where he does his managing," I said. "He's bound to show up here sooner or later."

I turned to get a better look at her. She had shoulder-length blond hair which was not her natural color, a pretty face, large breasts which were in imminent danger of spilling over the top of the tight dress and large hips which were firmly planted on the little bar stool. She looked like Marilyn Monroe would have looked if she had put on fifteen pounds. A lot of men would have found her attractive and sexy—certainly most Latin men would have, they tend to like their women well-rounded—but I thought that she was too heavy. Hell—I thought that Marilyn Monroe was too heavy. Really.

Obviously she was trying to get a job in the show and the manager was ducking her. Show business is a tough business anywhere in the world, but nowhere more so than in a tough town like Panama City. I felt sorry for the poor kid.

"Have a drink with me while you're waiting," I offered.

"Sure," she said. I liked that.

> **B**elmopan is the capital of Belize—the pace is very slow there. A few years ago, I interviewed a deputy minister of planning in his Belmopan office while his assistant slept nearby in a large easy chair. Large buzzing flies entered and exited his mouth, and still he didn't wake up. He was obviously used to it.
>
> ♦
>
> —George M. Guess, "Field Work in Belize"

I liked her, too. She was funny and fun. We had several drinks and the manager still had not turned up. I was getting hungry and I guessed that she was too—she certainly looked like she liked to eat—so I asked her to have dinner with me. We were still the only customers in the place and I didn't want to leave her alone up there waiting for a nightclub manager who wouldn't come.

I was right. She did like to eat, and to drink too. I reached my cut-off point halfway through dinner—I had to fly the next evening—so she did double duty from then on. She told me that she came from São Paulo and her name was Mary Rodriguez. Had I heard of her?

No. I hadn't spent any time in São Paulo.

She didn't work only in São Paulo, she said. She was on Brazilian television a lot and she made movies and she sang in stage musicals in places like Rio and Montevideo and Buenos Aires.

I felt even sorrier for her. Either she was making it all up, which was sad enough, or her career had taken such a nose dive that she was reduced to hanging around a dump like Panama City looking for a job in a hotel show and being avoided by a second rate nightclub manager. The poor kid was having a tough time. Even though she was too heavy for my taste I resolved to be nice to her.

Mary Rodriguez, it turned out, was way ahead of me.

"I don't want anything more to eat," she announced suddenly, pushing away what was left of her dessert, "at least not what they have on the menu here," she added, with a wicked chuckle. "Let's go to your room right now."

It was totally unexpected. My surprise must have shown.

"Don't worry," Mary said, with that wicked chuckle again, "I won't bite—at least not very hard—and I'll bet you breakfast that I can show you things in bed that you've never even imagined. I'm the best damn fuck in South America."

"I'm not worried," I said. Actually I was scared to death. My sex life in those days was decidedly conventional. I imagined going back to my Miami girlfriend covered with bites and scratches and a Brazilian flag tattooed on my rump or something. Still—the offer was highly interesting. I decided to buy some time to think it over.

"I'm no good on a full stomach," I said, which was the truth. "Let's go over to Ciro's for a while first."

Ciro's was a nightclub next to the hotel. It was built like a cockpit—the kind where they fight roosters, not my kind—with a small dance floor in the middle of a round room and tiers of little tables climbing the walls. The place was almost full. We were shown to a table in the top row. Mary and I sat next to each other with our backs to the wall and I draped my left arm over her bare shoulder. Under the circumstance I thought that it was time to establish contact.

That wasn't good enough for Mary. She grabbed my hand and stuffed it down the top of her dress. I found myself holding a large and pleasantly firm breast with a very erect nipple. Just then a waiter brought us a bottle of champagne that we hadn't ordered. Mary took hold of my wrist and held my hand firmly in place while he poured us two glasses.

"Compliments of the manager," the waiter said. Things were moving a little too fast for me.

In a moment they moved faster. Down on the little dance floor the orchestra leader waved to his band to stop playing and stepped into the center of the floor holding his hand mike.

"Ladies and gentlemen," he cried, "we have a very special guest in the room this evening—the star of stage, screen and television, the toast of South America, Miss Mary Rodriguez. Welcome to Ciro's, Mary." Then they turned the spotlights on us.

And there we sat, bathed in what seemed like a thousand candlepower, my left arm around the bare shoulders of the Toast of South America, my left hand stuffed into the top of her dress holding her left breast. I was told, later on, that I had looked like a deer caught in the headlights.

They left the damned lights on us for what seemed like minutes while the orchestra broke into a samba and Mary waved happily at the crowd with her free hand. There were cheers and clapping, and a good many whistles. I heard a voice that I thought I recognized say, "My God, that's our pilot!"

Then, blessedly, the terrible lights went out.

Mary and I finished the champagne before we left. She had to pour because I had only one hand available. Then we went up to my room to listen to the frogs. They never sang better. It turned out that Mary knew something about frogs and she picked up the beat. But she didn't stop when they did.

Marilyn Monroe was fifteen pounds too thin.

Joseph C. Diedrich is a retired Pan Am pilot who spends his time traveling, sailing, trekking, and "messing about." His work has appeared in numerous Travelers' Tales books, including The Adventure of Food, Travelers' Tales Central America, The Best Travelers' Tales 2004, *and* Hyenas Laughed at Me and Now I Know Why. *He and his wife live in Mallorca, Spain.*

*

A lot has been said about the attractive nature of Czech women. Forget anything you have been told. They are far more attractive. It appears as if the place is a breeding ground for models. The fall of Communism made a country of five million Victoria's Secret models free to explore. With little exception the women are flawless. Tall and slender with fair skin, the color of pastry dough. Even better, it appears the women have used up all the attractiveness of the country, leaving the men looking as awkward as an Eastern European mud fence.

—Jeff Neidt, "Slouching Towards Gomorrah: Libidinal
Misadventures in Eastern Europe"

KAYLA ALLEN

* ✳ *

Making Eyes in Paris

*A cure for existential despair exists
in the eye of the beholder.*

RAIN SHROUDS THE BASTILLE FARMERS MARKET IN
Paris and I'm flirting with a tall, chain-smoking ruffian who
looks like he hasn't slept in a week. He broods over aspara-
gus while making smoldering eye contact. Even though he's
a stranger, his glances imply intimacy. Something along the
lines of "I have a magnifying glass into your soul. I wish to
nibble your ear."

His rumpled profile appeals to me. I telegraph my thoughts
to him while considering cauliflower. "We share a beautiful,
tortured existence. I'll trifle with your arm hair."

I'm not a brazen hussy, just an average Sunday shopper
enjoying the frisson of flirtation. The art of coquetry is inte-
gral to everyday life in France. In fact, flirting is as much a
part of the culture as eating stinky cheese after dinner.

My late twenties brought a meltdown of cosmic propor-
tions. Despondency pervaded every corner of my being.
Occasional acting gigs in my adopted hometown of
Hollywood worsened my despair. I was too old to be a star-
let and too cynical to lie about my age.

241

In a supposedly near-breakthrough role, I played a stewardess with a speech impediment opposite Jim Carrey in "Ace Ventura: When Nature Calls." My part consisted of one word. "Peanuts?" I said, dropping the "t" and lisping the "s" as I offered the snack. I booked a ticket to Paris the day the royalty payment arrived.

I traded Los Angeles strip malls for the esthetic pleasure of the Place Saint Sulpice. Strolling aimlessly along the Seine, I struggled to recover my identity. I lingered at cafés and strayed deeper into nothingness. Poodle adoption became a consideration. Albert Camus's quote perfectly illustrated my state of mind: "Nobody realizes that some people expend tremendous energy merely to be normal."

Normalcy in Paris would mean learning the language. I enrolled in a free French course at the Sorbonne. On day one, a handsome, affable guy, Jean David, introduced himself as my teacher. The program used cultural references, rather than traditional grammar lessons, as tools. Jean David would screen an extract from a Truffaut film, then have the class interpret the dialogue. In the darkened room his attention turned to me. He shot playful looks that said, "There are many vineyards in my family. I have homes scattered across France, Switzerland, and Spain. I could have done anything I wanted in life, but I chose to enlighten others. I want to make love to you on this desk."

After a few days I warmed to the game. Feeling genuinely coquettish, I reciprocated Jean David's gazes: "I have angel's breath and a willing mouth. I cook a mean shrimp gumbo. You are a naughty boy and I like it."

Immersion in Parisian life helped erase the humiliating auditions that were the fabric of my former existence. The promise of connection fueled my bicycle rides to class. Jean David and I flirted every day for six weeks. I naturally expected he would ask me on a date when the course ended. For our class party, I prepared an apricot tart, hoping to impress him with my culinary skills.

The fete was in full swing when a beautiful, curly-haired girl appeared and Jean David presented her as "*ma petite amie*, Isabelle." My French was honed enough to understand this meant girlfriend. I was dismayed. How could he have led me on? Did he lead me on? He'd only provoked me with his eyes.

As he left, he offered me a long, expressive stare, one that said, "It is such a pity we won't make love, but I will always long for you." Meantime, Isabelle threw me a look that said, "I am skinnier than you and wear much nicer underwear." I slunk out of the party, empty tart pan in tow.

The secret glances that Jean David and I shared flashed before me as I lugubriously pedaled away from the Sorbonne. Something illusory, yet very real, had happened. Our ocular encounters weren't meaningless, they roused and inspired. I rode by a baguette-toting businessman who was exiting a boulangerie. With utmost formality, he electrified me with a sincere "I'd like to be a bicycle seat in my next life" look. My face reddened as I biked on. Then a cultural epiphany struck. American men flirt as a means to an end: to get laid. The French flirt because it is part of "la vie," a chance to transform an ordinary moment into a profound acknowledgment of elusive potential. Wow. Being anonymously objectified could be fun.

Armed with my new understanding, I cultivated the thrill of locking eyes across the sidewalk with a stranger and wallowing in the unknown. Such communication suited me more than one-side conversations with preening, wannabe actors in Los Angeles.

An unexpected exchange occurred at a hospital emergency room where I'd accompanied a friend with a broken ankle. As she waited to receive treatment, a disheveled paramedic entered, wheeling a bloodied body on a gurney. He turned to me and slowed his pace. His drawn out look said, "I am worn, battered, and need attention. Love me."

I returned with "I want to give you a warm bath and a foot massage. I'm wearing pink lacy culottes." The healing power of random connection outweighed my nihilistic tendencies and I actually started to feel happy. But I feared relinquishing my mask of angst, worried I might not attract as much flirt potential.

On an overcast afternoon when the Parisian clouds hung dramatically low, I hopped a bus along the Boulevard Saint Germain. The sandy-haired driver established eye contact with a frisky ogle in his rear view mirror. One that said, "my Ile St. Louis apartment is lined with books by obscure architects."

Clinging to my damaged persona, I demurely responded with "the Ile St. Louis is too touristy." But he was persistent. He penetrated with "my place is next to Bertillon and the view, magnificent." Always a sucker for good ice cream and a stunning panorama, I cracked a smile and sent a "chocolate is my flavor, what's yours" look. I decided to flirt with abandon. My stop was next: I'd never see him again.

His return grin sent me reeling with such intensity that my internal dialogue was hushed. Of the many memories I have of Paris, this one remains in the forefront. As I descended the bus, I whirled around and for that moment, enjoyed the sheer connection: the two of us strangers, radiating intangible delight in the other.

As the doors closed I was tempted to write down his bus number, or run ahead to the next stop and board again. But the actress Anouk Aimee's words were a reminder to love and lose: "It's so much better to desire than to have." I felt immense joy as he drove away, marveling at how my mediocre day changed into one of pure elation.

Kayla Allen is working on a novel started under the auspices of PEN West's Emerging Voices Fellowship. Rapture Dummy *is based on her years as a child evangelist ventriloquist in Shreveport, Louisiana. She divides her time between France and Louisiana.*

PHIL GORDON

* * *

The Fruit Salesman

Melons, bananas, mangos, and papayas—
it's all kind of sexy, isn't it?

THERE ARE MANY EXOTIC LOCAL FRUITS IN RURAL,
coastal Malaysia: star fruit, green wax apple, red wax apple,
watermelon, pomelo grapefruit, banana, yellow watermelon,
honeydew melon, and a host of others with names too difficult to pronounce. Succulent, juicy, refreshing fruits are exactly the kind of snack I needed after dodging potholes,
breathing truck exhaust, and bearing the 90+ degree March
heat during a three-hour circumnavigation expedition of
Penang on my underpowered, beat-up rent-a-moped. I was
delighted to happen upon a hilltop tropical fruit farm, and
even more delighted to be met in the empty parking lot by
my host for the afternoon, a slightly stooped, thin, and gray-
ing fifty-something-year-old host, Rigal.

In slightly broken English, Rigal welcomed me to his
farm and asked if I'd like the ninety-minute tour of the
grounds. As that involved far too much walking and too little gorging, I declined. Instead, we walked to a hilltop picnic area where I paid my 5 ringgits ($1.50) for a large fruit

platter. Rigal sat down next to me at the picnic table as I bit into a slightly sweeter, redder cousin of the star fruit and surveyed the panoramic views from atop the hill.

We were alone and I was mentally congratulating myself for finding such a great spot free from tourists and backpackers. Experiencing local culture, connecting with local people, eating the local food... yes, after two years of backpacking around the world, this quintessential experience was exactly why I'd left my job in high tech, given everything to Goodwill, and set out with no agenda and no real plan. Just me, unassuming low-key Rigal, and an unlimited supply of sweet, refreshing fruit.

I was halfway through a fleshy, slightly tart yellow watermelon tasting fruit I'd never heard of when Rigal scooted closer to me—just slightly on the side of uncomfortably close. He leaned in, and whispered coyly in my ear: "Mr. Phil, I have something I think you might be interested in." My mouth full, all I could do was mutter "Yeah?" and nod my head as I quickly tried to swallow. My radar and defenses went up, and my idyllic scene suddenly seemed a little less idyllic.

OK, here it comes, the high-pressure sales pitch for a bag of Green Wax Apples, I thought. He pulled from his shirt pocket a tiny, clear plastic bag containing something shriveled and dark brown.

I spit out the remaining unchewed fruit.

I was suddenly very worried: drugs in Malaysia are very serious and can subject the buyer and seller to the death penalty. I scooted further down the bench. "No, thanks," I said as I took a small bite of banana and prepared to make a hasty exit.

Rigal scooted closer and put his arm around me. Too close.

"You have penis problems?" he asked.

Way too close. I stood up and walked to the other side of the bench.

"Um, not that I'm aware of, Rigal," I said.

"This is better than Viagra. I'm selling it," he said, still whispering. I still had no idea what "it" was.

"Rigal, I'm twenty-eight not sixty-eight!" I protested. "I don't think I need any drugs, no thank you."

Rigal's laughed. "Drugs? You think I'm trying to sell you drugs? That's very funny." And he laughed. "No, Mr. Phil, this is a crocodile penis! You use this and your girlfriend have three, maybe four orgasm. You no shoot. You no shoot sperm. Guarantee."

I've always thought that the "shooting" part was the idea, though the "three, maybe four" part sounded pretty good. Entertained and intrigued, I decided to play along.

"Does it come with a girlfriend, too?" I asked.

"No, no, no, you no come! I tell you, you no come!" Rigal protested vigorously. Fully animated, he was no longer whispering.

Clearly, we had a language barrier.

"Well, I don't have a girlfriend now," I said, though I seriously hoped that would change in short order. I had just met a deliciously gorgeous Australian girl in the Galapagos Islands a few weeks back. Malaysia was a necessary, temporary stopover on my way to Sydney. In truth, the only reason I was in Malaysia at all was so that it didn't look like I was flying directly back from South America to see her. (My parting conversation with her a month earlier went a little like this: "So, I'm heading over to Southeast Asia for a bit soon. Hey, Australia isn't all that far, maybe I'll pop down for a visit...")

"No girlfriend? No?" he queried.

"No, no girlfriend, and even if I had one I wouldn't want to eat crocodile penis, I assure you." I took a bite of honeydew.

"No, you don't have to eat it, silly!"

He thought I was being silly.

"You put in a glass of water for five minutes and then drink water. You can use it over and over. You no shoot sperm. You no come. Guarantee. Only 100 ringgits."

I paused to consider the potential: "Just a minute, sweetheart, I need to drink my crocodile penis water so that you can have three, maybe four orgasms, while I exhaust myself to no effect."

He sensed my hesitation and shifted into hard-sell mode, "O.K., Mr. Phil, first time customer, 50 ringgits."

I liked his style. And though I had no intention of needing (or using) the sliver of crocodile penis, I countered with what I was intending on purchasing anyway: "Throw in a bag of star fruit, four waxy apples, and a banana."

As I left my gracious host and loaded the front basket of the moped with my bags of fruit, he tossed me an orange and thanked me for visiting his tropical fruit farm.

Two days later, eager to go down under, I was on a plane to Sydney. I ate several red waxy apples and a star fruit on the way.

Phil Gordon left a successful high tech startup company in 1997 and backpacked solo for the better part of five years to more than fifty countries on six continents. He currently resides in Las Vegas where he is a professional poker player. He is a two-time World Poker Tour champion, author of the best-selling poker books Poker: The Real Deal *and* Phil Gordon's Little Green Book, *and is co-host of Bravo's hit television show* Celebrity Poker Showdown. *Phil shares all of his travel experiences on his award winning website, www.philgordonpoker.com. Phil can frequently be found playing poker on www.fulltiltpoker.com, winning money to fund his next great travel experience.*

★

At the colonial, old-moneyed Manila Hotel, the cigar lady, petite and of unparalleled loveliness in a shapely floor-length dress with a slit up the side, floats through the lobby bar on the gentle wind of her own exquisiteness. She carries a mahogany box of hand-rolled Philippine Tabacalaras. Her smile says hello, welcome, I can't live without you, and a dozen other things to as many lonely gentlemen travelers.

She stops at your chair, presents the compartmented tray of elegant smokes of many sizes and textures and, in a voice that is liquid summer, suggests, "Cigar?" She takes the one you select, and places it capped-end-down into a snifter of brandy for a few seconds while she unsheathes a small scalpel. She removes the cigar and deftly incises the wet cap, cutting a small rabbinical v-shaped notch in the tip.

Then she strikes a match and ignites a small cedar twig. She holds the cigar close to the burning cedar, but not actually into the body of the flame. With nymphet grace, she rotates it evenly, toasting the foot of the cigar. She tenderly places the still-moist barrel between your lips and continues to hold the flame near as you suck slowly, evenly on the other end.

Rich, buxom smoke rises into the air. After it begins to burn, she asks, "May I?" And of course she may. Fingers of delicate femininity retrieve the cigar, which she examines to make sure it's evenly lit. If one area is burning faster than the rest, she wets her middle finger with her tongue and touches it to calm the fire on the part too intensely ablaze.

Even to Freud sometimes a cigar was just a cigar. Not so at the Manila Hotel.

—Larry Moffitt, "How to Light a Cigar
at the Manila Hotel"

DOUG LANSKY

* * *

Full Latex Jacket

A normal guy struggles to be a pervert.

I'M IN A BIT OF A BIND. NOT THE KIND THAT INVOLVES handcuffs and leather straps...at least, not yet. It's just that I'm faced with the rather daunting task of writing about my visit to Berlin's famous, erotic Kit Kat Club—while confining myself to tame, family-oriented words like "wild" and "group" and "fuckfest." I thought it would be interesting to find out for myself exactly what goes on there. And it was— starting with my first phone call to club owner Kristin, who told me I'd have to put on some kind of erotic costume if I wanted to get in.

This was more than a little intimidating because I'm an erotic fantasy novice, or beginner, or whatever the correct terminology is for someone who was completely ignorant about the details of kinky behavior.

When I arrived at the alternative clothing and fetish shop called Exciting, I introduced myself to the clerk, Jens, whose beard, leather vest, and beer gut gave him that middle-of-the-pack Hell's Angels look. He was wearing a baseball hat that said "Perv Police," and his English sounded like Schwarzenegger meets sex offender.

"I am eh stage und wideo pafoamer. Yoah noh vat I meen—S und M," Jens confided as he shook my hand. He gave me a quick tour of the tiny shop. I couldn't find anything that cost less than $100, except for a certain pair of shorts that I refused to even try on without modification. I held them up so Jens could see and said—I still can't believe I uttered these words—"Do you have these rubber shorts in my size, but without the synthetic genitalia?"

"No," Jens said, unfazed. "But meebee jou cun buy dose leda schortz." He pointed to the shortest leather shorts I had ever seen, not to mention the only ones with metal spikes built into the crotch.

I ended up getting a one-piece outfit resembling the uniforms Olympic wrestlers wear, except it was black, made of latex, and about two sizes too small. The only thing more outrageous than putting it on was paying for it: $120. To distance myself from the wrestler motif, I also purchased a rubber spiked collar with silver glitter: $30. This would raise a few eyebrows—besides the ones that belong to the IRS auditor when he spots this $150 "research expense."

I couldn't leave the shop without finding out what some of the little gadgets were for. "What's that?" I pointed to a little metal device that might be used to tune a carburetor.

I can't tell you what it was, but the words "nipple" and "clamp" were involved. Jens then added—a little too proudly for my comfort level—"Jou cun even hang veights off it!"

At that moment, a featherweight twentysomething guy walked in. Jens greeted him warmly, then introduced us. "Dis iz Fabrizio, from Italy. Fabrizio iz eh bondage mastah." We shook hands. Jens went on: "Ve vork togethah. Zometimes he appeerz in my show."

"Oh, really?" I said, trying to sound impressed. "That's great."

"Sometimes we make-a da spanking. You knowa da spanking?" Fabrizio asked.

"Oh yes, I know da spanking," I assured them in an effort to quell the conversation, although I wasn't at all sure we were speaking about the same thing.

I then pointed to a bottle on the top shelf behind the counter. Jens took it down. "It iz forah anal sex und fist-fahking." He undid the top and, before I had a chance to pull back, rubbed some of the clear liquid on my hand. "Zee," he boasted, "Dahrs no odah!" I didn't try to smell it.

"Go anda smell it," Fabrizio chimed in.

"I believe you," I said, but it was clear that this wasn't good enough, so I smelled it. And I am happy to report that it had no odor.

Standing there with anal sex and "fist-fahking" lubricant on my hand, I tried to think of an intelligent question.

Jens started going around the shop pointing things out with language that would embarrass Dr. Ruth. There were rings and clamps and handcuffs. Even a full-body rubber suit. It costs about $500 and has double layers so you can pump air between them.

"Pump it with air?" I asked in disbelief, a mental image of the Sta-Puff Marshmallow Man beginning to form.

"Sensory deprivation," explained Fabrizio.

Jens took down another bottle. This one for "cleeening out da asshohl afdah butt-fahking."

To change the subject, I asked Jens what kind of customers he gets. "Noarmal peeple," he said, "like me und jou." I had to bite my tongue to refrain from howling.

Almost on cue, a customer walked in—a hefty woman with multiple ear piercings. Another introduction. "She iz eh dominatrix," said Jens. We shook hands. What fantastic connections I was making!

Shopping complete, I went back to the hotel and got ready...for bed. (The club doesn't get going until 2 A.M.). At midnight, I donned the latex, then threw on some jeans and a sweater and made my way to the U-bahn.

I can tell you this from firsthand experience: latex doesn't breathe well. After only fifteen minutes I could feel sweat running down my legs and I began to wonder—purely from a dressing standpoint—if this is how it feels to be a superhero: wearing some constrictive, non-breathing, embarrassing costume underneath your regular clothing and trying not to fidget.

The entrance to the Kit Kat Club is a tiny staging area where you fork over your cash, strip down, and proceed through the next door into the actual club—a three-car-garage-size room with two toolshed-size rooms attached. The walls are decorated with comically pornographic glow-in-the-dark murals. Around the dance floor are two large swings and a freestanding wooden stockade.

The club was crowded, but not overly so. Maybe a hundred people. I can't describe the more outlandish outfits in the graphic detail they deserve without getting a bit ill, but about 15 percent of the crowd was displaying some sort of nudity. Another 40 percent (and I include myself in this group) had purchased overpriced outfits made of latex, rubber, and other materials not likely to decompose in the next millennium. Nonetheless, I felt most of the eyes turn toward me for inspection as I walked in. Did I look as ridiculous as I felt? I decided this was probably the case, and I proceeded to the nearest corner seat and tried to act as natural as possible under the circumstances.

After about twenty minutes, I made my way to the bar, pulled a bill out of my sock and bought a Coke. I'm not sure what it cost, but I got plenty of change, mostly in coins, which, for lack of latex pockets, I had to deposit back into my sock. During the evening, most of the coins worked their way under my foot, which may have accounted for the coin-shaped blisters I discovered the next morning.

With a little courage, I slithered my way onto the dance floor. I'm going to sound like a musically out-of-it person when I say this, but I'm not a big fan of house, rave, or techno (I'm not even sure if there's a difference between these styles) and I've never been sure how you're supposed to dance to it. Plus, I wasn't particularly inspired by my latex jumpsuit and rubber spiked collar. Some people were clearly under the influence of mind-altering narcotics. Others—as is often the case—were mimicking the dance moves of those under the influence of mind-altering narcotics.

A few people were making out, but not more than you'd see at a senior prom. And no one was having sex on the dance floor, although this supposedly happens every so often. The biggest surprise was all the people who weren't wearing anything special: guys wearing jeans and t-shirts and women wearing clingy numbers you'd see in any other nightclub. Reportedly, many are tourists who come to peek—or, perhaps, peek to come. How had these people gotten in? I guess it's hard to know how much clothing they'll take off after they've been admitted. Obviously, the Kit Kat needs more Perv Police.

Doug Lansky is a nationally-syndicated travel columnist, author of Lonely Planet Signspotting, The Rough Guide First Time to

Europe, *and* Last Trout in Venice, *from which this story was excerpted, and editor of the award-winning travel-humor anthology,* There's No Toilet Paper on the Road Less Traveled. *Doug spends most of his time in Europe with his Swedish wife, Signe, a medical doctor, and their young daughters.*

FRANK BURES

* * *

The Magical Miracle Tour

*When a German evangelist arrived in Africa to save
everyone from Satan and his evil witch doctors,
the author went along for the ride.*

A BOY IN FRONT OF ME HELD A SHINY BLUE BOOKLET.
"Can I see that?" I asked him.

He shook his head and shouted, "No!" He pointed behind me.

All around us, tens of thousands buzzed with anticipation.
We were waiting for German evangelist Reinhard Bonnke
to bless our dusty, East African city with his presence, since
his coming had been pasted to trees and cars and bars for
months.

So effective had his publicity machine been (made up of
every last born-again in the province), that it felt like the second coming. They said he could work miracles. They said he
could cast down witch doctors. They said he could heal the
sick. They said he was stronger than Satan.

Reinhard Bonnke and his Great Gospel Crusade were
here at last. *Witch doctors beware!*

Behind me, where the boy pointed, stood a Great Gospel
Crusade "Counselor" with a stack of blue booklets titled,
"Now That You Are Saved."

"Are they free?" I asked.

"Yes," said the counselor, whose name was Godwin, "but normally we ask you to fill out this card."

He opened the back of the booklet and showed me a "Decision Card." It was a tear-out form that declared my decision to accept Jesus as my savior, and would be used to register the number of those saved at the Crusade. The price, in other words, was my soul.

"Sawa." I agreed.

Godwin took my name, address and phone number.

"Do you attend church regularly?" he asked.

"Yes," I lied.

"Do you want a personal visit?"

"Definitely not."

He checked yes.

"Have you accepted Jesus Christ as your savior today?" he asked. His eyes wandered as though the routine were killing him. He'd probably asked the question a thousand times.

> **B**eware a naked man who tries to sell you a shirt.
>
> ◆
>
> —West African saying

"Not yet," I said, "but maybe after this."

"It would be a good idea if you did," he said and checked "Yes" again. He put the sheet in his pocket and gave me the booklet.

Looking over my "Convert's Copy" of the Decision Card, I saw Godwin hadn't even told me about some more appropriate choices, like "Has major spiritual problems," or merely, "Other."

Far across the field, several Germans wandered onto the stage and a murmur ran through the crowd. Under the giant banner that said, "Jesus Christ Sets You Free," the Germans looked small. The speakers crackled to life and a Tanzanian preacher named Mzee Muro came out to greet us with a rousing Swahili call and repeat cheers. Then he went backstage and returned when some bass guitars and a synthesizer launched into a happy African gospel tune. The ocean of people around me burst into swaying song and dance.

The stage, too, was packed with faithful dancing for Jesus—Germans and Tanzanians alike moving side by side, the Tanzanians in time, the Germans as if on wooden legs.

Then the music stopped.

Slowly, the stage cleared and amid the silence, Reinhard Bonnke emerged.

A cheer went up, and the show began.

It was a well-orchestrated scene that has played out again and again across the continent since 1974, when Reinhard Bonnke first took his show on the road in Botswana and allegedly healed five ailing believers. It was, according to legend, the fulfillment of a prophesy: When Bonnke was just ten years old, a woman came to him and said she had a vision of "a small boy with thousands of black humans following him."

Reinhard Bonnke was that boy.

Since accepting his destiny, Bonnke claims that in over eighty crusades across the globe he has preached to more than 40 million people, with 28,733,783 decision cards filled out. He mainly works among black humans in Africa, but lately he's branched out to brown ones in places like India, the Philippines, and Sicily. He routinely claims to heal polio, cancer, blindness, deafness, tuberculosis, and even to perform "supernatural reconstructive surgery." He can also heal your marriage and money woes. Bonnke says he's had more than 179 million "books" translated into 123 languages and dialects, and these are being printed in 53 different countries.

Bonnke was banned from northern Nigeria after his visit sparked riots that left 300 people dead in 1991. In 1999, he was sued by the families of sixteen Nigerians crushed in a stampede at his crusade in which hundreds of others were also injured. In 2001, HBO shot a documentary about Bonnke and his friend Benny Hinn in which they tried and failed to verify any of his healing claims.

But Bonnke's claims have only gotten more extravagant since then. Late last year, he says, he resurrected a dead man in Nigeria. This was a slight improvement on a dead baby he resurrected in a mother's womb not long before that. Fortunately, when the dead Nigerian man awoke, someone had a video camera handy, and now you can buy the whole thing (as seen on Benny Hinn's show) for $19.99. Miracles are also now available on Bonnke's website. Major credit cards are accepted. Bank drafts can also be arranged.

"Please be seated," Bonnke said. He looked much like his poster, with his pallid visage sneering at the devil, Bible in one hand, microphone in the other. He raised them both in an appeal for calm.

When we had quieted down, he made his first announcement.

"First," he said, "I want to say a prayer for those of you suffering under the curse of poverty."

That probably included everyone on the field.

"Because, even though I am no economist, I *pray* for God to *break* the cycle of poverty and provide jobs for those of you who are *unemployed!*"

Another cheer went up.

Bonnke's German-accented English was translated by Mzee Muro. When Muro's words boomed out, the crowd went wild. And as Bonnke went on and he revved up the rhetoric, Muro followed suit. Bonnke rolled into his sermon, flailing his arms and storming across stage, with Muro flailing right behind him. Bonnke shook his fist and raised his Bible. Muro shook his fist and raised his Bible. Bonnke jumped up and down to make a point. Muro jumped up and down to make the point. Bonnke dropped his voice to a whisper, then back to a shout, and Muro did the same. Through every step, every flinch, Muro was there, half a step behind, like a shadow. No detail was spared translation. It was eerie. The crowd loved it.

The men shouted.

"Amen!"

"Amen!"

"Hey!"

"Hey!"

Bonnke's sermon was on the theme of "Laws." The law of gravity. The law of sin. The law of salvation, and so on—an awkward blend of physics and metaphysics, of tangible and intangible, of hard reality and nebulous divinity.

The audience reveled. They clapped and cheered as his points were translated. They shouted back. They exclaimed. Bonnke knew how to work a crowd, and so did Muro.

With his sermon over, Bonnke began to tell us of a time, back in Jerusalem, when a group of true believers were suddenly so taken with the Holy Spirit that they started talking in a language even they didn't understand. And neither did the devil.

Only God.

Bonnke went into a long explanation of how, when he gave us the cue, we could close our eyes and speak in this language as well.

"But not yet!"

He shouted this again and again before going off on another tangent that eventually came around to speaking in tongues, which was a blessing we would receive.

To illustrate how we were to receive it, Bonnke called a young boy on stage and held up a 10,000 note (about $20). He bent down and handed the boy the note.

The boy grabbed the money, said "thank you," and ran off the stage.

Here was something everyone could relate to.

"That," he told us, "is how easy it is. Now raise your hands, close your eyes, and feel the *Holy Spirit* come down on you, just like it did in *Jerusalem!*"

I closed my eyes, raised my hands and felt nothing but the hot sun. All around me, though, thousands of converts began babbling with eyes closed and arms stretched to the sky, exactly as Bonnke had said they would.

That's not to say everyone was overtaken. Several children near me, whose parents stood enrapt, looked bored and confused. Various counselors roamed through the crowd and a few teenagers stood nearby with their arms crossed, apparently too cool for the rapture. The peanut sellers, too, managed to retain their senses.

But the most notable exception was Bonnke himself, who strolled back and forth across the stage, aloof from the babbling masses.

Mzee Muro, however, lost all power over himself, except enough to keep the microphone by his mouth. His holy gibberish thundered over the crowd.

Gradually people composed themselves—last of all Mzee Muro—and started speaking in earthly tongues. Finally order was restored and the meeting began to wind down.

But not before the healings.

This was what I'd been waiting for. Lately I'd been having stomach problems and had an old knee injury that had flared up. But up front, Bonnke informed us there were prerequisites. First, you had to be washed in the blood of Jesus Christ. Second, you had to come to the healing in faith. As far as I knew I didn't qualify for either.

The Lord's health plan was as bad as any.

The healing was anticlimactic anyway. There were no mass bonfires of wheelchairs and crutches, like there'd been in Kenya. Hardly anyone even fell down. No one was raised from the dead. Bonnke simply told us to check ourselves wherever we'd had a cancer, and that it would be gone. He said some blanket prayers for AIDS, sterility, goiters, malaria, rheumatism, arthritis, and other ailments.

Already people had started to trickle out of the field and back into the streets of the city. I decided to join them rather than get caught in the flood of converts and non-converts.

In the days after Reinhard Bonnke left, the town rocked in his wake. Especially in the days afterward the buzz was everywhere and opinion ran the full spectrum: Some were convinced they'd seen the Messiah, or the next best thing. Others wondered why their rickets hadn't healed or where all those new jobs were. A few saw a good business plan somewhere in there.

And still others just shook their heads at the crazy white man who came to Africa to give away books and money and to teach everyone a new language no one could understand.

Frank Bures is a writer whose work has appeared in Salon, Wired, Tin House, Audubon, World Hum, *and others. His essay "Test Day," was featured in* The Best American Travel Writing 2004. *He is currently working on a book about culture shock.*

* * *

Namaria, Island Nation

It's not about where he's going,
it's about where he's coming from.

"*KOOPISAUL?*" MY COUSIN WILL INQUIRED.

"*Koopisaul shou shey,*" I responded.

We were speaking Namarian, the indigenous language of Namaria, an island nation between Greenland and Canada that Will and I invented for our amusement—and out of necessity.

"Where you from?" That was the constant come-on from touts, hustlers, hasslers, time wasters, and conmen across Vietnam and Cambodia. In destinations like Saigon and Siem Reap, this inquiry was put to us dozens, nay, hundreds of times each day. A simple stroll down the street sounded like this:

"Cold drink, my friend? I have very cold drink. My friend, where you from?"

"Handsome man! Hello! Where you from? I have very nice Zippo lighter. Real Vietnam Zippo. Special price for you!"

"My friend, you want ride? Where you go? Where you from? I give you ride on motorbike. My friend!"

"You like ladyboy? I know very sexy ladyboy who very good for you. Wait! My friend! Where you from?"

The touts cross-referenced our response to this key question against a database of national stereotypes and then tailored their sales pitches accordingly.

The national stereotypes seemed to go like this:

"I'm British"   = "If it's not too much trouble, I'd like you to rip me off, please."

"I'm German"   = "My demeanor and banana-hammock may puzzle you, but I will gladly overpay for your bracelets."

"I'm French"   = "I'm rich and condescending, but I respond well to compliments."

"I'm Japanese" = "Yes, I seem gullible, but I will outsmart you. And I know jujitsu."

"I'm Israeli"   = "You cannot out-bargain me. You will sell me your finest hashish now, at cost, or else."

"I'm Australian" = "Sorry mate, I've only got the cabbage for seventeen more stubbies tonight."

"I'm American" = "Howdy. I'm a moronic billionaire. Let me finish my triple quarter pounder and then I'll throw money at you."

To avoid hassles, many Americans I met adopted the Canadian Defense, because:

"I'm Canadian" = "I'm a benign, indistinct soul without much personality or money. Did you know that Ottawa is the Capital of Canada? Wait...where are you going?"

I even met an American in Nha Trang who sported a maple leaf on her backpack. ("I'd rather punctuate my sentences with 'eh'," she said, "than have to defend our cowboy politics at every turn.")

I'm proud of the United States and I strove to be a good ambassador. But confessing my nationality to every flip-flop salesman across Asia was a waste of time—and not the shrewdest business move either. (Even a dumb American knows that a six-pack of fried tarantulas goes for 10,000 dong, tops.) So was I going to cop the Canadian Defense? Not a chance. Instead, Will and I invented our own nationality.

What to call it? I was gunning for Mikeastan or Hasselhoffia, but Will's proposal of Namaria sounded more legit.

Namaria was a foolproof tout baffler, with most encounters playing out like this:

Tout: "Hello! My friends! Where you from?"

Will & me: "Hello friend! We're from Namaria."

Tout (*nodding uncertainly*): "Namaria…Namaria in Europe?"

Will & me: "No. Namaria near Greenland."

Tout: "Greenland?"

Will & me: "Yes, Greenland. You know—Eskimos, fish popsicles, three months of darkness."

Tout (*looking at us with pity*): "Oh."

Will & me: "Don't you have something you want to sell?"

Tout: "Um, no. Goodbye, Namexicans."

The Namarian Defense also worked well on Europeans.

Many Europeans criticize Americans' lack of knowledge in the areas of politics, geography, history, diplomacy, style, current events, and, well, just about everything. And, for the most part, they're right. The average European will clobber the average American in any geography challenge. The average European probably knows *American* geography better than we do. But do they know Namaria?

One day on the porch of the Number 9 guesthouse in Phnom Penh, Cambodia, Will and I got chatty with a Teutonic blonde named Sabine. When she asked us where we were from, Will told her, "Namaria."

Sabine pursed her lips and rolled her eyes upward, as if referencing an atlas beneath her eyelids.

"It's the island nation between Greenland and Canada," Will added.

"Oh yes," Sabine said, nodding. "Namaria."

"Yeah, we were in the news a few years ago when we won our independence from Greenland," I said.

"What are you talking about?" Will said. "We're in the news all the time because we won't stop whaling."

"Namaria still slaughters whales?" Sabine gasped.

"Of course," Will said. "Whales are delicious. Namarians have been hunting whales for hundreds of years. You think we're gonna let Greenpeace push us around?"

"Whales are as fundamental to our culture as honey," I added.

"Honey?" said Sabine.

"Definitely. Nathaniel Sealcanoe brought Argentinean honeybees to Namaria in the early 1700s and now we're the sixth-largest honey producer in the world."

"We've got honeybees on our flag," Will said. "Along with an anchor and a hummingbird."

I struggled to think of a reason for the hummingbird, but Sabine changed the subject.

"You two talk so quickly," she remarked. "English is your first language?"

"We went to English-speaking schools," I said, "but we speak Namarian at home."

"*Koopisaul?*" Will said.

"*Koopisaul shou shey nosafia*," I replied.

Sabine considered our comments for a moment and said, "Well, it sounds like a lovely place. I'll probably visit some day. But I refuse to eat any whale while I'm there."

"But the honey," I countered. "You must try the honey."

"It really is the best in the world," Will added.

"There's nothing else like it," I said.

Will laughed and, imitating a Vietnamese street vendor, squawked, "Yes! Pretty lady! You try Namarian honey now. Where you go, pretty lady? Where you go?"

Sabine chuckled.

"My friend, special price for you," I added. "Today no lucky business day."

"Where you go, pretty lady?" Will continued. "Where you from? Pretty lady, where you from?"

Sabine laughed. "I'm from Scheißdreck," she said.

Will and I shot each other puzzled looks. I dropped the tout routine and said, "Scheißdreck? Where's that?"

Sabine winked and said, "It's the island nation between Greenland and Iceland."

Mike Pugh has never met a Canadian he didn't like, and he met a lot of them during a solo, one-year, round-the-world journey that he chronicled on award-winning Vagabonding.com. A Namarian, Mike lives in Chicago where he writes for an ad agency, builds his real estate empire, and plots another big getaway.

Index of Contributors

Acknowledgments

I'm fully prepared to disappoint Heather Grennan, Dan Buczaczer, and several other extremely important friends by not mentioning them in the acknowledgements this time around. They always wanted to be listed first instead of last, but for this book I want to keep things short and sweet. All my gratitude can be pointed in three directions.

To my family at Travelers' Tales—James O'Reilly, Larry Habegger, Susan Brady, and Sean O'Reilly—undying thanks for ten years of friendship, mentorship, money, sweat, and tears—you've built my career with this series of books, and I am forever grateful. I mean it, thank you. And yes, Susan, when I cash, you'll get your Manolo Blahniks.

To Sean Keener, Chris Heidrich, and the entire BootsnAll staff who've continued to believe in me and put their support in my websites. You've equally helped to build my name and fan base. I won't forget your hard work, love, and friendship.

And, to my guy, John Caldwell, the newcomer to the clan. Heartfelt thanks for your support, unwavering devotion, and thinking I'm funny. And also for taking me to Europe where the final edits of this book were made. No doubt, it's a better collection for having touched the cafes of Vilnius, Lithuania and Amsterdam, Holland.

O.K., one more very important thanks. To all the contributors in the past four books, the bookstore staff who've supported my author tours, and the fans that followed along on WrittenRoad.com. It's been a fun and funny, wild ride. May you keep having great adventures wherever you are now, and wherever the road takes you tomorrow.

"Love and the Bad Empanada" by Elliott Hester excerpted from *Adventures of a Continental Drifter* by Elliott Hester. Copyright © 2005 by Elliott Hester. Reprinted by permission of St. Martin's Press, LLC.

"Lust in Translation" by Jim Benning published with permission from the author. Copyright © 2006 by Jim Benning.

"The Butt Reading" by Essa Elan published with permission from the author. Copyright © 2006 by Essa Elan.

"Be Grateful, Not Hateful" by Julia Weiler published with permission from the author. Copyright © 2006 by Julia Weiler.

"Day Trip to Chechyna" by Tamara Sheward published with permission from the author. Copyright © 2006 by Tamara Sheward.

"Pumpkin" by Donna DiMenna published with permission from the author. Copyright © 2006 by Donna DiMenna.

"Skymalling" by Susan Orlean excerpted from *My Kind of Place* by Susan Orlean. Copyright © 2004 by Susan Orlean. Used by permission of Random House, Inc.

"Birthday Boy" by Conor Grennan published with permission from the author. Copyright © 2006 by Conor Grennan.

"Total Immersion" by Gil Gevins published with permission from the author. Copyright © 2006 by Gil Gevins.

"Fear of Floating" by Tim Cahill reprinted from the August 2004 issue of *National Geographic Adventure*. Copyright © 2004 by Tim Cahill. Reprinted by permission of the author.

"Pissing on Dave's Feet" by Janna Cawrse published with permission from the author. Copyright © 2006 by Janna Cawrse.

"Trying Really Hard to Like India" by Seth Stevenson reprinted from the September 27, 2004 issue of *Slate*. Copyright © 2004 by United Media. Reprinted by permission.

"Your Ambassador to Butaritari" by J. Maarten Troost excerpted from *The Sex Lives of Cannibals Adrift in the Equatorial Pacific* by J. Maarten Troost. Copyright 2004 by J. Maarten Troost. Used by permission of Broadway Books, a division of Random House, Inc.

"Little Fish that Eat You" by Sean Presant published with permission from the author. Copyright © 2006 by Sean Presant.

"El Max" by Gary Buslik published with permission from the author. Copyright © 2006 by Gary Buslik.

"The Most Tenacious Turd in Nairobi" by Scott Turner published with permission from the author. Copyright © 2006 by Scott Turner.

About the Editor

Jennifer L. Leo is a magnet for misadventure and always ready to gamble on having a good time. She is the editor of the best-selling Travelers' Tales women's humor series, including the award-winning *Sand in My Bra*, *Whose Panties Are These?*, and *The Thong Also Rises*. Her writing can be found in several books, magazines, and websites. Her blog, WrittenRoad.com, was named one of *Writers Digest's* 101 Best Websites for Writers, and a favorite among the editors at Frommer's.

In 2005, Jen moved to Las Vegas to watch the 2005 World Series of Poker and fell in love with both the poker world and a poker player. Now she is the author of *Night + Day Las Vegas*, VivaLasVegasBlog.com, and a columnist for *BLUFF* and *Women Poker Player*. She aspires to be the Rachel Ray of the gambling world, and bounces between Los Angeles and Las Vegas enjoying her fabulous poker scenester life.

Check in with JenLeo.com to find out what she's up to next.